# Anxious Am I?

# ANXIOUS AM I?

## A Pseudo-memoir with Some Fiction and a Bit of Truth

Alan A. Block

RESOURCE *Publications* • Eugene, Oregon

ANXIOUS AM I?
A Pseudo-Memoir with Some Fiction and a Bit of Truth

Copyright © 2022 Alan A. Block. All rights reserved. Except for brief quotations in critical publications or reviews, no part of this book may be reproduced in any manner without prior written permission from the publisher. Write: Permissions, Wipf and Stock Publishers, 199 W. 8th Ave., Suite 3, Eugene, OR 97401.

Resource Publications
An Imprint of Wipf and Stock Publishers
199 W. 8th Ave., Suite 3
Eugene, OR 97401

www.wipfandstock.com

PAPERBACK ISBN: 978–1–6667–9335–2
HARDCOVER ISBN: 978–1–6667–9334–5
EBOOK ISBN: 978–1–6667–9333–8

FEBRUARY 14, 2022 12:08 PM

To Emma
and Anna Rose
my inspiration and my hope

*And if no one reads me, have I wasted my time, entertaining myself for so many idle hours with such useful and agreeable thoughts?*

MICHEL DE MONTAIGNE

# Permissions

Permission has been granted to quote from the following works:

Lyric from the song "Turning Toward the Morning," ©1970 Gordon Box, BMI

Lyric from "It's Alright Ma," Bob Dylan, *Blonde on Blonde,* Universal Music Publishing Group 1966.

Lyric from "Not Dark Yet" Bob Dylan, Universal Music Publishing Group *Time Out of Mind,* 1997.

Lyric from "Every Grain of Sand" Bob Dylan, Universal Music Publishing Group, *Shot of Love,* 1981.

Lyric from "Bob Dylan's Dream," *The Freewheeling' Bob Dylan,* Universal Music Publishing Group 1963.

Lyric from "My Back Pages" Bob Dylan, Universal Music Publishing Group *Another side of Bob Dylan,* 1964.

Lyric from "Honest with Me" Universal Music Publishing Group Bob Dylan, *Love and Theft,* 2001.

Lyric from "Silvio" Bob Dylan, *Down in the Groove,* Universal Music Publishing Group 1988.

Lyric from "Red River Shore" Bob Dylan, *The Bootleg Series Vol. 8-Tell Tale Signs: Rare and Unreleased 1989–2006,* Universal Music Publishing Group 2008.

Lyric from "You're Gonna Make Me Lonesome," *Blood on the Tracks,* Universal Music Publishing Group, 1975.

Lyric from "Stuck Inside of Mobile (With the Memphis Blues Again)" Bob Dylan, *Blonde on Blonde,* Universal Music Publishing Group 1966.

Lyric from "Mary Ellen Carter," Stan Rogers, SOCAN, 1979

Lyric from "The Kid," Buddy Mondlock, *On the Line,* 1987.

Lyric from "1000 Lovers" Lynn Miles, *Love Sweet Love,* Red House Records, 2005.

Lyric from "The Gathering of Spirits" *The Gathering of Spirits,* Carrie Newcomer, Shanachie Records, 1998.

Lyric from "Show Me the Road" Harvey Reid, *Of Wind and Water,* Quahog Music, ASCAP, 1988.

Lyric from "The Wallflower's Waltz," Wendy Wall, *The Road to Paradise,* Tumblestone Records, 2009.

Nathan Zuckerman, Phillip Roth's fictional creation, accused Roth of deceiving the reader in *The Facts*, the work intended as Roth's autobiography. Zuckerman accuses Roth that by writing "only the facts" he has edited out "the one percent that counts—the one percent that's saved for your imagination and that changes everything."[1] Zuckerman complained that in *The Facts*, Roth has assumed too much propriety to be truthful, that he had presented himself as too well behaved and modest to be taken also as being honest. Of course, I think that the opposite might also be true: to only write what is impolite and immodest about oneself is equally false and does not offer a wholly honest perspective on reality. Autobiography is a presentation of the personal, and I think that writers of these books dress for the role. As for myself, I have a wardrobe filled with handsome attire. I aspire to write a memoir. I would be known to be truthful, but I also want those truths to be expressed elegantly. Wittgenstein writes that "No one can write objectively about himself because there will always be some motive for doing so. And the motives will change as one writes. And the more one is intent on being 'objective,' the more one will notice the various motives that enter in."[2] The autobiography ceases to be fact and becomes well-spoken opinion and the latter always has subjective motive and debatable veracity. In the autobiography, I am who I want to be, or more accurately, who I have decided I want to be! In writing the autobiography I become who I would be.

The autobiographer controls the presentation of self and chooses those elements of the life that justifies that presentation. Now I'm writing an autobiography and inventing, in part, a life. The novelist Jeanette Winterson says that we are much better to think of our lives as fiction rather than fact. I believe that what she means is that a life—my life— is not to be defined by the concatenation of facts, but as the responses I have made to the events I have referred to as facts. Facts are events with the life taken out of them!

1. Roth, *The Facts*, 172.
2. Szabados, *The Journal of Aesthetics and Art Criticism*, 6.

## Anxious Am I?

Facts are the record of the wavelengths of the various colors, meaningless when I view the particular blue of the sky at any single time of day. Virginia Woolf's Mrs. Dalloway walks through the flowers at Mrs. Pym's emporium: "White, violet, red, deep orange; every flower seems to burn by itself, softly, purely in the misty beds; and how she loved the grey-white moths spinning in and out, over the cherry pie, over the evening primroses."[3] How would the knowledge of the various wavelengths—those facts—offer any greater delight to Mrs. Dalloway than her joyous and sensuous pleasure? We know Mrs. Dalloway not by the colors she names but by her responses to the colors named. And those responses have a history only one of which can be told.

My living awakens digressive responses to events in which I have engaged and to thoughts that I have had, and when all goes well my presence in life inspires emotions and feelings that I forgot that I had remembered; those memories enrich—give substance—to my existence. For example, this morning at the gym after my shower and after I had finished running the hair dryer about my thinning head of hair, I reached for the jar of Q-tips. I suddenly remembered my fourth-grade teacher Mrs. Seaman's caution that the only thing that should be put in the ear is one's elbow! Of all the directives I have received in my life I wonder why it was that I held onto this one. Almost sixty-five years on, I see gray-haired and thin Mrs. Seaman still. But maybe she wasn't gray-haired except in the eyes of this eight-year-old. And then from that particular memory of Mrs. Seaman's health directive another memory rose to consciousness. I recalled that I first entered her classroom when the school year had already begun and on that first Friday Mrs. Seaman was giving a test and despite my late arrival to the unit, she insisted that I participate. One question I recall concerned the legacy of the Phoenicians, and before I knew my response as a clichéd joke I answered confidently that they invented the Phoenician blinds. I think Mrs. Seaman was polite enough not to laugh out loud, but she did place next to that question a decisive red X mark. And then from that memory I recalled that in that same fourth grade I gave Marjorie Eisenberg my ID bracelet. I will say that dear Marjorie had been my first crush: in my mind now she looks like an older version of Charlie Brown's sister, Sally. But on the day following this troth, I retrieved the offering from Marjorie, afraid I would have to explain to my mother where the bracelet had gone. Alas, I might now with this troubled (and troubling) interaction recognize a very

---

3. Woolf, *Mrs. Dalloway*, 13.

early instance of the anxiety-filled relationships with women in which I have engaged, or in which I have avoided engaging. With a hint of Oedipus thrown in for seasoning.

Tristram Shandy says that when a "personage of venerable character and high station" becomes an author, all the devils in hell turn against him in order to "cajole" the writing. Though neither venerable nor of high station, I am in this memoir-writing beset by all the devils in hell as I sit at my desk. The OED says that "cajole" means "to prevail upon or get one's way with by delusive flattery, specious promises, or any false means of persuasion." I want the writing to go my way, to do what I want it to do . . . if only I could be certain what it is that I want. I change this or that word, move this or that sentence or paragraph, delete sometimes whole sections that I then save in a separate file just in case . . . Even now I have moved this whole section from page 62 to its current location. I tease the writing, assure myself that it is insightful and beautiful, that it dresses me up in the finest clothes and jeweled accoutrements and puts this memoirist up for view. I flirt and I cajole. But in fact, the process is like trying to dress a five-year-old who won't stand still, or who refuses the first dozen offered outfits and after the struggle is finally concluded and she is properly dressed, then slips down in the mud or dribbles strawberry jam down her front. Tristram says, "So that the life of a writer, whatever he might fancy to the contrary, was not so much a state of composition, as a state of warfare; and his probation in it, precisely that of any other man militant upon earth, —both depending alike, not half so much upon the degrees of his wit, —as his resistance."[4] For Laurence Sterne, the word probation might have meant "the testing or trial of a person's conduct, character, or moral qualifications," or it might have meant "the act of showing or proving to be true." By either definition, writing becomes not the romantical image of an author transcribing reality peaceably and effusively at her desk, but of an individual beset by demons and devils attacking her on the field and demanding submission to their will or else to simply cease writing.

These devils offer the possibility of a quick retreat from the struggle: "Get up from the desk, fool," they urge. When I write I am beset by untold outside influences—indeed, by all the devils in hell. Distractions are myriad and only increase daily in this too-technological age. That assault leads me to question everything about the work in progress. With every word I put to paper, a doubt arrives with it. Every thought has its antagonist, and every

---

4. Sterne, *Tristram Shandy*, 262.

statement set down contains a question that must be addressed before the work might proceed. And what about my children? Are they happy and thriving? And the state of the world? O God, I could be bounded in a nutshell and count myself a king of infinite space—were it not that I have bad dreams. I grow more anxious. I eat too many chocolate chip cookies and dust too many surfaces. I had to purchase a new vacuum cleaner that was easier to take out and carry about the rooms.

As a writer also I am not unconcerned with the size and nature of the anticipated audience that sits not before me but atop my shoulders or grasped onto my back. That audience speaks its demands into this writer's ear, insists on certain emendations, corrections, and additions that I think sometimes compromises the integrity of this writer and his writing, though very often these imagined audiences actually do improve the work. Yes, writing is a battle. I remember reading somewhere in Roth's corpus that he could write for a full day—eight hours—and produce a yield of a single page that at the beginning of the next day's effort he might choose to discard.

Sterne addresses this difficulty by inventing his reader—the writer's audience. The narrator—Tristram Shandy himself—speaks directly to the reader who is identified sometimes as a woman and sometimes as a man. This type of address might have been a convention of 18th century literature, but Sterne offers at least one motive for this direct address: he can inform his reader how to read the book! Tristram sometimes addresses a reader's concerns and sometimes questions and advises the reader what he and she might expect from the narrative (such as it is); he offers explanation for his direct address. For example, Tristram chastises the reader (this time a woman) for not paying sufficient attention to his narrative. "How could you, Madam, be so inattentive in reading the last chapter?" he censures her. The reader objects, "You told me no such thing, Sir." And Tristram insists that she go back and reread. The reader's inattentiveness, Tristram accuses, is a result of the acquired habit of reading for plot and not for meaning. Tristram expresses hope for his admonitions: "I wish it may have its effects; —and that all good people, both male and female, from her example, may be taught to think as well as read."[5] Should reading be merely to follow the plot in strict linearity or is reading the enjoyment of digression: the movement away from focus on the linear plot and into imaginative and ruminative flight? If the former is true then perhaps books might be made shorter: as Joe Friday demanded, "Just the facts, Ma'am." Tristram complains that his

---

5. Sterne, *Tristram Shandy*, 40–41.

insistence that the reader go back and reread rebukes "a vicious taste which has crept into thousands besides herself—of reading straight forwards more in quest of the adventures, that of the deep erudition and knowledge which a book of this cast, if read over as it should be, would infallibly impart with them."[6] Digressions, then, become the stuff of thought. Daniel Mendelsohn suggests that the structure of *The Odyssey* is constructed not unlike that I have found in this much later novel, *Tristram Shandy*. Mendelsohn writes "the forward push of the plot, the backward pull of the flashbacks, of the backstories and digressions without which the main narrative would seem thin, insubstantial."[7] A reader might learn to follow the white pebbles not toward home but outward to somewhere she does not yet know. It is not a long step to Thoreau's dictum that a good book requires one to stand on her tiptoes to read it! I have always wanted strong calves.

I think the same might be said of a life. If it is organized by a plot then perhaps it lacks meaning, but if structured with digressions then that life has deep context and character. Mendelsohn writes of the structure of *The Odyssey*, "And so ring composition, which might at first glance appear to be a digression, reveals itself as an efficient means for a story to embrace the past and the present and sometimes even the future—since some "rings" can loop forward, anticipating events that take place after the conclusion of the main story. In this way a single narrative, even a single moment, can contain a character's entire biography."[8] In *A Week on the Concord and Merrimac Rivers*, Thoreau writes, "The most glorious fact in our experience is not anything that we have done or may hope to do, but a transient thought, or vision, or dream, which we have had."[9] Tristram's digressions argue from a similar position. Without them, he avers, there is no book: "That tho' my digressions are all fair, —as you observe,—and that I fly off from what I am about, as far and often too as any writer in Great Britain; yet I constantly take care to order affairs, so that my main business does not stand still in my absence."[10] The story must go on, but the story lacks substance and even direction without the digressions.

To subvert the linearity that would obstruct the possibility of creative thought, Tristram interrupts his narrative with digressions. The steady (and

---

6. Stern, *Tristram Shandy*, 41.
7. Mendelsohn, *An Odyssey: A Father, A Son and An Epic*, 55.
8. Mendelsohn, *An Odyssey: A Father, A Son and An Epic*, 33.
9. Thoreau, *A Week*, 153.
10. Sterne, *Tristram Shandy*, 51.

anticipated) forward movement of plot suffers continual interruption and the reader must therefore attend carefully to her or his reading because the reader can't expect to know exactly what is to come next. Tristram says, "I set no small store . . . that my reader has never yet been able to guess at any thing. And in this, Sir, I am of so nice and singular a humour, that if I thought you was able to form the last judgment or probably conjecture to yourself, of what was to come in the next page, I would tear it out of my book."[11] A digression stops the movement of story because the digression occurs outside of the narrated events; the digression fails the idea of plot because it does not explain causation or motive of the events past or present. But the digression offers history and depth to the event and provides for it perhaps some context. The digression might be somehow inspired by events, but the digression has no place in them. The digression puts an end to the plot and vice versa: the plot puts an end to digression. The digressions provide character to the plot by giving it color and context and therefore, richness; the plot needs the digressions so that it might aspire toward (and even achieve) some honesty. The author has to be attentive to "keep up the spirit and connection of what they have in hand." The bird in the hand, it is said, is worth two in the bush, but I think that those two birds in the bush sing so beautifully.

    I remember once walking in a nature reserve in New Paltz, New York. I had traveled there with my friend Ed who had a cabin on the boundary of the reserve; there were no neighbors and no intruding noise from traffic, human or automotive. Upon arrival he immediately settled in for a quiet nap, but as a city dweller whose Nature had been entirely curated in the City Parks, I wanted some sun and a relatively untended Nature in which to warm some lingering, chilling anxieties. The sun shone brightly—it was an early summer day, and I set out to saunter. Thoreau declares that it is a great art to saunter and I thought to exercise my talents. I carried a copy of Thoreau's *A Week on the Concord and Merrimac Rivers*, my journal and a fountain pen. At some point I paused not to rest but to just imagine, and climbing upon a rock embankment I looked about me out onto a small stream down below. I felt at peace. I opened the book and read for a time. I annotated the text with care and copied some lines into my journal. In a while I arose and continued my saunter. I followed a meandering path and stepped without conscious intent or meaning into a copse of trees. I love the sound of the word "copse," and I love the idea that the small group of

---

11. Sterne, *Tristram Shandy*, 57.

trees formed a community. And as I entered the copse (there, I got to use the word a second time!), I became aware of the cacophony of a chatter of birds from above me, and I suddenly wondered if they were warning the community of my presence, or if I just at that moment had noticed the chorale in the trees. I could have been satisfied with either possibility. One definition of irony posits it as the necessity to choose between two options, neither of which is adequate. I took the road less traveled. Sauntering might be inspired by the question without the necessity of heading toward an answer.

I have for a time considered that opening a new book enacts a moment of estrangement, and that perhaps the reticence to read we sometimes observe in children and even in some adults (and even often one such as me!) might be due to the discomfort that entering a strange world and meeting new people presents. Opening a book the reader enters a world that might be somewhat familiar but ought not to be wholly so, and the characters are, indeed and for the most part, strangers to her. A reader enters warily, with caution and even suspicion. Beginning a new book feels somewhat like jumping into the cold waters of a lake: it originally shocks the system but the temperature soon becomes acceptable and even somewhat comfortable. Or sometimes setting out in a new book is like entering a darkened forest filled with lions and tigers and bears; and sometimes it is like joining a party already in full session in an unfamiliar house with nothing but strangers in attendance. "Who are these people? Where am I? Who invited me, after all? What am I doing here?" Sometimes rather than enter, the reader will turn and flee.

Sterne appears to have prepared for this possibility by offering the reader entrance into the book. Sterne recognizes this relationship between reader and writer, inviting the reader to an intimacy that must be developed over time and page. Tristram says, "In the beginning of the last chapter, I inform'd you exactly when I was born; —but I did not inform you, how. No; that particular was reserved entirely for a chapter by itself; —besides, Sir, as you and I are in a manner perfect strangers to each other, it would not have been proper to have let you into too many circumstances relating to myself all at once.—You must have a little patience . . . As you proceed further with me, the slight acquaintance which is now beginning betwixt us, will grow into familiarity; and that unless one of us is in fault, will terminate in friendship."[12] This invitation (and caution!) not only creates the reader but

---

12. Sterne, *Tristram Shandy*, 6.

also directs him or her as to how the book has been written and therefore, how it might be read. The reader is warmly welcomed and early cautioned not to remain blithely passive.

Ah, who is the reader of this memoir, my work, I wonder? Of course, the writer is always the first reader, and so I am reading as I write. But at some point I must create the opportunity for others to join me. I think I have always read to belong. Reading regardless of the genre joined me to a community that existed first in the book and then spread to those others who had read and were yet reading the book. "What are you reading?" I like to ask of my intimates. Reading connects me to the community for whom the book might serve as a communal space. And some of my dearest friends and comrades are the books that sit on shelves that line the walls of my home. I call them friends because with them I have shared a precious intimacy. They are my chosen, and I have offered my life to them. I have stood naked with them and written my soul's secrets on their pages, and they have offered me their private thoughts and given me entrance to their most intimate confidences. I have lain with these friends during my brightest days and my darkest nights; in the lonely moments of my soul they have comforted me and been my companion through until morning. These friends and I have together laughed and wept, bemoaned and celebrated our individual state and that of the world; we have together in joy studied and frolicked. These friends have drunk with me my coffees and my liquors. I have stained their pages with my carelessness, and they have often served as *valet de chambre* and wiped my face when I was too untidy. These intimates have entered the cloistered spaces into which even my children have had no access; they have suffered without complaint the stench of my ordure and enjoyed the sweeter smells of my private fragrances. The books have kept the splatter from my desktops and my lap and often screened my face from the muck and mire of the world; they have often borne the blows that were aimed at me. And they have often invited me into societies and worlds that have provided me great pleasures, provocations, and comfort.

*Tristram Shandy* might serve as one context of this memoir. Both, perhaps, are books as much for reading as they are about writing! But I think that *Tristram Shandy* is also about how a life might be lived: with tolerance for our contradictions, our foibles, and our virtues. Tristram says to his audiences, "Now I love you for this—and 'tis this delicious mixture within you which makes you dear creatures what you are—and he who hates you for it—all I can say of the matter, is—That he has either a pumkin for his head—or a pippin for his heart,—and whenever he is dissected 'twill be found so."[13] I have aspired to this tolerance and this love, falling short too often of the achievement but never abandoning the attempt. This volume is a record of that effort.

I have also long read Montaigne and his thoughts, too, punctuate this memoir. In his wonderful essay "Of Presumption," Montaigne defines that term as "an assumption, a belief, a guess or hypothesis." In this essay Montaigne offers his idea concerning two vainglorious stances that he describes as "presumption." The first stance concerns how we esteem ourselves too highly: "It is an unreasoning affection, by which we cherish ourselves, which represents us to ourselves as other than we are . . . It seems to me that the nursing mother of the falsest opinions, public and private, is the over-good opinion man has of himself."[14] *Mea culpa*. Of course, as I have learned in therapy, it is all, all more complicated than that. The second presumption concerns just the opposite: how we do not esteem others highly enough. *Mea culpa*. That, too, I have learned in therapy is all, all more complicated. Montaigne's essay is confessional and concerns mostly the sense of his own inadequacies—how much and how little he presumes. But in an essay criticizing so many of his traits—Montaigne notes that he is ugly and too short and that though he can behave like a stoic, he often acts like a fool—in fact, Montaigne expresses contentment with himself and his life. Acknowledging his many faults, he minimizes them. Montaigne does not complain or bemoan his fate. Like Prufrock, he seems not a little lost, but unlike Prufrock, Montaigne seems not to care; he portrays himself as a happy man. "For I have come to the point where except for health and life, there is nothing for which I am willing to bite my nails, nothing that I am willing to buy at the price of mental torment and constraint . . ."[15] Quite content with the life he has constructed and with those things that Fortune has offered him. Montaigne lives a full and productive existence. "The only ability I have needed is the ability to content myself with my lot, which, however, if you take it rightly, requires a well-ordered state of mind, equally difficult in every kind of fortune, and which we see by experience is more readily found in want than in abundance . . . as with our other passions, hunger for riches is sharpened more by the use of them than by the lack of

---

13. Sterne, *Tristram Shandy*, 255
14. Montaigne, *The Complete Works*, 584.
15. Montaigne, *The Complete Works*, 591.

them, and because the virtue of moderation is rarer than that of patience."[16] It is the lesson Thoreau will learn in the cabin at Walden Pond: to front only the essentials of life so that when it came time to die he would not discover that he had not lived. It is a goal I continue to seek as I finish now my seventy-fourth year. Montaigne says, "I think my opinions are good and sound . . . ," and offers as proof of the soundness of his opinions the low esteem he holds of himself and a lifetime of essays.

And this must now suffice as my preface.

---

16. Montaigne, *The Complete Works*, 592.

# STARTING OUT

S HE asked if I had anxiety.
Yes, I answered, my God, I do. I worry about climate change and nuclear wars, about failed economies and aging infrastructures. I am anxious about my psychic health and await anxiously for the next therapy session. I worry about my children's well-being even though they are no longer children and seem to flourish, though I recognize that they are haunted by anxieties of their own. *Mea culpa*! And I am anxious that in my retirement from the classroom and academia, now that I am mostly out of view, I will slip into academic oblivion and no longer be acknowledged or remembered. I remain anxious about my legacy and wonder what effect my work has had on anyone. My books appear somewhere near the bottom of the Amazon lists.

Do I suffer anxiety? she asked. Yes, I answered, my God, I do. I worry about the state of the world, especially now and always then. I still worry about my mother who suffered from dementia and who died in 2015. I am anxious that I, too, will end up sans language, sans dream, sans thought. Until she slipped into the oblivion of dementia, my mother was always an unhappy woman. I recognize that she probably suffered from depression though her sense of propriety would have kept her from ever acknowledging that state. I still discuss her in regular therapy sessions even as I confront her in my daily interactions with women. My father died of lung cancer in 1979. He had smoked Chesterfield unfiltered cigarettes throughout his life, but having characteristically left his cigarettes somewhere else or having neglected to purchase a pack of his own, when the urge would come upon him he would beg a cigarette from anyone in his vicinity, even strangers, and then he would proceed to tear the filter from it so he could better suck in the dirty smoke. I worry about him still: by his own reckoning, he lived an unfulfilled existence of work and love. I do not doubt that he, too, suffered from depression though I am certain the word was to him unfamiliar. I confront him daily in my interactions with men, and I suspect he appears in the lives of my daughters as well. I wonder what part of my parents, Roberta and Sidney, am I? I discuss this in regular therapy sessions. Prevalent racism and the rise again of anti-Semitism in the world makes me anxious. I worry about the spread of fascism across the globe and that threatens our democracy in the now-ended but not-finished reign of Donald Trump. In addition to everything else about which I am anxious, today I worry about the incidence of plague and pandemics. Oh, and yes, I worry about the children, and often about those who are not even mine! I am anxious about so many things, even about those over which I do have some control.

    She asked if I had anxiety. Yes, I answered, my God I do suffer from an almost ceaseless sense of angst! I often wonder what thinking person doesn't suffer from anxiety in this world. I know that she had asked this question so as to confirm the normal presence of her own anxious state, but I was perhaps little comfort to her in my response. I acknowledged that perhaps there is no escape from anxiety as long as we continue to think and feel. Of all the sane men I have ever met or considered, Henry David Thoreau has always seemed to me a quintessential exemplar of self-contentment. Walden has served me for a long time as a guide for the perplexed offered by one who seemed to have found his own way out of the confusion. And yet . . . though Thoreau's time at Walden was a glorious experiment, it seemed not to have produced a man free of the world or from the anxiety that derives from living in it. In his narrative that addressses the burning of Breed's hut, Thoreau admits, "I lived on the edge of the village then—" [he was at Walden] "and had just lost myself over Davenant's Gondibert, that winter that I labored with a lethargy . . . "[1] Thoreau attributes this state of lethargy with which he suffered to heredity, a family complaint, he avers, or more amusingly and dismissively to his "attempt to read Chalmers' collection of English poetry without skipping." But despite his rationalizations regarding the origins of his emotional state, I am certain that what he acknowledges suffering from is the very condition of depression that has led to the ubiquity in our modern-day of a wide assortment of psychotropic drugs.

    She asked if I had anxiety. Yes, I answered, I do, as I suspect do you! And yet if there is no escape from it then perhaps there might be the possibility of some relief. Thoreau continues to offer me hope that despite our anxiety, of which he, too, had experience, we need not be condemned by it. Thoreau declared that in his life he had meant to journey not in cabin

---

1. Thoreau, *Walden*, 281.

passage but rather "to go before the mast and on the deck of the world . . . " It was just such a motive, I think, that led Ishmael to board the Pequod as a cure for his hypos, his restless anxieties. It was just such defiance of resignation that kept Bulkington at sea so as not to crash to complacency upon the Lee Shore. I have learned, often painfully, that it is not easy to stand so before the mast, and that the wind up there blows cold and hard. I suspect that to be alive is to suffer anxiety and to learn to live with this unsettling, uneasy condition. We all seek to find relief from our hypos. Perhaps it is just this effort that might also be the source of whatever creativeness and joys we possess. Ralph Waldo Emerson advocated for the presence in our lives of a bit more insanity. He wrote, "As insane persons are indifferent to their dress, diet and other accommodations, and as we do in dreams, with equanimity, the most absurd acts, so a drop more wine in our cup of life will reconcile us to stranger company and work."[2] I have kept my wine bottles filled and readily available, and I sip from them deeply and often. Emerson advocated here not for an escape from reality but for a more nuanced stance toward it that both he and more recently psychoanalyst D.W. Winnicott has encouraged. Emerson had desired that we approach our realities with a bit less solemnity in order that we might better follow our own business and desires. Winnicott had counseled that we are poor indeed if we are only sane, and that if all we ever do is that which is expected of us by the social order; if out of our debilitating anxieties and paralyzing fears we never enjoy the opportunities to enact our creativity, then we are indeed poorer for our sanity. I think of Polly in the film, *I Hear the Mermaids Singing*, who keeps her photos hidden rather than offer them to the world and take the risks of judgment. Her photos hang silently and unseen on the wall of her apartment.

And, oh, yes, I added to my response to her, I am forever anxious about my health to which as a practicing hypochondriac I devote an inordinate amount of time and energy. I have recently come across the opinion (with which I strongly concur) of Gottfried Wilhelm Leibniz who said, "I am not astonished that men are sometimes sick, but . . . I am astonished they are sick so little and not always." To be specific, my long-term and very patient family physician and I refer to my annual physical exam as the Alan Block Death Watch. For over thirty years now, we have kept vigilant guard. Currently, I do what I can: expend excessive sums of money on supplements, vitamins, and organic foods. Long ago I swore off consuming flesh (except

---

2. Emerson, *Complete Writings I*, 533.

turkey on Thanksgiving, *mea culpa*) and I exercise rigorously. I believe that each day I work out ensures my survival to see another morning. I do suffer immoderate episodes of anxiety in the course of those sedentary days. I am a devoted follower of WebMD, an obsession I share with a few others of my acquaintance who, too, suffer their hypos.

My therapist suggests that perhaps my somatic concerns occur as I attempt to move my psychic conflicts and sufferings onto the physical body. Well, that is one answer. I tell that to my daughter who has those anxious tendencies as well. But another rationale for the motive and persistence of my hypochondria might be ascribed to the assumption I learned that with the acknowledgment of illness, be it real or imagined, I can at least in knowledge assert some control over a body that often feels out of control. I certainly didn't possess a sense that I had control over anything during my years growing up in my family and much less any control over my body. But I remember gaining an appreciation as an adolescent when nothing about my life seemed to be in my power that in the throes of some even imaginary ailment I could yet possess some sense of control. In the absence of any actual markings on my body, my illnesses allowed me to order my actions and the attentional behaviors of others. Hypochondria was a stratagem for asserting control. Or alternatively, maybe my hypochondria derived from an anxious awareness that the body is out of control. Hypochondria, then, for me—as perhaps it might be for you, my daughter, *mea culpa*, —might have been either a strategy to control a sense of helplessness, or it might have been itself the expression of that helplessness. In either case, anxiety over the state of my body's well-being has persisted. Of my hypochondriac tendencies I have long identified with Yossarian in Joseph Heller's *Catch-22*. "There were too many dangers for Yossarian to keep track of... There were lymph glands that might do him in. There were kidneys, nerve sheaths and corpuscles. There were tumors of the brain. There was Hodgkin's disease, leukemia, amyotrophic lateral sclerosis. There were fertile red meadows of epithelial tissues to catch and coddle a cancer cell. There were diseases of the skin, diseases of the bone, diseases of the lung, diseases of the stomach, diseases of the heart, blood and arteries. There were diseases of the head, diseases of the neck, diseases of the chest, diseases of the intestines, diseases of the crotch. There were even diseases of the feet. There were billions of conscientious body cells oxidating away day and night like dumb animals at their complicated job of keeping him alive and healthy, and every one was a potential traitor and foe."[3] I caution my two daughters that this awareness is enough to make a person shiver with fear and trembling. I remember once reading that hypochondriacs are never wrong: they are just early. I never arrive late. And it strikes me now that perhaps my hypochondria was also a means to control anxiety rather than to exacerbate it. I tell that also to my daughters.

**ONE ORIGIN STORY**

I narrate this story to identify a motive for the onset of my tendency to hypochondria and the anxious concern that accompanies it to the following event, aware that this identification essentializes a complex history and even might represent an imaginative flight from the present. I know that the time of year in which it takes place must have been early Fall because in my memory I see me wearing shorts. School was then in session and so the incident must have occurred on a weekend or a school holiday: in those days the wearing of shorts in school was forbidden except for attendance in gym classes and participation in after-school sports. I am certain that on the day in question I was not wearing Bermuda shorts because that style was identified as an attire of older men—like my father—who wore those shorts with socks of color that often rose upwards to their calves. I don't remember ever wearing Bermuda shorts until well after I had graduated college and even then never with calf-high colored socks. Now, of course, I only wear Bermuda shorts and never short shorts because the latter are identified as a style for the young, and anyway, I no longer possess a figure that would look anything but absurd in that style. I do maintain an assortment of Bermuda shorts but wear them only with white crew-necked athletic socks. I grow old, I grow old . . . I shall wear the cuffs of my trousers rolled.

Along with the shorts I must have been wearing a white T-shirt, probably a Hanes, on my feet tennis sneakers and white cotton athletic socks, the ensemble a sort of uniform at the time. I was slender and not at all muscular, and I must have been standing expectantly and anxiously somewhere in the infield pounding my fist into my Rawlings baseball glove that had been regularly oil-anointed and carefully shaped by nightly inserting a hard baseball in the deep-well pocket and enclosing the mitt over the ball with a thick rubber band. I haven't any idea if this made the baseball glove more effective or improved my capacity to be a better player, but it was a *de*

3. Heller, *Catch-22*, 171.

*rigueur* practice amongst the baseball crowd with whom I associated. Every evening I would ritually season and shape what was commonly designated as "my mitt!" On this particular day of which now I speak I wasn't wearing a hat of any sort: this apparel was not deemed appropriate anytime except when playing in full uniform regalia, say, for a Little League game where I played an infield position for the Maple Leafs and donned an official league-sanctioned and parent-purchased baseball uniform. As a player I was more adequate than exceptional (though I wanted desperately to be the latter I performed mostly as the former), and I stood nervously in my position anxious that the ball would actually come to me and I would have to adroitly execute a play. Sometimes I even succeeded.

Or maybe on this day it was a pick-up game on a warm weekend afternoon. We rarely if ever had two full teams of nine players each, and so we often played without a catcher and often even without a pitcher. The shortstop would double as a third baseman, and whoever played second base would also cover the terrain in short center field. Of course, there was always a first baseman and a right and left fielder. I don't remember on that day with whom I played: pick-up games consisted of whoever was on the field at the time. Sometimes we even stayed for a double-header—heat and time were as irrelevant then as they are crucial now. And unlike now, we never tired.

Or maybe on that particular day it was just simply a game of catch-a flyers-up. In this exercise, a batter hits the ball up into the air in the direction of a player in the field. I haven't the slightest idea what the actual name of the activity meant or from where it might have derived, or even if I have named it correctly. Catch-a-fly seems to be the significant root of the name, however. I remember that on that day it was a very high fly ball and I carefully positioned myself under it as it descended. "I've got it," I called out, and spread my arms out wide to give myself plenty of room to get into the right position: I didn't want anybody crowding my space even though I knew that nobody had even attempted to come close. I punched my fist into the prepared glove center, but I must have lost the ball in the sun or, more realistically, I had misjudged my position and my expertise because the next thing that I remember was the sound of a loud clunk and the experience of a sharp pain as the ball hit smack in the middle of my forehead. I fell to the ground fully conscious and not a little embarrassed.

## Starting Out

**I DIGRESS**

Now, I don't remember having any aversion to school—my God, since then I've spent much of my life in them—I think that learning in schoolrooms nourished a curiosity that my home life couldn't and wouldn't foster. It was in the classrooms that the world seemed to open up, even if I came to that opening fraught with my own personal homegrown anxiety. In the books that were assigned and which I always read, there were even things that cast some light on what my home lacked and suppressed. But there also existed in the school clouds of judgment: grades were often a measure of character and the competition for them complicated even the possibility of relationships much less an actuality of them. And for me there was always the awkward social interactions.

At Jericho Junior-Senior High School the social circle with which I associated was aggressively competitive and very competent. These boys and girls were the school and class presidents, the stars on the football and wrestling teams, school cheerleaders and members of honors classes. Some of the boys even had girlfriends. I was none of those things. I then had not the skills, or at least did not think I possessed them. With these acquaintances I struggled to play catch up, but I often missed the ball. I was forever anxious. Believing that for them I was not good enough, I think I wore myself out trying to be what I thought they were already. At first I announced that I was going to be a doctor because medicine was a prestigious profession to which to aspire especially for young Jewish boys and certainly amongst the group of friends and acquaintances with whom I socialized, but I soon learned that I really had not that talent and besides, I didn't like the sight of blood. Another smaller segment of my crowd declared their intention to study for the law, at the time also a high-status career. I had watched a great deal of Perry Mason but couldn't imagine myself in the role. Nevertheless, I wanted to be like them and continued to seek enrollment in the honors classes to which they were assigned but to which I was usually denied access. I learned anyway. Over fifty years later when I sat in company with these same boys at a reunion, I learned that they had, indeed, become the doctors and lawyers that they had back then intended to become and that I had taken a completely different road that they seemed to look at with some disdain. I had stayed at school, I had become a teacher, aspired to scholarship, earned a doctorate, became a university professor and published academic books. And I have since realized that if I thought then that I was not smart enough, I have certainly become so now.

## Anxious Am I?

If I wasn't comfortable in either the hierarchies of school or my social circles, I did in the classroom nevertheless love learning and even some of my teachers: Mr. Meissner, the biology teacher whom I and my lab partner Christine called Peeps; Mr. Tobin, the English teacher who once had been a police officer; and Mr. Matienzo, who named me his favorite existentialist when he inscribed my yearbook. I know that Mr. Bartul, an American history teacher, taught me to do academic research and introduced me to the idea that it was wise not to trust everything I read in the textbooks. One early assignment asked us to read our textbook for its biases! I believe that it must have been this latter experience that made me receptive several decades later for a deep immersion into Marxism, deconstruction, and post-structuralism. I think Mr. Bartul taught me also about the intimacy and authority that learning could possess for the individual who engaged in it; the idea that learning was about the present that was informed by the past and wasnot divorced from it; and that how we felt about events mattered and us. I have never forgotten that on the Monday after we returned to school following the funeral of the assassinated president, Mr. Bartul stood in the front of the room and began to speak. He stood underneath the American flag that hung in the front of every classroom and with his right hand he reached up and shook the cloth. "I have been trying in our work to give you some sense of the meaning and significance . . . " but his voice broke and he began to tear up and could not continue. In a few moments he apologized and said he didn't think he could go on as if today could be normal in light of the events of the past three days, and that perhaps we could take the remainder of class to be silent and consider the events through which we had just lived. Mr. Bartul then sat down at his desk in the front of the room. We sat quietly in our rows, all except Leona Weiss who tore happily into her math homework. I sat awed by the emotion Mr. Bartul's response revealed and that he allowed to be visible in the classroom.

When I think of high school it is of these teachers and the study in which we engaged of which I think, and it is to them and their inviting engagement with their subjects and attentions to me that I attribute my eventual decision to turn to academia and then to the study of literature. To this day I attribute a certain fascination with the French Revolution to my reading of *A Tale of Two Cities* in Mr. Tobin's ninth-grade class; with my strange affection for Edith Wharton's *Ethan Frome* (and to Lionel Trilling's wonderful essay on that book) to him as well; and my immersion in existentialism and the theater of the absurd to Mr. Matienzo. I found in literature a community of readers outside my family of non-readers; confirmation of the emotions I felt but that my family refused, disallowed, and would not display. I found in literature people in whom I could believe and who experienced and suffered some of what I did. They were all, all anxious people.

And then, even more than a wish to join the medical or legal professions, I believe that I aspired to become a beatnik. I had read *On the Road* and perhaps I wanted to be Jack Kerouac, albeit traveling on a different road. In high school I envied the daring of Sharon Reinhart, Sandy Wasserman and Sue Green, girls who traveled out from the confines of middle-class white suburbia and headed to the Village and to alternative experiences. I went to Greenwich Village, as well, though I was perhaps less courageous that were they, and my experiments there were less radical. Perhaps I was not so brave. It was not drugs, alcohol or abandoned sex that I had sought in the Village, though I think at least some engagement with the latter might have been nice. Rather, I traveled to the Village on weekends often alone, and found comfort in Washington Square Park and walking up and down Bleecker and MacDougal Streets. I found many of my formative books on those streets and in the bookstores there: *Been Down So Long It Feels Like Up to Me; Howl and Kaddish, Soul on Ice, Manchild in the Promised Land, Catcher in the Rye* and *Franny and Zooey, Another Country,* . . . There was even an establishment down there called Allan Block Sandals: in that Village I felt as if I was home!! I think I became a successful beatnik—Renee, my dear friend and high school love, remembers me in black turtlenecks and chinos—then as the times evolved I progressed into a competent hippie, if that description is not an oxymoron. In the sixties and into the early seventies the coffee houses, book and poster shops of Greenwich Village were my happy places, and it certainly served as one location where I learned to be me.

It wasn't in the libraries where I usually fell asleep or in the school laboratories where I moved about befuddled and perplexed, but on the streets of Greenwich Village where I found inspiration and community. I had become captivated with folk music and Greenwich Village was the place where it played. I was drawn to the musicians and writers who called the Village home. Sometimes I would actually meet one or two of them walking the same streets with me. At first, from the reclusiveness and alienation of suburban Jericho, I could travel on the Long Island Railroad into New York City and ride on the downtown subway to the West 4$^{th}$ Street Station; later, from my parent's apartment in Queens it was a relatively brief subway ride and short walk to the intersection of Bleecker and MacDougal and to the coffee houses and folk clubs that dotted the streets. It was a few steps down into The Gaslight where I would hear on different nights Tom Paxton, Phil Ochs, Eric Anderson, and Judy Collins. At the small round tables there I drank Coca-Cola—even had liquor been on the menu I was not eighteen years of age, then the legal drinking age. Down the block on Bleecker Street I did drink coffee or hot chocolate at Café Figaro sitting again at a small round table and looking out of the window at the street teeming with people, some of whom even looked like me! I didn't understand the music of Tuli Kupferburg and The Fugs, but I attended a show of theirs across the street from The Gaslight at the Café Wha? Next door to Café Wha? was the Café Wha Not? where a different show played. I frequented The Bitter End but for me it was only a beginning. The Village felt like home to me and when I returned to New York, I always made my pilgrimage to the Village.

## HOMELESS, HOMELESS

Early in my life I experienced an episode of homelessness, and I have since maintained a troubled relationship with home. For the last two years of my high school, I did not live in the same community as my family: under economic pressures, they had moved from the house in Jericho, Long Island. They were in a downward slide because once again my father had run out of money and business and at the time my mother did not work at a job outside the house. Come to think of it now, I don't recall when she started working at a job inside the house: I grew up with African American live-in maids who did everything but cook for the family, and that was probably because my father insisted we keep a kosher home and he was sure that the family's domestic hires wouldn't know how to maintain this discipline around food. I remember specifically two live-ins, Annie and Sadie, the former a large and older woman, and the latter a young woman fresh from the South. Sadie taught my siblings and I how to eat an orange as it was practiced in her rural Southern family. First, she said, you roll the orange on a flat surface or even between the palms of your hands to break the fibers and release the juice. And then you bite off a small hole at one end of the fruit and drink the orange dry. When we had sucked all the juice from the orange, we would split the orange with our fingers into halves and devour the meat. It was messy, and perhaps that was in part its pleasure.

## Starting Out

For the first several of my adolescent years, from when I was thirteen to when I might have been sixteen years of age, I shared a downstairs suite with Sadie. Her bedroom adjoined mine and we shared a bathroom. She was young and attractive, a woman no more than twenty-five years of age, though I realize that perhaps she might have been even younger. Once I remember awakening in the nighttime, walking into an upstairs bathroom and discovering an African American man bathing in the tub. I think this event remained a secret between Sadie and me, though I don't remember the two of us ever talking about it.

I know that there were other hires: my mother sought candidates from an agency that brought young African American women from the South to work in homes of upwardly mobile white families. My parents aspired to upward mobility, but alas they had not the skill. When a housekeeper didn't satisfy my mother, she would return her back to the agency as she might return to the place of purchase a defective utensil, garment, or a bad piece of fruit. I remember my mother once petulantly complaining that while serving my parents dinner, one young newly hired girl moaned that she had felt ill and nauseous. This upset my parents' meal and the next day my mother sent the girl back to the agency. It seems to me now that this woman who could not have been much beyond teen-age years was just looking for a little motherly nurturing and sympathy; she was probably lonely and missed her family, but my parents could only see in her eyes their reflection and their disturbed dinner. I suspect they treated us children not very differently.

When my father failed in business and the family had run out of money, we transported ourselves (with some shame, I recall) to Rego Park, a Queens middle-class neighborhood. Down the 65$^{th}$ Street hill and across Queens Boulevard my mother earned employment at what was then known as New York Bell Telephone. She liked to refer to the company as Ma Bell, and that company nurtured her better, I think, than she nurtured us or perhaps than she had been nurtured in her girlhood. That job saved our lives financially and later saved her life when the salaries and stock purchases and investment plans she enjoyed helped support her stay in Assisted Living and Memory Care Units until her death in 2015.

My parents had married right after my father's discharge from the army after World War II. Actually, they had eloped for reasons that were to me never clear. It was not that my mother was pregnant because though they married in February 1946. I, the eldest of three children was not born

## Anxious Am I?

until August of 1947. I can only speculate that one family must not have accepted the other. Ironically, my parents lived first in Manhattan in relative close proximity to both sets of their parents. But, my mother and father spoke not at all about their early life apart or together or even where they had been residing when I finally did enter the world. But the City was a place out of which they were supposed to move. Queens would have served as the next stop on their exodus. We left Manhattan and settled into a garden apartment in Flushing, Queens, a place name I absurdly abhorred for its association with toilets and excretory functions. We lived next door to the Mann family: Fran and Manny and their two children, Michael and Amy, names with which my parents then gave over to my siblings. The Manns also had a dog that I envied and when my brother was born I offered to trade him to them for their dog. They graciously refused. Manny illustrated greeting cards and for some years made an adequate living; Fran worked as a housewife. At some point Manny's card business failed and my father gave him work in the factory. Manny became one of the continuing array of employees that my father referred to as schmucks and who became unemployed when the business failed. And then, as with so many of their friends over the years, my mother quarreled with Fran and the relationship abruptly ended.

On their way eastward my parents next moved my brother and I from Flushing to a first-floor apartment in a duplex in Little Neck, Queens, right on the border of Nassau County. From their windows they could see the Promised Land. Of Little Neck I remember almost nothing, though I do recall our neighbor, Jake Sirulnick, who if memory serves drove a city bus. He smoked a cigar and was a fan of the Brooklyn Dodgers. I was an avid devotee of the New York Yankees. He and I would argue incessantly . . . well, as cogently as an eight-year-old could debate seriously about almost anything. In 1955, the Dodgers beat the Yankees in the World Series and Jake glowed albeit politely, but for Halloween that year I knocked on his door for Trick or Treat dressed as a Yankee ballplayer with a sign hung around my neck that read, **Wait 'Til Next Year**. Jake was married to Ray, a tall, thin redhead whose thick eye frames could not mask her sparkling gaze. She possessed a joyous, raucous laugh and a strong, husky voice. . . . as I recall. I think she represented to me an energy my mother lacked. Jake and Ray had two daughters, the eldest, Claire, might have been my age. I don't remember the younger one at all, though there exists a shadow image in my consciousness that might approximate her or that might be an amalgamation of a host of young girls with whom I once came into contact. I must have been enrolled in some elementary school there, but I have no memories whatsoever of any attendance. I don't think we lived in Little Neck very long, but my sister was born there. She was brought home in January 1955 in a rented ambulance during a winter snowstorm. We moved from Little Neck when I was in fourth grade, or when I was eight years old.

As I have suggested, Long Island represented the Promised Land and Little Neck had been the mountain top from which that Land could be viewed. To continue with Christian imagery, the City of New York, that included Manhattan, Brooklyn and The Bronx was Hell, and Queens served as Purgatory. (The borough of Staten Island was as distant to my parents as any foreign country would ever be.) I believe that with the rest of the returning white and Jewish soldiers and wives, my parents believed that if they were good enough then these Pilgrims would be blessed and head to Paradise—and with the help of the GI Bill and racist housing policies, they entered the Land and were admitted to Long Island. Eventually my father accumulated enough resources (or perhaps it was the hope of sufficient resources that he would earn in the future: he always spent a dime more than he possessed in the anticipation of earning another one with the next dubious deal) to leave Queens and enter Paradise: rural Long Island, the final destination of white, Jewish, aspiring middle-class families.

We moved to Jericho which at the time was still potato fields. For the first few months in residence, I recall, I rode my bicycle to the local post officefor our mail because there was no home delivery. There we lived for eight financially troubled years and where my desperate father eventually suffered a nervous breakdown. On one sunny weekday morning he left for the City but never arrived there. We somehow discovered that he had boarded a plane from LaGuardia Airport and flew for some unexplained reason to California. We soon learned that his factory had closed and he really had no place to go in the morning. When he came home on a return flight, he took to his bed and his older brother, Harry, who was a lawyer and a rabbi, was enlisted to help. He sat by my father's bedside and coaxed him up out of bed and offered him some counsel. Therapists were never considered an option; as far as my parents were concerned psychiatrists were for crazy people and they were perfectly sane if only a bit troubled. My father's other older brother offered him a position in the rather successful (and lucrative) family business, but my father seethed there. He and his twin brother were the youngest sons. Both of them wanted to make it on their own. I guess I never learned of what 'it' comprised. I think I still don't know. Whatever it might have been, both men failed in the pursuit of it and my father's twin, Milton, died of a heart attack at forty-four years of age. My father failed in business miserably but thankfully managed to avoid criminal prosecution for some illicit business activities. His factory was finally sold at auction.

Of course, the move back to Rego Park seemed a regression, a return to Purgatory; no one, and especially my mother, was particularly pleased. As for me, it was proposed that I stay on in Jericho and finish high school there. This decision led my parents to search out room and board for me for the final two years before my graduation from high school. I seem to recall that the whole scheme had been presented to me at some point though the details of the proposition are not part of the memory. I acceded to the self-exile, and recently I have been considering that this seeming exile has had a greater effect on me than I previously had understood. This separation might have been a significant source of my ocnophilia. Ever since then I have been troubled by the existence of home. Especially now and often then I do not take well to leaving home, and the energy I must mobilize to make the move out into the world is often fraught with anxiety and requires an energy that is sometimes more than I can muster. I invent reasons to stay in place and seek excuses to avoid travel. When I do travel, I tend to look at homes passed along the way and think longingly that if I lived here, I'd be home now. The entire first movement of my *Symphony #1 in a Minor Key: A Meditation on Time and Place* explores in some detail the idea of home. Home is from where I will depart from those whom I know to go to those whom I will leave. Life is constant movement. We start by moving away from home, and then continue on until we get there. But where *there* might be remains unspecified and exists in my mind as that unknown bourn to which traveler neither arrives nor returns. I don't believe that we ever do arrive. Once I imagined that I had never been homeless, but things have changed.

During that first year of roughly voluntary exile and homelessness, I stayed with friends of the family: I recall sleeping on a pull-out couch situated in the den. I imagine that this must have been a surreal time for me because I don't remember anything about it: not meals, not conversation, not homework. I do know that I was not invited back for a return stay. During the second year I boarded with an older couple whose sons, both doctors, had attended Roanoke College in Salem, Virginia. It was through them that I even heard of Roanoke, and so, in a very bizarre way I have this exile to thank for a joy that I have experienced and for which my life at Roanoke College has prepared me. There is much joy here in my present. But I have no idea how I ended up for my senior year at the Hirsch home. Until arrangements had been made, I don't think I even knew who they were, in fact. Ironically the family's last name was the same as that of my maternal grandparents, Hirsch, and the man's first name was that of my maternal grandfather. In name alone I was living with my grandparents! At their home I had an upstairs room to myself, and I think inside the room there might have even been a television. I think that because while I nervously waited for college acceptances to arrive (I wonder now if they were sent to the Rego Park or the Jericho address) I stayed anxiety-ridden awake watching *The Tonight Show* starring Johnny Carson. Outside of that, I cannot recall anything of my time in the Hirsch household. Perhaps I met their sons but of that event I have no memory. I do not recall meals or conversation, and I know that no one visited me there and I visited no one. Not even my dear Renee with whom during that year I established an important relationship, platonic though it remained. Renee is the only one with whom I now maintain any contact. Her Italian grandmother insisted that she ought to marry me, but alas, Renee marched to the beat of a different drummer that I was then incapable of hearing. I think then I demanded that she be someone other than she was, someone who would satisfy my image of myself. Nevertheless, she was an anchor for me not only in my imagination but in reality as well.

In the alienated world in which I then lived, both before and certainly after my family moved to Rego Park, and in a world in which I seem to have floated without any sense of stability or security, Renee offered me some sort of haven. She sat next to me in Mr. Matienzo's senior English class, and she explored with me the cultural scenes from Greenwich Village to the theater district. Renee was my date in 1965 to the Joan Baez concert at the Hempstead Arena and then later to the performance of *Jacques Brel is Alive and Well and Living in Paris* at the Village Gate. She and I went to Broadway shows and even once saw Sammy Davis, Jr., at the Copacabana. She reminds me we frequented the Gaslight. Renee was the only one who knew me as the beatnik I wanted to be before I was the hippie I became and maybe still remain. I took Renee to the Senior Prom, but that night at least I think she liked Trini Lopez better than she liked me. I recall discussing with her the disparate merits of versions of "Lemon Tree" as sung by Peter, Paul and Mary compared to that offered by Trini Lopez. Recently Trini Lopez died of coronavirus and from different ends of the world we remembered. First loves are always loves even if they remained unrequited.

Roanoke College seemed as good a choice as any other at the time. My parents hadn't a clue how to help me in post-secondary application and my guidance counselor was incompetent, something I learned from my experience as a teacher in a school that engaged a functioning and skilled guidance staff. Jericho High School permitted seniors to apply to only three colleges, and though I was accepted into the class of 1969 at Boston University and the University of Buffalo, I elected Roanoke for now indefinite and unclear reasons, and the consequences of this decision was then and remain now significant. In Salem, Virginia, I moved into a culture as different from the one in which I had grown up as a mule is distinct from a thoroughbred. When my mother's friend, Fran Mann, learned that I was planning to attend Roanoke College, she was appalled: Fran had been born in Salem and had escaped from there as soon as she was capable of doing so. That I was voluntarily heading to that place from which she had desperately fled seemed to her a dreadful development.

I had long felt homeless even before I actually became relatively so, and Roanoke College and Salem, Virginia, was as far from home as I had in fact ever been before. Salem was a rural setting in the South and I had grown up in a suburban, white middle-class world in the North. Roanoke College was definitely a bastion of white supremacy and anti-Semitism in a Southern society. Salem represented the South of which I was somewhat frightened—I knew about the lynching of Emmet Till, the murders of Medgar Evers and Goodman, Schwerner and Chaney; I saw the photos of the Freedom Riders and the hosing of protesters outside of the segregated Woolworth counters; the photos of tobacco-chewing officials Sheriff Rainey and Deputy Sheriff Cecil Price, who it was asserted facilitated the murders of the young civil rights workers. Socially conscious folk music had kept me apprised and engaged. Bob Dylan, Joan Baez, Carolyn Hester, Pete Seeger, Phil Ochs, Tom Paxton, Judy Collins, Peter, Paul and Mary, Buffy Saint Marie, Patrick Sky, Eric Anderson, etc. etc. The struggle for civil rights was all around me and I was receptive. I went South nevertheless, and when I arrived at Roanoke, Judy Collins sang at the first concert in the school gym. As her encore she sang "We Shall Overcome." I sang the song I had learned so well and thought that if Judy Collins would choose to sing here, then maybe I could stay here, too. In fact, I never really considered that I could actually leave. I had not the skill, but Judy Collins's presence gave enough me justification to stay.

When I arrived at Roanoke College there were no Black people on campus save for the custodial help and Arillia Crump, the cook in my fraternity house and whom we all called Lee; Jews, too, were in very short supply and at a minimum, considered somewhat distasteful. Religion had been a required category on the original application, and so I assume that I was admitted under a quota system. The South and Roanoke College was steeped in a Christianity about which I knew very little, but what I did know was that Christians didn't much like Jews and Roanoke College was no different. The college was a Lutheran-affiliated institution, and everyone was required to be in attendance at every Sunday chapel. I did not stand for prayer; but chapel attendance was assiduously taken, though the more savvy among us knew the ways to be recorded present even when they were not. I had never been in an environment in which Jews were not present everywhere and though I lived in a nation that prided itself on being Christian, I had never before been in a place where Jews were not in the majority and where they were an open object of derision and hatred. I remember dear Dr. Wise defending Shakespeare's *The Merchant of Venice* of the charge of anti-Semitism by defining the play as a comedy with Shylock as the comic figure who would not adapt and change. On campus there were fraternities from which I was excluded membership. I learned to keep my mouth shut.

I don't remember how I was transported to Roanoke College that first year, but I am certain my father was in attendance because rather than leave me to become acclimated to the place and to meet people with whom I would live for the next four years, he pulled me away from campus and chaperoned me into the city of Roanoke to make sure I had accommodations for the Jewish High Holidays. I also do not remember how on the evening of Rosh Hashanah I was transported from campus to the synagogue, nor do I recall with whom I was bivouacked, but I do know that it was the last time I took residence in the city of Roanoke during the Jewish holidays. Of Southern and Jewish hospitality I remember very little, well, almost nothing, but this might be a result of my own psychic discomfort of being twice removed: from my parent's home in Rego Park from which I felt estranged and then from campus to which I had recently arrived and where I certainly felt a stranger. The next year I owned a car that broke down permanently on its first Thanksgiving trip home, stranding me somewhere in West Virginia.

But in that second year and for the first time in my life I drove to services on the holidays. During that second Yom Kippur at Roanoke College, I kept a purchased bottle of vodka in the car because following the blowing of the shofar signaling the end of the fast, I would leave for a date with Linda Soltis. She had been a member of the advisory group for which I served as leader during her freshman orientation. She was attractive and I was attracted, but during our date I drank too much on an empty stomach. More important to Linda, I belonged to the wrong fraternity. This confluence of events resulted in this being my only assignation with dear Linda, well, with anyone else of her style on campus for almost three years. I do remember a flirtation with a girl named Flo. She attended Hollins College, a woman's school also situated in Roanoke. But Hollins College coeds preferred the boys from Washington and Lee, and the flirtation in which I floundered was brief and unrequited.

But to return to alienated and alienating Jericho: the home at which I boarded during my senior year of high school had requested that I not remain in residence during the weekend, and so during most weekends I returned to Rego Park and left whatever social life I experienced behind me. On Friday afternoons I would be somehow transported to the Hicksville station of the Long Island Railroad and took the train to Jamaica, Queens. From there I descended the platform, walked through the ticket booth waiting room and carried my suitcase filled with the week's worn and dirty clothes. I had not been assigned any semi-permanent dresser space nor access to laundry. During the winter in the cold wind and rain I lumbered up Sutphin Boulevard to the subway. I boarded the express F train to Woodhaven Boulevard where I would change for the R local that in several stops would deliver me to 63$^{rd}$ Avenue and to Rego Park. Then I would lug the suitcase up the station stairs, walk two blocks on Queens Boulevard, turn up the hill on 65$^{th}$ Street to the apartment house on Wetherole Street. There I would spend every weekend alone in the relatively cold bosom of my family or mostly alone on the streets of Greenwich Village. I don't remember engaging in any social events with school chums during that last eighteen months of my high school life other than my dates with Renee and the Senior Prom; when I returned home from college during breaks I did not go out to Long Island to see anybody and they did not come in to see me. I figure it was because the trip was too expensive. For whom, I now wonder? On Sunday I would be driven back to Jericho by my father in the family car.

I had in high school been reading a great deal about alienation. For my senior term paper for Mr. Matienzo, I studied the Theater of the Absurd and read Ionesco, Sartre, Kerouac, Albee, Jones, Beckett and more. Martin Esslin's study *The Theater of the Absurd* was the first purchased text that I annotated. I sought out Dostoevsky in the Underground and Ishmael aboard the Pequod in search of the White Whale. I was then an angry existentialist and wore black turtleneck shirts, tight black chino pants or Levi dungarees that in the early 1960s one had to manually distress with hard work, sandpaper and multiple turns in the washer. I read Kurt Vonnegut, Joseph Heller, John Barth, George Orwell, Nathaniel Hawthorne and Charles Dickens (especially *Great Expectations* and *A Tale of Two Cities*). The works of Ralph Waldo Emerson, Henry David Thoreau. Walt Whitman and Ralph Ellison addressed my life; I discovered homosexuality for the first time in James Baldwin's *Another Country*; later I would discover *Go Tell it On the Mountain* and Baldwin's political writings. I read *The Autobiography of Malcom X*, Claude Brown's *Manchild in the Promised Land*, and Piri Thomas's *Down These Mean Streets*. I read Jerry Rubin and Abbie Hoffman but did not steal either book! I had hopes of becoming me. (And as I write that list of authors, I am not surprised but certainly appalled that there were no books by female writers included in my canon—well, in 1965 in almost any legitimated canon. All I remember reading then written by a woman was Edith Wharton's *Ethan Frome*, a work I only appreciated much later when I read Trilling's essay concerning moral inertia; Shirley Jackson's short story "The Lottery," and some poetry by Emily Dickinson). I listened to the songs of the Weavers, Pete Seeger, Bob Dylan, Joan Baez, Phil Ochs, Peter Paul and Mary, and Judy Collins. I still do. I watched the Huntley-Brinkley report. I knew where I was. I knew something about alienation.

That high school experience in alienation has been one great force influencing my reticence to now not want to leave my home. I plant myself in my current soil and am reluctant to move. I remain alienated. If I had possessed any ambition, I regretfully lacked the energy to uproot and realize it. I worked from home. Over the years I have set down my roots as has the huge cottonwood tree outside the window where now I write. Like it, I might bend in the wind but I do not move. I love that tree: it is tall and stately. Where I have shrunk with age, it has over its years risen nobly. In the late spring it casts its cotton-y seeds abroad blurring the view out of my window screens; during the summer months its branches are so thick with leaves that I cannot see the building behind it nor can the building's occupants peer into my windows; in winter the tree is bare, humbled but unbowed.

I think my experience of homelessness drew me to a respect for and fascination with trees. In addition to the cottonwoods outside my window, there are several other trees that have had significance in my life and that help keep me rooted. Christmas trees which as a Jewish family we did not possess come immediately to mind. Despite living in a predominantly Jewish environment as a child, the absence of the Christmas tree was always obvious because those trees were everywhere else—all over the television screens in advertisements for Christmas shoppers and in Hallmark holiday specials and Christmas movies: *Miracle on 34th Street, A Christmas Carol; It's a Wonderful Life*. On Thanksgiving day in New York City the Christmas trees from Vermont and New Hampshire were brought into line on the streets of the Upper West Side and made the air redolent with the winter fragrance of pine. I loved walking the streets then amidst these trees and their caretakers. Once, I almost purchased a very small shrub-like tree, but at that time though I had attempted to betray so much of my past I couldn't take this next step. One particular Christmas tree stood very tall and centrally located at Manhattan's core, in Rockefeller Center. I think I remember once visiting that tree, maybe even with Renee, even as I remember watching on the television the appearance of Santa Claus at the end of the Macy's Thanksgiving Day parade. His arrival always announced the start of the Christmas season to which as a Jew I was excluded. Later, indeed, much later, I studied a book titled, *The Battle for Christmas* written by Jewish Stephen Nissenbaum who explained that his fascination with Christmas derived from the experience of his exclusion from it. My maternal grandparents were married on Christmas Day and we celebrated the event at my Aunt Phyllis's house: she had a Christmas tree and the pretense of honoring the anniversary allowed us to exchange gifts that had been placed under it.

When I accepted a position at the University of Wisconsin-Stout in 1990, we moved to Menomonie, a semi-rural environment. I had come from New York City where outside of Central and Riverside Parks trees were in short supply. The four-acre property in Wisconsin to this New York Jew was as capacious as the Ponderosa! But on our property there existed no trees, no lawn, nothing but bare hard earth. I remember that as a joke a friend purchased for us a lone plastic pink flamingo for decoration, but

## Starting Out

the ground was so hard that the flamingo couldn't stand. We hadn't the slightest idea how to landscape our property, and so at some point early in our residence, a man named George, a real estate agent who on the side sold shrubbery, etc., advised us on landscape designing. In truth he was not a landscape architect, and George randomly threw a few bushes and three trees about our home. Of the bushes we purchased, I recall very little except that at some time too late I understood they required pruning care. In season and along the perimeter of their beds they had looked to me all green, but below their surface they were quite dead. (And there might there be an apt metaphor for something!) But the poplar tree George advocated grew healthily on the front lawn, and begun as a mere sapling, it grew finally to a height of thirty feet or more. I recall that the ground into which I placed it was very hard and I didn't (or couldn't) plant the sapling deep enough, and so its roots grew up through the surface and terraced the surface of the lawn and made grass cutting on my riding mower a very bumpy affair during the all too brief (thankfully) growing season. After almost thirty years, the poplar died. Coincidentally, I suppose, at its death I also vacated the premises. (Another metaphor?) George also recommended two maple trees: they grew very slowly, I recall, and one of them suffered a strong windstorm injury and became (pun intended) truncated!

There were eventually other trees in the backyard, a mountain ash I believe, purchased by my father during one of the summers when he and my mother visited Wisconsin from their retirement home in Florida. Wisconsin always surprised my father. The first time my parents visited us in the Midwest the plane landed at Minneapolis-St. Paul airport, and as we drove along I-94 toward Menomonie he looked out of the passenger window and wondered aloud at the farms along the way. He asked in all seriousness, "Do they have electricity out there?" I responded, "Yes, and indoor plumbing." That mountain ash began small and weak but over the years became strong and full. It was this very tree that our cats climbed bravely and then, having become stuck atop, cowardly whined and waited for me to climb the ladder and help them descend. Later, two black walnut trees, a gift from friends in honor of my father upon his death in 1999 grew in the backyard.

During the two years she spent in the Secret Annex, the solace Anne found in her chestnut tree provided a powerful contrast to the Holocaust unfolding beyond her attic window. I feel rooted by that tree. As the war narrowed the world for Anne and her family, her tree became a vivid reminder that a better world was possible. I have thought often of Anne Frank and the Secret Annex. I have two Jewish daughters. After twenty-five months hiding in the Secret Annex, living a life of horrific circumstances which defy my understanding, she ended her journey at Bergen-Belsen dying of typhus. I turn the last page of her diary—ah, and read, "Anne's diary ends here." What was all of her suffering for I asked myself. The incredible, almost impossibly inhuman physical discomfort, the perpetual terror of being discovered, the absolute, horrible claustrophobia of her existence defies my ability to conceptualize it. That hiding was supposed to be a journey, but where did it lead; what was it for? Never in over two full years to have gone outside to breathe the air, to play in a park, to walk to the store for food or candy or ice cream but only to finally exit into the stench of the camps and the horrible smoke coming from the crematoria. For twenty-five months to never live a moment without paralyzing fear and then to exit to that fear's real existence.

That chestnut tree somehow gave Anne comfort, even perhaps as Moses' view of the Promised Land which he would not enter after forty years wandering in the desert comforted him. From her view of the chestnut tree, Anne gained strength and hope. Somehow she drew strength from that tree outside her window that she would never touch, nor inhale its scent, nor hear its leaves rustle in the wind. I am reminded of O. Henry's story, "The Last Leaf." On her sick bed the dying young girl, Johnsy, stares out at the leaves fluttering down from the trees. She sighs and says, "I want to see the last one fall. I'm tired of waiting. I'm tired of thinking. I want to turn loose my hold on everything, and go sailing down, down, just like one of those poor, tired leaves."[4] She intends to die with the fall of the last leaf. But unbeknownst to her, the artist Old Behrman had climbed up that tree and painted a beautiful last leaf that does not fall and that restores Johnsy's will to live. And as she recovers Old Behrman dies from exposure to the cold he suffered atop the tree painting that last beautiful leaf that did not fall. There was for Anne Frank no Old Behrman and no last leaf.

I feel rooted and calmed by those trees outside of my window. Regardless of weather conditions though they bend they do not complain. They stand quietly and I think patiently. I have sometimes felt enfolded—somewhat at home in the environment of these trees.

---

4. O. Henry, "The Last Leaf," https://americanliterature.com/author/o-henry/short-story/the-last-leaf.

## Starting Out

### HEADING FOR HOME, MAYBE NOT TO ARRIVE

That digression into one tangle of roots has to now return to the origin story with which I began some pages back . . . On that baseball field back then I played at having skill until what seemed like the sky falling on my head proved to me otherwise. I think that I continued playing even after the ball struck my forehead. But maybe I slunk home: I really don't remember, or I have conveniently forgotten. In either case, I must have felt embarrassed. What I do know is that soon after that event I began to complain of experiencing fatigue and headaches. In all honesty (an empty phrase that reminds me of Holden's statement, "If you want to know the truth . . . "), I don't remember actually suffering any of these conditions. I think I just wanted to kvetch. And I wanted to lie in my bed during the day and read and listen to music and not have to go to school. I stayed home one day, two days, three days . . . at which point my parents called the doctor who lived down the block. As was the practice then, he had an office in his home where he daily received patients, but after office hours he would make house calls carrying his traditional black leather doctor bag. Perhaps when he examined me he shone a light in my eyes, but really of the experience I don't recall very much. Dr. Schmirer was a competent doctor and a kind man, and I was determined to convince him of my supposed symptoms. Perhaps he understood the necessity of believing me, and after a while he must have shrugged his shoulders, closed his bag and declared that I probably had suffered a mild concussion, and he advised continuous bed rest. I was satisfied. I would stay home from school for a while longer reading books and listening to music.

I ascribe to this occasion the onset of the effectiveness of illness and my turn to hypochondria. As I said, from my present distance in time and place I don't believe that I actually experienced any of the symptoms of which I had complained; the complaint itself was enough to give me a sense of independence. Being sick was empowering. And if I did not (ever) receive in my home the notice I desired and required, I did for a while control their attention and I did manage to stay home from school and away from the anxiety I suffered there. In any case, the account of my baseball experience is a nice story and helps me construct an interesting narrative of my life.

Until I broke my ankle in 2005 this so-called concussion was the most serious medical event I had experienced in my life though it did alert my consciousness to the efficacy of bodily harm. Prior to this occasion I had never really suffered an actual injury despite the complaint of a concussion.

## Anxious Am I?

When I was three or four years old, my mother had insisted on cosmetic removal of birthmarks on my eyebrow and lips and then in my early teens an excision of some dark moles on my chest. None had bothered me but about them she was obviously troubled. Sometime before I was ten years old, I had my tonsils and adenoids removed, and enjoyed several days of ice cream feasts. Once I included my finger in the cut when I sliced through a bagel— this resulted in six stitches for the finger and cream cheese for the bagel. I've had the occasional root canal work and a few painful tooth extractions. Aside from my hypochondriacal tendency, I acknowledge that I have seemed a somewhat healthy and aging specimen. I continue to consume large doses of mega-vitamins and for a long while outside of these supplements, I required no other medications.

And then I broke the ankle while running in the early morning hours in the month of March in the year 2005. There was nothing hypochondriacal about this event. During the day the ice on the roads melted but then refroze overnight. As I ran in the early dark morning, I lost my footing on some patch of ice, slipped, upended, and came down somehow with a foot twisted horridly awry. Without thinking I attempted to twist it back, as if I had merely to screw it back on to repair the damage, but I had no success there. My running companion on that morning then ran what he claims to have been a sub-four-minute mile back to our starting point where we had parked our cars and he drove above the speed limit back to where I remained sitting and moaning on the ice. He packed me into the front seat of his pick-up truck, and with him moaning in sympathetic misery we raced to the nearby hospital. By the time we arrived at the emergency room, there was a swelling the size of a tennis ball on the inside of my right ankle.

Interestingly, I did not suffer great pain: some said it was the result of my endorphins, others that it was due to psychic numbing. Even when I had tried to turn my foot aright, I had felt nothing. I simply lay there anguished that there would be no more running for some time; I could not imagine how I would psychically survive this abrupt cessation. At the time I had been running for thirty some odd years and had never rested for more than four days in a row, had never paused any longer than that from taking my thoughts and my anxieties out on the road. I now envisioned too many troubled months ahead. I decided to schedule an appointment with the psychotherapist.

I had to have surgery on the ankle, during which they placed pins and plates and other implements of construction into the broken bones.

## Starting Out

In recovery, I could hardly move. Every event had to be carefully planned. Whereas before I had been completely mobile, now I had become completely immobile. I could not easily get up from my chair to get an extra pencil; to find a book from the shelf; to walk into the bathroom with any ease. Once my hypochondria had served as a means of psychic motility, and now I moved about only with physical supports. I couldn't carry my laptop about with me, nor plug it in to what had now become an inconveniently located outlet. I could not arise from my labors easily to make another cup of coffee—not because I could not get to the stove (though it was certainly a chore to maneuver there on my crutches), but because I could not return to my desk on those crutches and also carry the filled cup. I found myself imagining such inventions as secure hooks onto which one could hang things like stoppered (!) coffee mugs, or mini-shelves to carry buttered hunks of French bread and sliced green apples or a plate of chocolate chip cookies. Such attachments would free my hands to still maintain balance on the crutches and permit travel. Suddenly, the world had to be rethought and reorganized from the position of immobility. For example, the simple trip to the bathroom demanded energy to lift the computer from my lap and find some temporary resting place for it, reach then for my crutches, lift myself out of my chair, schlep myself to the toilet—upon which for ease I now would sit—and then schlep myself back to my chair, awkwardly opening assorted doors along the way. I preferred to remain in the comfy chair, albeit sitting a bit uncomfortably. I thought that I might use the return trip from the bathroom to grab a breakfast repast in the kitchen through which I would pass to return to my seat. I would dine standing at the counter. Conservation of energy.

Whereas I was once completely independent, suddenly I felt completely dependent. This condition had rendered me in exactly the opposite position of my hypochondria: over my body now I had no control! Oh, I do not mean to exaggerate nor romanticize my condition—I remember, that I yet controlled at least my bodily functions and maintained all of my F-A-C-U-L-T-I-E-S, and, of course, I still could hobble about on crutches. But I could not, as the cliché went, eat and chew gum at the same time. I could move on crutches into the next room, but I could not also carry my book along with me. I could still enjoy a dish of Ben & Jerry's ice cream cone, but not while I was walking on my crutches down the street or even into the next room.

So many unassuming acts now had acquired assumption. I was forced to rest wholly and completely. I could neither run nor walk. I could not drive nor swim. I could not cook nor clean. I was consigned to my chair, desk and books. I had to remain immobile. Oddly enough, I learned, there is a privileged sense of freedom if not control in that restriction.

Today in addition to my hypochondriacal tendencies I have actual health issues. I think it interesting that people preferred to hear more about the imaginary than the real though I would rather suffer the former than the latter. I had been diagnosed with an aortic aneurysm and hypertrophic cardiomyopathy. It took me several years to learn to say the latter abnormality much less understand it. The conditions were discovered in a CT scan ordered for an issue wholly unrelated to my heart. Indeed, were it not for this unrelated issue—having to do with my lungs, actually—I wouldn't have learned that I had an enlarged aorta and a bicuspid valve and would have then remained innocent of imminent mortality as opposed to living anxiously with a neurotic anticipation of same. Having learned that I had an enlarged aorta, I suddenly felt the weight of mortality and I physically and psychically felt substantively different. I was the same, but I was also not the same. The aortic aneurysm was a structural issue: there were no pills or therapies that can cure it. Surgery remained the ultimate treatment. I returned to the psychoanalyst.

After a lifetime characterized by periodic outbreaks of hypochondria, the occurrence of an actual medical condition had cast a strange light on life. The hypochondriacal tendency had offered to me a perverse control over the body and events in which it should engage, but this too real medical condition suggested an actual lack of control. Its presence resulted in serious angst for which Xanax was the cure. What about this knowledge that made it so threatening recalled to me the story in *Genesis* of Adam and Eve and the Tree of Knowledge. That knowledge was of sex and death, I guess exactly the realities that that other tree might have made unnecessary. The knowledge of death made life precious exactly because it guaranteed that it would end and so the work outside of the garden from which Adam and Eve were now banished had to be done now. For years I have believed that leaving the Garden started their lives. In the Garden there was, indeed, nothing to be done. It was outside the Garden where the work had to take place; outside the Garden, life was hardly perfect and the world (young as it was) was in need of repair. This knowledge of an enlarged aorta and my inevitable death endeared me to life and the work of tikkun olam. I recognize that it is a cliché that awareness of our mortality makes life the more precious—the conclusion of the television series *The Good Place* seemed based on this premise. But this knowledge of the condition of my heart opened a new perspective on my life in which my mortality played a greater part and has had a greater influence.

It has now been at least fifteen years since the first diagnosis and my condition is yet unchanged. This aortic enlargement is in a stage right now that though it is still psychically troublesome yet remains today consistently stable; it may not require further attention for another several years or even another decade or two. But somewhere down the line, when I want to live longer, they will have to fix my heart! Ironically, it is a repair I have sought for years.

## ANOTHER ORIGIN STORY

Along with wanting to be a beatnik and then a hippie, and certainly more than becoming a doctor, I wanted to be a writer. I read voraciously and being an author seemed a most glorious way to spend my time. To create new worlds into which others might venture; to offer characters with whom others could commune and from whose lives one might draw comfort and direction seemed to me valuable work. Ironically, I have no memory of journaling during my adolescence. I may have at one time received a journal complete with lock and key as a gift, but I have no recollection of ever writing in one, and if such tome exists it has not survived. No such volume exists anywhere in my archives that are now kept safely at the university library. However, I began to keep extensive personal and reading journals steadily from my early twenties and have continued to do so for the past half-century. For a number of years, I carried about with me an assortment of notebooks and pads into which I would deposit bits of my consciousness that I would then incorporate into a piece of writing. Often the insights and thoughts were connected to what I was reading or viewing at the time. I spent a great deal of time at the cinema, and I composed not a few unpublished movie reviews. During some years I purchased large and rather heavy accounting registers to record my reading notes and personal ruminations. In order to transport such volumes, I discovered I needed larger and larger bags—this before the ubiquity of daily backpacks—and so began the search for what I would later refer to as ManBags. And I also began to purchase banker's boxes to store the journals when the pages of each had been filled. Thus also began the cluttering of spaces in my various apartment and house dwellings.

I have been from an early age enthralled with learning, and that learning became associated with the process of writing. Driven by a seemingly insatiable, indiscriminate curiosity, I sought to know—Come Watson, the game's afoot! I wanted to know everything. I remember once as a prepubescent—I don't think I was past the age of thirteen—deciding that I would write a history of the world. My ambitions then were not slight. At my student desk in my downstairs bedroom, away from almost everyone, I began this opus by copying out word for word just such a narrative from the history of the world entry in the World Book Encyclopedia that my parents had purchased from a door-to-door encyclopedia salesperson. These volumes were intended specifically for the use of their children for I am almost certain that neither mother nor father ever opened a single volume. Perhaps the purchase was part of the rituals of middle-class life on Long Island in the post-World War II world to which my parents longed to belong. In that attempt my father even once joined the Republican Party because he thought it would be good for his business. The move was a fruitless exercise because he regularly drove himself (and others) out of business. But ironically, whenever my father entered a voting booth he always voted for the Democrat fearful that if he touched the other lever God would immediately strike him with a bolt of lightning!

I wanted to learn and I wanted to be known as an author. I seemed somehow to have understood that writing was the means by which to learn and by which to establish some presence in the world. I was convinced that my history of the world, plagiarized thought it would be, ought to lead to that knowledge and to that position. But admittedly, as I copied the narrative out of the white leather-bound tomes, I must have imagined I was doing something consequential. Alas, my history of the world didn't make it very far; my hand began to cramp somewhere just prior to the Middle Ages. But in the process I came to understand that I wouldn't finish my history of the world because the world kept on keeping on even as I wrote; and more alarmedly, I began to understand that even if I did finish my history of the world I still wouldn't know everything. Or maybe know anything at all. That doubt would carry into my engagement with postmodernism when I even called my Self into question. This realization, however, must have been a first step toward my present ironic stance. And I think I found pleasure in writing and I found that learning did accompany and was inspired by it. I continued to purchase pens and pencils—I write now mostly with fountain pens—and I purchase Moleskin books for journaling. But I did come to understand that writing was hard work and that its rewards were hard wrung. The ink in the fountain pens sometimes dries up or runs out.

I remember my next serious attempt to become a writer. For a high school English class we were assigned to write a short story—I seem to recall a seven-to ten-page limit—I chose as my form what I had learned as satire. It was a story that spoke against capital punishment and concerned a man awaiting execution for smoking a cigarette. A bit prescient, I think now. Then the only smokers I knew were my parents, and I recognize now in my story writing not a few deeply oedipal issues. The story itself has long disappeared from any known files, but I remember vividly that when I proudly showed the story about to my small circle of friends they laughed derisively at it. Aside from the judgments I regularly faced from my parents, this was the first public experience of ridicule for a literary effort. I suffered an anxious shame from which I do not believe I have really ever quite recovered. They were cruel or just insensitive, and I placed too much weight on their opinion. Back then, I think, I suffered from too much sanity—I have since put more wine in my cup—but I believe also that I have never quite recovered from that first harsh dismissal, misspoken as it was.

I persisted nevertheless, and continued to write and to explore, to write and to learn. In my classes and at college I enjoyed writing papers. Throughout undergraduate and graduate education, I elected always to address not the suggested topics but one of my own choosing. I enjoyed the tortured process of writing my ideas down on paper, of thinking through ideas and creating sentences that followed reasonably from the previous ones and that led logically to the next. It was wonderful to see what I thought and to shape my thought by what I could write. I have since written ten books and dozens of articles and book chapters and I continue to fill journals that fit into an assortment of ManBags. I have kept a blog for sixteen years. I'm even at work now on this pseudo-memoir!

# BEFORE THE MASTS

## GOOD TROUBLE, SMALL REBELLIONS

JOHN Lewis, who died of pancreatic cancer in 2020 after a lifetime of civil rights activism and public service, and who from 1986 served as a member from Georgia in the U.S. House of Representatives, urged citizens to engage in what he referred to as "good trouble." I think that by good trouble Lewis meant that which is undertaken in pursuit of a more just society. Good trouble is a necessary trouble. Lewis urged, "When you see something that is not right, not fair, you have a moral obligation to say something, to do something." Good trouble is action in the pursuit of freedom; freedom was not a final destination but an act. He said, "Freedom is the continuous action we all must take, and each generation must do its part to create an ever more fair, more just society." I think that good trouble occurs from a belief in the possibility of a society where the measure of a person's worth is not dependent on money, or skin color, or gender or sexual preference; good trouble fights against inequality and against domestic and foreign oppression.

I don't know what catalyzed my belief in good trouble: perhaps it was the assassination of President Kennedy which introduced into my consciousness the existence of evil in world; perhaps it was my growing awareness of the civil rights movement and the violence that ensued and that led to the murder of four young girls in the cowardly bombing of the Birmingham church. I had been raised in a wholly segregated intentionally white environment. Perhaps I was horrified by the shooting of Medgar Evers and the beatings of the Freedom Riders and the marchers across the Edmund Pettis Bridge; perhaps it was my developing horror at the structural inequalities built into societies and especially that of the United States; perhaps it arose from my immersion in folk music that often spoke of social injustice and the necessity of good trouble that had been already undertaken and that which was still to come. Or perhaps it was the developing sense that things were not right in my home and that to maintain a semblance of order I had had to suppress my dreams. There was there no space for happiness, no notion even that happiness should be sought for and hard-won.

## Anxious Am I?

Certainly, in my home I experienced no freedom: I had been trapped in their nightmares. But out there I saw that there were people doing what Lewis would call good trouble, and I thought that I might become a part of some movement that was so engaged. I could disrupt and maybe realize some freedom.

I was not conscious during high school and college of engaging in anything that approached the actions of good trouble; then I might have characterized my behavior as merely rebellious, but mostly I was trying to keep from drowning. Mine were small rebellions. I was oxymoronically a cautious rebel: I frequented the coffee houses where socially conscious and political active folk music played, but I avoided attending with Sharon Reinhart and Sandy Wasserman the venues where played the Rolling Stones. Once the two returned from a concert in possession of what they said were T-shirts given to them by Mick Jagger and Keith Richard. I enviously imagined how they had acquired those prizes! I wore the buttons but hadn't the authority or the courage to ride the buses. I read *Do It!* and *Revolution for the Hell of It*, but I didn't actively join any movement nor really engage in anything that could be known as good trouble. But I began to slowly recognize that there might be a difference between the trouble that I thought was in me and that made me as I thought disagreeable, and the trouble I could cause because I was all right and could engage in doing something true and moral. I read Thoreau's "Civil Disobedience" and studied Sartre's *Anti-Semite and Jew*. I read everything I was assigned and more! I adopted existentialism as a personal philosophy and understood the absurd as reality. I began to understand that I could be disagreeable and not only in opposition to an unjust society and in the service of justice and social equality, but also in the assertion of personal release and freedom from my family and culture of origin. When I joined my parents at their dinner tables loud and rancorous arguments took place about almost everything. I accepted a moral obligation to right some wrongs and cause good trouble and I wanted my independence from their lives. I began to rebel in greater ways against my parents, my school, and my government. At some later point I joined the Marxist Society and there studied *Capital* with Michael Harrington. It took years for that rebellion to finally birth a man; I think that I am still busy being born.

I think about the kid in Buddy Mondlock's song who admits, "I'm the kid who has this habit of dreaming/Sometimes gets me in trouble too." I have learned the habit of dreaming, and at least one thing that I learned from my dreams was that sometimes the product of my dreaming could lead to an engagement in good trouble. At the beginning I was not terribly brave and I marched to the beat of someone else's steadfast drum, but a moment did finally arrive when I felt compelled to do something that was not familiar to me. At the time, and it remains so even still, my world was the school and in study, and it was there that eventually I undertook to engage in what I might now call good trouble. In November 1969, two months into my first teaching position, on an early Friday morning, I called in sick so that I could travel to Washington, D.C., and join the November March on Washington. I think now that this was a small move into the public world of protest. I had spent much of my college years with my fraternity brothers considering ways to avoid the draft: allergy shots, physical disabilities, mental illnesses of all sort. Now I felt compelled to go to Washington, to carry the name of a soldier killed in Vietnam to the coffin set before the White House—shout his name out loud, we were advised— and to march the next day along Pennsylvania Avenue in a show of mass protest. Sayville, where I taught, was a conservative district despite its proximity to Cherry Grove, the gay community on Fire Island. Sayville's politics supported the war.

I wasn't at all sick but perhaps I was getting well. I remember the phone call I made immediately after arising in the morning hoping to sound desperately ill and being terribly worried that the ruse wouldn't work. I think that in those days we had to actually speak to a live person and probably it was the principal, Mr. Limouze, to whom I moaned and rasped. I thought I might have been convincing, but then the black arm band and buttons declaring the war unjust that I wore after that weekend might have suggested otherwise. Also suspect was my refusal to lead my homeroom class in the Pledge of Allegiance every morning. Perhaps the last straw occurred at a high school basketball game when I and the newly hired and long-haired math teacher, Jeffrey Wasserman, chose not to stand for the national anthem. Behind us were sitting two board of education members. At the end of the year I was informed that my contract would not be renewed. My evaluations thus far had been exemplary, and so I wondered aloud why I was being fired. The principal, Mr. Limouze, looked at me disdainfully and said, "Think about it." I have thought long about it since then.

Dreaming does sometimes get me in trouble. After Sayville and unemployment and a carefully executed failure at my draft physical exam, I accepted an unfortunate position in my father's clothes factory making very inexpensive ladies and children's wear. I was appalled at the minimum salaries paid to the workers—rats ran through the factory and within the walls from which the smell of death emanated—and as the union contracts came up for renewal I argued for awarding considerable raises. I became a favorite of the union representative. Eventually, my father's abysmal business sense and my socialist urgings drove the company to bankruptcy, and I was released from a form of imprisonment. I consider now with some horror that but for that failure, I might have spent the rest of my life in a business for which I had no interest and no real ability. I returned to the classroom first at Eastern District High School in Brooklyn, New York, serving as a reading tutor, and then in 1974 I was hired at North High School in Great Neck on Long Island, where over the next fourteen years I engaged in different kinds of good trouble. I thought that school and learning could be both fun and socially responsible and I organized a curriculum that promoted those goals.

For me, as I have said, school had been fraught with anxiety. I had had companions but perhaps not friends. I was the outlier aspiring to belong but sensing that I would always be adjudged as falling just short. I wasn't considered smart enough, athletic enough, politically astute enough, social enough. It was a traumatic life back then. But as now a teacher I wanted to create spaces where others need not suffer those anxious feelings. Perhaps I hoped that my students—and over the years there were many of them—would experience high school differently than I had. In my first year at Great Neck I organized an all-day Shakespeare Festival that transformed the entire school into a celebration of the Bard's birthday. The event disrupted the normal workings of that school day. Teachers dressed as their favorite Shakespearean character: I wore a suit of inky black and for a short while I could be Hamlet, a play from which I was excluded in high school from studying because I was not deemed intelligent enough. On Shakespeare Day, while I recited Hamlet's soliloquies (in a style I hoped that aped that of Richard Burton's Broadway performance) and Carolee played Ophelia; and Larry in his robe and politically incorrect black face wept because soon he would murder Desdemona, the school became Elizabethan. The music department sauntered through the halls singing madrigals; the home economics department baked Elizabethan goodies. The school principal, dear Red Noyes, paraded the halls as Shakespeare himself! I recall this as a glorious day though there were not a few faculty who disapproved vociferously and refused to join the festivities.

Another time I organized an all-day Saturday festival that began with a concert of folk music offered by student musicians, that was followed by a catered fried chicken dinner. Following the meal that had been served in the school cafeteria, we moved into the gymnasium for a traditional square dance called by an authentic and well-paid professional. At another time and along with several politically active and astute students we founded and I advised the North Star, a left-wing publication of political and social comment and critique that was written and edited wholly by students. For several years I advised the school yearbook and served as sponsor for the senior class. In this latter position, I proposed a few nontraditional options for activities. As an idea for an egalitarian and affordable senior prom I offered the possibility of a lobster bake at Jones Beach rather than the traditionally extravagant affair of gowns and tuxedos, orchids, expensive restaurant dinners and all-night parties. I was overruled. And then again: once the expansive lawn in front of Great Neck North High School was divided by a concrete path to keep students from taking the easiest route to the street by trudging across the grass that had then each year to be reseeded. After our study of Walden, we considered that the cement pathway seemed to be nature despoiled, and my English classes petitioned the school board and the principal for monies to plant flowers to border and grace the concrete. They surprisingly agreed and several days later the class had graced the walkway with color. Small rebellions but rebellions nonetheless. I was still learning and dreaming.

My classes remained free of seating assignments; I thought of the room as open space where the measure of achievement was not grades but engagement. I had come to think of the classroom as most sacred ground, and I dreamed that I could bring others to the prayer that was study. I thought of Thoreau's beanfield: *Walden* was a book I taught every year to every class. It was not the yield of beans that was significant to Thoreau but his engagement in the activity. Thoreau sought study and the bean field became the place for that endeavor. Our study, I hoped, would open the world to awe and wonder and makes us holy. Our study might lead to engagement in good trouble. I urged my students to join me in the quest. Though Great Neck provided sufficient materials for our classrooms, I wasn't so much interested in teaching anything specific so much as inspiring curiosity and the love of learning. I wanted to seduce students to the delights of study and activism. Another dear principal, Bernard Ludwig, once entered my classroom during a discussion of Thoreau's *Walden* to find students sprawled about in their chairs and on the floor and myself seated atop a file cabinet, French scarves wrapped about my neck and a hat labeled Thoreau atop my head purchased for me by a student who found it at the bookstore of a college she was visiting. During our post-observation discussion, Bernie told me that were this any other classroom he would have been concerned, but that he recognized a good teacher when he saw one, and that I was engaged in a good trouble.

These were all small rebellions, I recognize now, but at the time I was listening for the beatings of my drum. I intended to effect good trouble...

But, oh mother, things didn't always go so well. When I went to the university my efforts too often inspired only strong complaint and caused me real trouble. I recall a regular critique offered by students over the years:

> Don't ask him a question and expect an answer. All he'll do is ask you another question. Terrible teacher!

I had believed that the question kept the conversation open whereas the answer closed it down. I did ask a great many questions and did not offer many answers. But over the years as students were transformed into clients and our lives in academia became ever more quantified and organized by the numbers, students as customers came to expect satisfaction and ease. In the United States the mantra has long been that "the customer is always right!" And my students became wholly focused on the good grades for which they had paid. Sometimes, it got me in trouble.

> I had Dr. Block when I attended Stout for my undergrad. I found his course to be extremely challenging and very hard to understand. Somehow, if I remember correctly, I managed to get an A. From experience with him during that time I did not wish to have him again for this program, which is why I specifically asked a representative from UW-Stout if any other teachers taught the courses listed in the sequence besides the ones listed on the information pamphlet.

And this:

> I was not going to say anything, but since several students in the class have expressed an overwhelming stress re: the amount of coursework expected—both reading and submittal requirements, as well as a lack of response from instructor re: student coursework questions and feedback on assignments submitted. Most of us work full-time and for the most part the students are answering their own questions through the discussion format and that

is part of the objective, but the time we spend helping each other with course organization questions means less time reading and discussing the assignments which are increasing in volume every two days(two days being the same as one week in the regular class format).

But at other times there were other and differing opinions:

Curriculum Theory has been a different class than what I am used to. I took this online class because I assumed it would allow me to go on during my hours of convenience. However, this is not the case. I had to lower my work hours to spend more time online just for this class. This class requires a lot of time, which was not expected. Maybe I went wrong here thinking so. My online courses that I took over the years are nothing compared to this class. This class has been a struggle and challenging course. The material is hard to grasp, but once you understand some part of it, the material is very interesting. Makes me feel like my entire schooling years have been fake/unauthentic all along. The class is moving and has some high standards because of the students. This course is a challenge.

And sometimes I could no more stop dreaming:

Dr. Block has generated the kind of learning environment I dream of generating as an educator. He's caused me to really examine what I do as an educator when it comes to curriculum theory and to realize that there are no simple answers. He's done this in a matter of weeks and I know I'll be forever changed and (more importantly) better because of this learning experience. The reason this has worked so well is that Dr. Block has allowed me to realize this on my own; subtly he led me there.

And this:

In all of my efforts as an educator and student, I have never experienced any instructor that has been able to bring the philosophy and theory of their writings to the class with such success. In fact some of the instructors in my undergrad teacher preparation were well versed in textbook educational methods, yet did not bring those teaching strategies to the classroom. When Dr. Block's paper on "Curriculum as Affichiste" describes learning as building new meaning from materials that are already present it sounds great theoretically. Then when we are given the opportunity to do just that with his "Complicated Conversations" assignment, we see that it is possible to bring obtuse educational concepts to our teaching! In his book *Talmud, Curriculum and the Practical,* Dr. Block argued not that answers be discovered, but that discovered answers be interrogated. In our discussion posts, and our Complicated Conversation assignment, this was regularly and positively encouraged. It is my assertion that this is an example of enlightening teaching, by a model teacher.

I think that maybe each and other responses are correct, but I have a habit of dreaming, and sometimes . . .

Dreaming I had learned and hoped to teach didn't lead to Truth but was itself truth. And dreaming often led me into good trouble. Good trouble came from dreaming. The dream, however, is sometimes somewhat inarticulable, and when I struggled to fit the dream into words or actions, I experienced anxiety. I sputtered at times, and I was not always comprehended. Thoreau admits, "I would give all the wealth of the world, and all the deeds of all the heroes, for one true vision. But how can I communicate with the gods who am a pencil-maker on earth, and not be insane?"[1] We are poor indeed if we are only sane. Thoreau's humility humbles me and reminds me that my dreaming might appear marked by folly but is ultimately wisdom. I know that Thoreau certainly dreamt, and it often got him in trouble. And I do not think he was afraid of appearing absurd; his drummer beat a different tune. I think of Pip in *Moby-Dick* who fell from the decks of the Pequod and before he was rescued had sunk into the ocean where lived the White Whale. Hauled back onto the ship, Pip had become insane. Ishmael writes, "Pip had seen God's foot upon the treadle of the loom, and spoke it; and therefore, his shipmates called him mad. So man's insanity is heaven's sense . . . "[2] I pour a bit more wine into my cup.

Ironically, Thoreau, whom many would have described as not quite sane, had been, indeed, a pencil maker in the family business and had been a rather skillful one at that. At work in the factory, he developed a method to make pencils that were equal and even superior in quality to those made in Europe. He studied German and French techniques, and in that endeavor had even learned some German and French. Thoreau pencils came to dominate the United States market, but he left the pencil-making factory to become a teacher, a career he cut short when he was required to cane students. I have myself not caned a single student though I have too

1. Thoreau, *A Week*, 170.
2. Melville, *Moby Dick*, 413.

often whipped them with grades. *Mea culpa.* I do, however, continue to employ contemporary exemplars of Thoreau's pencils in my intellectual and emotional pursuits with the awareness that all of Thoreau's pencils would be insufficient to the task: even if there were one true vision and I could speak it, my shipmates would call me mad. But I know that I would be poor indeed if I were only sane. I think it is my willingness to welcome such insanity that allows me to create. Adam Phillips says that "Creativity, what Winnicott would later call creative living—involved the search for, and attempt to establish a medium, an environment, a relationship that could survive the person's most passionate destructiveness."[3] Such a medium, an environment, and relationship can be worked into something new and imaginative. This progress might often look like the activity of an insane person, might even be so, as in the case of Vincent Van Gogh. But I think such activity might be understood as the mark of a greater sanity. I, too, have the habit of dreaming.

Psychoanalyst Adam Phillips says that our capacity for creativity as akin to an insanity that he refers to ironically as the condition of the deeply sane. I have long happily engaged in questioning my sanity. Ironically, so too have not a few of my dear acquaintances. Phillips assigns such anxious creativity to what he calls "the deeply sane," to those who maintain their integrity and self-reliance despite the pressures and even the calumnies of the social world. The deeply sane are those who march to the beat of a different drummer and who adamantly refuse, often at some personal and social cost, to live lives of quiet desperation. The deeply sane enjoy the presence of conflict for the provocation it offers for engagement and growth; they do not seek harmony, consistency, or redemption, but neither do they resort to fighting or violence. Sometimes it gets them in trouble, too. *Mea culpa.* The deeply sane experience no need to be believed, though they do insist on being heard. D.W. Winnicott says that it is a foolhardiness to insist on being believed; I have at times indulged in this stupidity and sometimes even with the ones whom I loved the best. I have become anxious. But the deeply sane are comfortable not only with their own doubts but with those of others.

I have learned that wisdom sometimes matures at great cost. The deeply sane enjoy that effort though it doesn't come without anxiety and even some pain. When they are dissatisfied, the deeply sane are inspired to act and not to complain: they get pleasure from the problems that life presents and they do not retreat from the challenge; they do not blame

---

3. Phillips, *On Kissing, Tickling, and Being Bored*, 39.

others for the vexing situation. The deeply sane seek out situations that will challenge them; this often gets me in trouble. Says Ishmael, "Know ye, now, Bulkington? Glimpses do ye see of that mortally intolerable truth; that all deep, earnest thinking is but the intrepid effort of the soul to keep the open independence of the sea . . . "[4] It is an insanity to avoid the safety of the Lee Shore, but Ishmael knows that though the winds blow him towards home, the ship will founder on that shore. Freedom exists in the dangers of the open waters and in the search for the White Whale.

**THE OPENING SEA**

Sometime in the latter part of the 1970s, I traveled to France with two confreres. I have put my journals in the university archives and so I am unsure of the exact dates of this journey, but we three men were public school English teachers in Great Neck, New York; we were not friends, just colleagues, I suppose, but in conversations (probably in department meetings), we discovered a common desire to travel to France. Our plan was to spend some time in Paris and then to rent a car and travel south to Dijon. Or maybe we didn't rent a car but instead purchased a relatively inexpensive Eurail Pass. I don't remember. In any case, it was our intention to spend a week in Paris and then to head south.

We arrived at Orly Airport and took the tram into the city arriving somewhat after noon. We had found—I don't remember how— a garret room contiguous to the Luxembourg Gardens. Jim and Fred lay down to nap, but I was too excited to sleep. I was intent on the voyage. Leaving them asleep I headed down to the Seine and the Left Bank. I wanted to find Shakespeare and Company, the bookstore known for its friendliness to the American expatriates and for the support it gave James Joyce in the publication of *Ulysses*. Then, this English language bookstore had been owned by Sylvia Beach, but now its proprietor was George Whitman, a distant descendant I learned, of the poet, Walt. As I strolled leisurely along the banks of the Seine, I passed a varied array of stands selling all manner of things; I think I might have then purchased a thin, cloth scarf, or perhaps two or three scarves, that I then wore regularly over the next several years. Across the river towered the Cathedral of Notre Dame. But I knew that it was not yet time to enter that edifice; that visit would wait for another day. I was at the moment on a different search.

4. Melville, *Moby Dick*, 105.

## Before the Masts

During the Spring semester I had enrolled in a graduate course on Joyce's *Ulysses*, had read and studied that novel, and excitedly now was in the environs in which Joyce had roamed and where he had found finally a publisher for his controversial book. And now even as I turned about and away from Cathedral of Notre Dame, I saw before me the painted yellow sign: Shakespeare and Company. The shop (I am loath to refer to Shakespeare and Company as a store!) seemed tucked into a corner; outside and along the river in front of the door there were carts and shelves of used books stacked on tables and carts. Shakespeare and Company had been and remained even then an establishment heavy with English-language books. I resolved to purchase at least one book there. For a while I browsed through the shelves: mostly I was interested in the work of the American expatriates. I had been studying them at the time in graduate school, fascinated with their apparent abilities to leave home, a struggle with which I was then engaged. I can't remember how I managed to identify the owner, George Whitman, but I screwed my courage to the sticking place and approached this thin, bearded, white-haired man. "I understand that you have an original volume of Joyce's *Ulysses*," I said. "I wonder if perhaps I could see it." He looked at me, shook his head and denied any such ownership. I persisted: "I know that Sylvia Beach helped publish the book and I heard rumor that an original volume may still exist here." "No," he said smiling, "no such thing exists here." And he turned away from me.

I was disappointed but not forlorn. I was, after all, still in Paris and at Shakespeare and Company. I returned to the filled shelves. And after some minutes I was approached by an attractive young woman. "Would you like to come upstairs and have a cup of tea?" she asked. I was a bit stunned; these kinds of invitations did not usually occur to me. With women I was particularly shy, probably, as I have learned since, a result of an anxious home life and a depressed, narcissistic mother. But this young woman smiled beautifully, and added, "I have something I can show you." Here seemed an offer I couldn't refuse, and I followed her up a set of stairs and into a small room over the bookstore. This was not a bedroom, but in my memory, it was also not an office. I think George lived there, actually, and this seemed a kind of living room. She led me to a chair and on the table before me was indeed, a blue bound text of Joyce's *Ulysses*. At least I remember now it was blue though of course I might be mistaken, but the volume was certainly Joyce's *Ulysses*. I opened the book and read: "Stately plump Buck Mulligan came from the stairhead, bearing a bowl of lather on which a mirror and a razor lay crossed." It was the first sentence in this very difficult and to my sense wonderful book. I paged gingerly and silently through the volume, drank my tea and engaged in I suppose some small talk with the beautiful young woman. I returned not a few times to Shakespeare and Company, but I never saw either the sacred volume or the young woman again. In the end, however, the experience served as a wonderful beginning to the voyage aboard my Pequod. From the shelves I pulled a copy of Ford Madox Ford's novel, *The Good Soldier*.

I don't know what had inspired me to engage with George or the unnamed woman at Shakespeare and Company. It was not a life-changing event, and it did not dramatically alter my existence. I had always been a somewhat timid individual and have remained so since. I suffered then and now from too much anxiety. It wasn't even that this was my first trip abroad: I had almost fifteen years previously traveled for ten weeks in Europe with a somewhat difficult companion and had later taken holiday in Israel when my sister lived there and to where my brother traveled from his semester abroad in England to tour the land for a bit with me. But this time in France I felt like I had chosen to sail before the mast: I think I considered that I was finally leaving home and I had landed in this voyage first in Paris and at Shakespeare and Company. It was a tentative start to a lifetime of leave-taking and arriving. This whole trip with two relative strangers was an adventure. And I had entered into the trip overly optimistic of my capacity to sail. But there were complications. By this trip's end the tensions in the relationships had created some unpleasantness between us three, and I spent greater periods of time wandering by myself through streets and passageways though not really feeling alone.

And during the next summer I returned to Europe for six weeks intending to travel solo. Then I was in the throes of other dreams, sometimes drug-induced, but sometimes I found myself experiencing ironic moments that pierced through my sought-for anonymity. I was again trying to leave home but on three separate occasions as I traveled to three separate locations I encountered recent students, one busking on the streets of Paris, one at a youth hostel, and one on the streets of Florence, Italy. As was I they were no less surprised, and as was I were they visibly dismayed by the meetings. While in Paris, I roamed through Père Lachaise Cemetery paying respects to various visionaries interred there. Oscar Wilde. Honoré de Balzac. Marcel Proust. Abelard and Heloise. Jim Morrison. At that time Morrison's gravesite was unprotected and about the site there was debris and celebrations of different sorts. Cards, illustrations, emptied liquor bottles, half-smoked joints. There were also handwritten notes scattered about the gravesite; the one I recall so vividly read in French, "Jim, he loved the colours." I have thought often of that note. I, too, love the colors. I drank Pernod at La Coupole with two Canadian sisters and listened to a rehearsal of Fauré's *Requiem* at the Cathedral of Notre Dame. I did my morning runs in Jardin du Luxembourg and enjoyed coffee in the afternoon at a café. One night I attended a performance in French of Ionesco's Rhinoceros, though I didn't understand very much of the dialogue. I had read the play in English for my high school term paper, and so I had some sense of what was occurring.

Another night I took the subway out into the suburbs of Paris for a concert by Lou Reed in a high school gym: it seemed that even in Paris I found my ballast in the school. There I had brought some marijuana and I shared the joints with whoever stood next to me. On another day I signed into a tour at the Cinematèque Française that to my dismay was led completely in French. Behind me was an Italian man who recognized my frustration and undertook to translate the tour as we moved on. After the tour Vieri and I had coffee and he invited me to visit him when I got to Rome. Vieri lived in a very large rooftop apartment that his father had purchased for him, a very bourgeois perk I thought at the time, but remarkably every day a housekeeper would arrive to clean and arrange it and Vieri paid handsomely for the service. Vieri Razzini was employed by RAI television to purchase American television shows for Italian viewing. He knew a great deal about cinema and on one of his buying trips we met at a townhouse where he was staying in New York City. While visiting with Vieri in Rome, I spent most evenings with him and his friends at nightly potluck dinners. Vieri always brought a risotto, and though I did not understand very much at all of the conversation held wholly in Italian (what else?), the regular gatherings of left-wing newspaper editors, writers and actors taught me about a community that I would come to desire to create for myself.

Eventually I left Paris and headed to Monet's gardens at Giverny. On that journey I traveled with a lovely Italian woman who was returning home from California and a failed marriage. This is how that happened: We met accidentally (if such things are ever truly accidents) in the Jardin du Luxembourg on an early morning. I was sitting on a bench hoping that my wet, showered hair would soon dry and I could make my way to a café for coffee and croissant, and suddenly a lovely young woman sat down on the bench next to me. She told me her story and said that she, like me, was also unsystematically traveling about France before she would arrive back home to Italy. I impulsively invited her to join me the next morning for a trip to the Normandy coast. I was surprised that I had made the invitation, and even more surprised and then anxious when she tentatively accepted it. The next morning I waited anxiously for her outside her hostel thinking that she had decided not to travel further at that moment, but soon the door opened and Licia bubbled to my side. We headed for the highway where her gender helped to facilitate a hitched ride north. The driver traveling from Denmark in a VW microbus flirted with Licia, but she chose me. When we arrived in Normandy a heavy rain was falling, and I suppose we huddled in the hotel lobby though to be honest I don't remember how we might have passed the time. But when the rains cleared we walked about the town—and we then returned to the inn and celebrated a lovely dinner of steamed mussels (a first and last for me) and bottles of red wine followed by a wonderful night of lovemaking. We never did get to either the gardens or the Normandy beaches and that was just fine with me. Licia was adventure enough. I have since enjoyed other such occasions, but few rest in my memory as warmly as that evening in Normandy with Licia from California making her way back home to Italy as I was attempting to run away from mine in New York.

After France I took the train to Switzerland to visit with Fritz whom I had met in Washington, D.C., in another escape from home during a spring break. He lived with his father in Berne, and Fritz and I hiked in the mountains where I stayed in a hostel while he returned home. I then traveled to Italy to see Vieri. I think I returned home to New York a freer man than when I had left, though I still had a great deal to learn about freedom. Perhaps since then I have learned some things. At least one thing I came to know was that all my life has led me to the present moment where I experienced happiness, and so despite the ever-presence of anxieties I wouldn't have wanted to change anything. During that one solo summer trip, even in my inevitable moments of loneliness, well, I felt I was a free man in Paris and very much alive. Indeed, I might say now that during that summer I was the freest I had ever enjoyed, and maybe ever have felt since, but that experience taught me about a freedom that I continued to seek and even have sometimes in moments found. I think I have engaged in my share of forbidden things and sometimes been in trouble, too. Some of those forbidden things have made me a person for whom I have more respect. And though I suffer my portion of anxieties I hold onto remarkably few regrets.

Today that earlier sense of careless abandon that I then enjoyed in Europe during that summer has weakened; I have grown older and more brittle. I wonder whither has fled that visionary gleam? I do not move effortlessly nor with so much freedom; I do not travel far from home and when I engage in mild ventures I do so without ease. I have become more watchful of my movements. Chiron had asked for death when he understood the terms of his immortality. I am not yet near that appeal, though at my back I always here time's wingèd chariot. I am not a wayfaring stranger ready to cross over Jordan, but I know where the river is on a map.

**OH, DEATH!**

Often over the years I have written about death: the entire second movement of my Symphony explores that subject. The movement itself is written in the form of what I understood to be a funeral march. Death remains for me the greatest mystery, even more so than the mystery of God whom I also cannot comprehend but whose incomprehensibility makes sense. But death—the absence of everything I have held valuable, yes, even of my aging, parchment-like skin—represents the opposite of everything for which I have lived and loved and worked. The idea of death as "no more" I find inconceivable. Obviously, death is all around me, but I understand it none the more because it is so proximate. I am familiar with its ubiquity but fail to comprehend its reality. It is non-being, and this makes no sense to a being. Someone dies, and they lie as if asleep, but they will not awaken nor do they know that they are not merely asleep and so will not ever awaken. Having always awoken from my sleep, I cannot imagine what not to awaken must be like. Of course, this implies a consciousness of not waking, and the dead do not possess such thought. Or so I think. The dead do not dream, so I believe. And so it is that they do not even know that they are dead. We are, indeed, only a too, too solid flesh and that is all we ever will be, soon to melt, thaw and resolve itself into a dew. Dust to dust. But having acted with consciousness and sometimes with even a false or double consciousness all of my life, I cannot imagine the absence of consciousness that must be the truth of Death. No more. Nothing. Absolute nothingness without even the knowing of the nothingness. The notion appalls more that it frightens though it frightens by its complete absence of credibility.

Spinoza says that the free man thinks least of all of his death. Alas, I am not so free. The Torah keeps describing death as a return to kin; death is a reunion. Hamlet calls it an undiscovered country from whose bourn no traveler returns. Death is a place. Rage, rage against the dying of the light, Dylan Thomas urges his father. Death is a darkness. But sometimes death is portrayed as a brilliant pure light; death is blinding illumination. Death where is thy sting: death is a poisonous creature inflicting pain and suffering, though ironically the suffering of the dying is relieved by death: it is the living who would feel death's sting. Death be not proud: death is a vain and haughty being.

There was a poster hanging on the wall in a basement niche opposite the house furnace and the cat litter boxes and food dishes. My workspace then lay on the other side of the room. On some cold winter mornings as I happily wrote, the air about me hung warm and pungent from the presence of cats. The poster pictures a shirtless, well-built older man (he appears well past the age of fifty, I'd say), a man whose appearance suggested a well-practiced use of free weights and body-building apparatus and regimen. He stands in the poster bare-chested staring defiantly out at me, his muscles flexed and poised and his fists clenched, wearing a pair of tight and worn jeans, aka dungarees. And underneath him the poster pronounces, "Growing Old Is Not For Sissies." I know that this man had been working out for years in preparation for his aging. I had purchased the poster when I was not as old as I am now, but when I was certainly older than before my getting older was ever a conscious issue. I admire the man in the poster, but I think I require more than the caution he offers me. In fact, I want more explicit direction. Having never done this before, I don't know how to get old, and the generation that raised me didn't talk much about it: they just died. Their sixty-five was the new one hundred and fourteen or thereabouts, I am told. I graduated high school in 1965. I know there are no rules for living, but I think I could use some signposts. For example, is the soreness in my shoulder arthritis or charley horse? Do I have costochondritis and need a regimen of Advil, or is that pain a hint that I need either a new bed mattress or a new heart? Am I really overworking or am I more tired from the same amount of work? Is what I tell my children the result of long-suffering wisdom or mere ornery cantankerousness? What am I to make of my anxiety coming upon yet another set of stairs and the increasing frequency of urinations in what is already troubled sleep?

Of course, these are rather silly questions, but I mean them quite seriously. It is naive nonsense to say that I haven't followed any maps up until this moment, so why I wonder should I be desirous of them now on my way to dusty death. Indeed, I acknowledge that not to follow an available and proffered map is not at all to be free of maps; there are charts all about and always have been so. I marched to the beat of a different drummer, I boasted, but it was a drum that beat, nonetheless. Perhaps the issue that I consider now has more to do with the impress of time: I once behaved with a greater boldness, leisure, and complacency when I permitted myself to get lost. Then I had no concern for time's passage: time seemed illimitable and I immortal.

Montaigne says that to philosophize is to learn how to die. He writes, "He who would teach men to die would teach them to live."[5] I suspect that for Montaigne learning to die means studying what to do as one readies oneself for death's occurrence and such study would mean learning how to live. My hypochondria doesn't debilitate me, but it does keep sounding time's winged chariot drawing near; nonetheless, I choose to move forward carrying my medications, my vitamin supplements, my books and journals inside my ManBag. Montaigne wonders why anyone should bother to teach somebody how to die when it would be so much more productive to teach them how to live. Death requires no teaching because it only happens once and for all time. He says, "Wherefore it is as foolish to lament that we shall not be alive a hundred years from now as it is to lament that we were not alive a hundred years ago." And so, in the process of learning to die, Montaigne keeps the idea of death about him all the time to remind him that he is not dead and that he still lives. He will remain active. I suppose this might be one reason why I daily read the obituaries in the *New York Times*: while I read them, I am not in them. Montaigne writes, "And there is nothing that I investigate so eagerly as the death of men: what words, what look, what bearing they maintained at that time, nor is there a place in the histories I note so attentively." Their deaths teach me how to live. Because to learn how to die which is to learn how to live frees us from the slavery that fear of death imposes. Montaigne would be about his business without ever forgetting that death occurs and will occur even to him. While I write about death I do not think of my death. To learn how to die is to remain engaged

---

5. Montaigne, *The Complete Works*, 75.

in life, for death will come when it will, and as Dylan reminds me in "I'm Alright Ma (I'm Only Bleeding)," "He not busy being born is busy dying." Montaigne knows full well that death is not life, and that life is action. "I want a man to act, and to prolong the functions of life as long as he can, and I want death to find me planting my cabbages, but careless of death, and still more of my unfinished garden." Whatever is unfinished remains still to do and death will make irrelevant that which is uncompleted.

But for now, I think that the counsel that getting old is not for sissies seems to me to be just the reassurance I need to keep on keeping on. This effort takes patience and determination. I remember that when I ran long distances I would devote my Sunday mornings to a long, tiring twenty-mile run, fully aware that on the following Monday morning I would early awaken and go out to run again. No run ended running. It was never the speed that I valued in the running but the persistence. Living was to remain, to make mistakes and learn from them. Learning how to die is, yes, learning how to live. For the immediate present, I go to plant some cabbages with my seed bags filled with ambition, honest angst, and some hypochondria.

**THIS IS STUPID STUFF**

I don't remember in whose class I first read the poetry of A.E. Housman, but I am looking now at the text that Henry Taylor assigned in the course entitled Modern Poetry. In the anthology many of the poems by Housman are ink-dotted and so I assume that mark means that they had been assigned and that I must have read them. I took that class at Roanoke College in 1968, I believe. In 1986 Henry Taylor won a Pulitzer Prize for poetry.

I'm thinking now specifically of Housman's poem "Terence, This is Stupid Stuff." Terence is the poet, A.E. Housman, and in the poem his friends berate him for the dolorous, depressing views of life expressed in his poetry: "It gives a chap a belly-ache" they moan! Pipe us a tune to dance to, Terence, and give up singing these dismal bits of poetry that are so sad they even killed the cow to whom these poems were first chanted! But Terence responds: If it is good cheer you want, friends, there are sources more appropriate than poetry; liquor seems to Terence the most effective antidote to depression and despair.

> Ale, man, ale's the stuff to drink
> For fellows whom it hurts to think:
> Look into the pewter pot

## Before the Masts

To see the world as the world's not.[6]

Inebriated beyond consciousness, fallen drunk into a stupor, the world appears pleasant and hospitable until, alas, one rouses up from his drunken stupor and realizes that the happy tale was all a lie: "The world, it was the old world yet,/I was I, my things were wet . . . " And so would begin another day. Some years later Samuel Beckett will have Pozzo pronounce something similar: "But—but behind this veil of gentleness and peace night is charging and will burst upon us pop! Like that! just when we least expect it. That's how it is on this bitch of an earth."[7] We live in troubled times and I am often anxious.

I have often wondered whence derived my cynicism, perhaps an anxious and negative flavor of irony, but I am certain it blossomed before my confrontation with Housman's poetry that served only to confirm my distrustful stance. I was raised for cynicism. My father had never had dealings anywhere with anybody who he believed was capable; I assumed that I was included in that grouping of incompetents. My mother never ceased to complain about her lot in life; if I and my siblings were any joy to her, she hid her pleasures well. My parents communicated their displeasures and fears to us more clearly than they expressed their love, and we heard and probably accepted their criticisms as fact. The world for them was a frightening and dangerous place: she told us that if we left the refrigerator door open the appliance would explode. She told us that if we swallowed watermelon seeds we would develop appendicitis. When they moved into an apartment that did not allow pets, they put down our beloved dog but told us that they had taken it up north and to a farm where it would be well cared for. There was little room for pleasure. Perhaps they both had reasons; I have at this time no intention to judge, though there were not a few years when all I did was criticize and blame. Neither of them ever told us that everything would be well then or ever or that we were loved. Anxiety became me.

And then, too, I was raised during the era of the atomic bomb and was taught in school to crouch under my desk, away from the windows with my arms covering my head. And to remain silent! I guess the latter was a caution that would prevent the bombs from finding us. I learned later that any one of these actions, indeed, all of them together would have been meaningless in the event of a nuclear attack. And I lived during the McCarthy

---

6. Housman, in Sanders, *Chief Modern Poets of England And America*, I-91.
7. Beckett, *Waiting for Godot*, 26.

hearings, ("Have you no decency," lawyer Joseph Welch said to McCarthy, and the senator didn't); the Vietnam War conducted under a blanket of lies; the assassinations of Medgar Evers, Emmet Till, the Kennedys, Martin Luther King and John Lennon—oh, the list is too long and painful—; the United States' support of the plot to assassinate Patrice Lumumba; the CIA organization of the Chilean coup by dictator Augusto Pinochet and the subsequent murder of the duly elected president, Salvador Allende; illegal and immoral subterfuge in the Iran-Contra affair. And then arrived Trump and the Republican prostitutes. Cynicism and anxiety were present in the air I breathed.

And so I think it was my cynicism that originally drew me to Housman's poetry. The poet's pessimism nestled into a fertile bed that my experience had prepared. I believe that I had been nurtured by and fed on the cynical: Mark Twain, Joseph Heller, Kurt Vonnegut, John Barth, Ford Madox Ford, Edith Wharton, Samuel Beckett, James Joyce, E. L. Doctorow. I have spent not a little time with unreliable narrators and I read the news today! And cynicism opened a path to irony which suggested that it was wise to question and despair of the identity of everything, even that of the self. Cynicism suggests as the Grateful Dead sang, "[W]hen life looks like Easy Street, There is danger at your door."[8] Seneca wrote, "Whatever can happen at any time can happen today."[9] I remember once insisting to the owner of a video rental store that the film I had reserved to pick up the next day had to work because I had scheduled it for viewing as a significant part of a class. He promised me that he would test it that evening, and I believed that he would do so. I was grateful, but I knew that just because he found no flaws in the product did not mean that it would screen flawlessly for me. I was hopeful, but I had my doubts. Ultimately, the film worked just fine, but I sat anxiously awaiting the moment when the tape would break or the deck explode. Best to expect the worst and to prepare. We would be rarely disappointed by the occurrence of the former and can be fortified by the activities of the latter. The cynic expects to live but knows that even in the summertime the living won't be easy. Cynicism holds that whatever meaning might be discovered bodes no one well. The cynic trusts no one and no thing. Or rather, the cynic expects the thing and the relationship either to fail or at a minimum to cause trouble. That's how it is on this bitch of an earth.

8. https://genius.com/The-grateful-dead-uncle-johns-band-lyrics
9. Seneca, *Letters from a Stoic*, 117.

Terence offered a very guarded and even oxymoronic cynical optimism. In response to his friends' complaint concerning his poetry, he advises them that though the world contains much good, there is, in fact, much less good than ill, and that his friends would do well to live their life expecting and preparing for that ill rather than hoping for and awaiting the good. Of his poetry he cautions his friends, "Tis true, the stuff I bring for sale/Is not so brisk a brew as ale . . . If the smack is sour, The better for the embittered hour."[10] We toughen ourselves with small doses of the bitter that we would be not destroyed by it when it powerfully and inevitably assails us! There was a king in the East, Terence says, who knew how easy it was to poison the food upon which he would feast, and so each day with each meal the king would add a small portion of "all that springs to birth/From the many-venomed earth." And as "they" added arsenic to his meat and poured strychnine into his wine, his would-be assassins sat aghast at the failure of their poisons to affect any harm. They "shook to see him drink it up." But the king had made himself immune to the poisons by imbibing a bit of them every day. "I will tell the tale I'm told," Terence says, "Mithridates, he died old." I guess that is one answer. I remember also Housman's poem, "To an Athlete Dying Young," in which the poet suggests that there is benefit to dying before the athlete's renown is forgotten and his medals rusted and decayed. I suppose that is another answer.

Hilary Mantel says that in her novel of the French Revolution, *A Place of Greater Safety*, she has "as far as possible" used the real words of the characters—from their recorded speeches or preserved writings. Her central protagonists are George Danton, Camille Desmoulins, and Maximilien Robespierre, architects of the Revolution, from whose words and works she draws significantly. I have been long interested in the French Revolution, an interest derived I suppose from my reading of Dickens's *Tale of Two Cities* in Mr. Tobin's ninth-grade English class; from the events of the Reign of Terror; and from my reading of Edmund Burke during college courses in 18th-century literature. And I read this in Mantel's novel taken from the private notebooks of Maximilien Robespierre:

> What is our aim?
> The use of the constitution for the benefit of the people.
> Who are like to oppose us?
> The rich and corrupt.

---

10. Housman, in Sanders, *Chief Modern Poets of England And America*, I- (Shakespeare)ll.

What methods will they employ?
Slander and hypocrisy.
What factors will encourage the use of such means?
The ignorance of the ordinary people.
When will the people be educated?
When they have enough to eat, and when the rich and the government stop bribing treacherous tongues and pens to deceive them; when their interests are identified with those of the people.
When will that be?
Never.[11]

Robespierre, the revolutionary, is a cynic. He expresses high ideals but maintains an awareness that they will never achieve realization. Robespierre's words sound threateningly familiar, because they describe the situation that has existed in the United States since its inception and had been only exasperated under the reign of Donald Trump, the man who would be King, and his Republican sycophantic and pusillanimous horde.

I was sitting atop my stationary bike in my spin cycle class one morning and the instructor in the front of the room was shouting at us to increase our pace by five RPMs and to raise our Watts by twenty percent, and saying something about the lessons of adversity and pain, and I, weary and out of breath, spun my legs as fast as I could manage, which was not very fast at all, and what came to my mind was that Mithridates, well, he died old. I pedaled a bit harder, but only hard enough to inure me to the embitterment I would face outside.

## ON IRONY

I believe that the deeply sane (a community of which I now would consider myself an humble member) do not seek out recognition (admittedly, a state I did sometime pursue but did not achieve, *Mea culpa*) because they understand that the need to be special requires the setting of aims and objectives for oneself that are often based only in a relation to the behavior of others—thus, a superficially sane person who organizes his behavior to be special does not participate with others, in fact, because he is always in competition with those others. I have at times suffered from this need and the competition that resulted from it. The effort has usually added to my levels of already-present anxiety. *Mea culpa*. Equally, I acknowledge

---

11. Mantel, *A Place of Greater Safety*, 642.

that the demand to be believed is madness, and the deeply sane achieve recognition because they have obeyed the urgings of their own creativity and not the need for approval. I have too often complained that I have remained unrecognized and unknown, and I have even had some moments when I accepted that perhaps the obscurity was appropriate. *Mea culpa.* But despite my doubts and anxieties, I also have come to acknowledge that in the end as at the beginning I thought and wrote out of my own Desire. I acknowledged that it was my choice to write, and that after the writing was completed, the judgment was out of my hands and I would soon return to the pen and paper. I remember a short film I used to show regularly in my high school English class called "Why We Create," by Saul Bass. One final section of the film focused on the judgment by the critics of the artist's creation. It was a pitiless sequence: the artist responded to the attacks of the critics as if he were being shot! That might be one response. Humor would be another. After the publication of *A Week on the Concord and Merrimac Rivers* which did not sell well and for which he was responsible the cost of printing, Thoreau quipped, "I have a library of one thousand volumes, nine hundred and ninety of which I wrote myself!"[12] Tristram Shandy chides himself: "Is it not enough that thou art in debt, and that thou hast ten carloads of thy fifth and sixth volumes still—still unsold and art almost at thy wit's ends, how to get them off my hands."[13] As for me, too many copies of the books I have written with my own hands, now ten in number, remain on my shelf.

The demand to be believed is one that comes from the superficially sane: they avoid conversation for the performance of the monologue. And as long as the superficially sane speak they do not have to listen. To listen stems from empathy that might be love. I have, alas, spoken too often and loudly to listen. Thoreau says that the intimacy of conversation often requires silence. Only then can one truly hear. I wonder for what a deeply sane person would listen. Certainly, it would not be evidence that she had been understood: I think that when someone says that they understand me, what they might mean is that they have summarized me. I don't want to be understood, a situation that is both impossible and intolerable; what I want is for someone to listen to me and then to pose a question. Thoreau suggests that to hear that most intimate society we have with ourselves requires not that we be alone but that when in company we would stand so far apart that

12. Thoreau, *Journal*, V, 459.
13. Sterne, *Tristram Shandy*, 384.

## Anxious Am I?

we cannot possibly hear our own and each other's voice. It would be then that we can surely listen!

Sometimes when I speak, I don't always know all that I have said. I think that I often mean more than I say and say less than I mean. I don't always know what else I have said. Language is remarkably imprecise and heavy laden. Sometimes when I had spoken to you, my daughters, I was speaking not to you but to myself, and I think that sometimes you must have overheard. I am sorry. I remember with horror my behavior at a concert that I attended with you and several of your friends and at which my actions and language embarrassed you. And I remember once demanding your return home from an impromptu sleepover invitation for no other reason than I insisted that you do so. I think I have often misspoken. Sometimes when we were together you saw in me the child, at other times the adolescent, sometimes, and I hope mostly, you dealt with your father, the deeply sane adult. Perhaps then you couldn't name the difference, but I am hopeful you might have felt it.

The deeply sane understand and invite irony into their daily lives. Traditionally irony has been defined as a figure of speech in which what is meant is the opposite of what is said. Famous examples of such irony are Antony's description of Brutus and his co-conspirators as "all, all honorable men" during his funeral oration for the assassinated Julius Caesar; or Jonathan Swift's modest proposal that the overflow of children and the excess of poverty in Ireland might be managed by selling the children of the impoverished to wealthy families for food. Mark Twain's *Huckleberry Finn* depends on the irony that exists in the gap between the innocence of its narrator, Huck Finn, and the reader's experienced awareness of the world Huckleberry describes. Everything Huck says has to be qualified by the reader's knowledge of the world behind (or would it more properly be described as beyond?) Huck—even, I might add, extending to Huck's use of the N-word. Huck's resignation that he will go to hell for protecting Jim must be understood by the reader as evidence of Huck's morality that would endear him to heaven rather than be an act that would exclude him from it. Similarly, Leopold Bloom's wanderings through Dublin on June 16, 1904, might be viewed ironically when compared to the heroic wanderings of the hero-soldier Ulysses trying to get home to his wife and son following the victory in the Trojan Wars. Though I know that one can read *Ulysses* without having read *The Odyssey*, the experience of reading Joyce's novel gains depth when the reader has knowledge of Homer's epic and appreciates, perhaps, the irony of Bloom's helpless wanderings through modern Dublin as he makes his way home when they are compared to the heroic wanderings of Homer's here, Ulysses who, too, makes his way home.

Irony also acknowledges that I am always less than finished and thus, often subject to the ridiculous and the absurd. Like Mrs. Bates, in Austen's *Emma*, I often do act the fool. For example: for almost forty years I was a compulsive runner, searching out the roads not only for physical health but for mental well-being as well. By compulsive I mean that barring some dire physical ailment, like broken ankles, I ran distances six or seven days a week regardless of the weather or time of day. I kept running journals recording distances, times and experiences of each run. I ran in the early mornings, in the mid-afternoons, and early evenings. I ran in Central Park on its four-, five- or six-mile routes. Occasionally I chose the path around the reservoir, but I found it difficult there to maintain some solitude and my considered thoughts. I ran in Riverside Park as far uptown as 181$^{st}$ Street and as far south as 72$^{nd}$ Street. I ran anywhere and everywhere I happened to be. I once counted the number of states in which I had run and was surprised the total was as high as thirty-six. There are some states I have refused to ever visit: Texas, Mississippi, Missouri, Alabama, maybe Kansas. And there are a few I can't imagine touring: Idaho, perhaps, Arkansas, and maybe North Dakota! I ran for pleasure, and I ran for my sanity, though that quality might have at times been indiscernible, and I ran also for physical well-being.

But on this one particular day which I even now recall with cheer, I ran down 97$^{th}$ Street toward Riverside Park from my studio apartment. I don't remember the season, but it was not winter because it was raining and not snowing. However, it wasn't just raining: it was torrentially pouring and though I was not oblivious to conditions I was without care. My compulsion to run overrode any other concern. I recall that the temperature was warm and so it must have been spring or summer, and my attire was running shorts and T-shirt I had earned from some road race. By the time I had arrived at Riverside Drive, not more than a block and a half from the front door of my apartment building, I was quite soaked through. There might even have been thunder and lightning, but I wasn't deterred, and I was alone. And remarkably I was content and though impelled by anxiety I was not at the time anxious! I turned that day not into the park but onto the sidewalk that ran alongside the park, and I headed up the sloping drive toward Grant's Tomb. My Asics running shoes squished every time they hit the pavement, but I was determined that I would finish this run. From behind me I sensed the existence of the blue and white police car that had also turned onto Riverside Drive. I heard the police speaker switch on; I couldn't imagine I was going to get arrested for running and singing in the rain, but, well, I had in my time learned to distrust the police. Loud and clear the voice called out from the speaker, "Are you crazy? Go home!" I had to acknowledge that I probably was if not crazy then certainly not exactly at the moment entirely sane. I waved my right hand in acknowledgment, but I continued uptown on the slow incline, and the officers in their patrol car left me to my drenched solitude. I finished the run in the heavy rain, logged the experience into the running journal, and opened a bottle of beer.

I am often subject to a power that I attempt to control; the effort sometimes gets me in trouble, too, and keeps me humble. I know only a little; I make mistakes, Oh Lord, what mistakes I have made!. I hold fast to the belief that I have learned from my mistakes today, but I recognize that tomorrow undoubtedly, I will commit other blunders. I might even make the same mistake today as the one I committed yesterday. I would always like to speak the truth, but the best I can do is speak truthfully. I have learned to consider irony my lifeline to the world because I have found hope in irony. And I have thrown that lifeline to my daughters. That irony filled with hope refuses the world as it is; knows that every truth exists briefly if at all; it says that meaning cannot be tied down and therefore, becomes infinite. It is irony that ties me to my adoration of Thoreau's transcendentalism and Heschel's spirituality: there is always more day to dawn!

I am not a wealthy man and yet, as do the fathers in Jane Austen's novels, I have daughters whom I love. I often wonder what I might leave behind to them, and I have long considered that what might best serve my daughter's lives is a sense of irony, a bit of insanity and the willingness not to call things by the same name as others; an ability with little exception not to take anything spoken at face value. I hold that a sense of irony will stand my daughters well in the world. I have offered the hope I have found in irony to them both in our reading, our enjoyment of the cinema and the theaters and in the concert halls. Hope, I believe, resides in that space that these activities create between the present and the future. It is irony with which I am concerned because it is irony that I think must be my most valuable legacy to my beautiful daughters. At times I think hopefully that that have accepted my offering.

To take an ironic stance in the world will, I still believe, offer my children hope; and to be somewhat dramatic, it might even save them. Not keep them from harm but permit them to accept difficulty, learn its inevitability, and understand how to resist hopelessness and despair. I acknowledge that this will not make for a calm or even comfortable existence, but I believe that it will leave much room for creativity. As Yossarian makes ready to escape the war Major Danby asks him, "How do you feel Yossarian?" and he answers, "I'm very frightened." And Danby says, "That's good . . . It proves you're still alive."[14] The fear is a challenging measure, but it may be a sensible gauge of aliveness. Do I have anxiety? Oh God, yes, of course I do. And it is reasonable that they do too. As Yossarian jumps out of the window to make his escape from the ward, Nately's whore who was hiding just behind the door, brought down her knife missing Yossarian by inches. And then Yossarian heads away from the Lee Shore and out to sea. I imagine he had a smile on his face as he heads anxiously into his future.

[Do you not see, my dears, how I cannot talk without the books and the texts with which we have surrounded ourselves? You will see how I cannot speak outside of the texts with which I have immersed myself in life.]

And an ironic stance also acknowledges that our understanding is always limited and that we will be always wrong. Nathan Zuckerman in Philip Roth's *American Pastoral* says that being wrong is how we know that we are alive. There is always more day to dawn. Our lives depend on our decision-making processes, but how to decide is always problematic: accepting one path shuns the other. I recall Frost's ironic poem, "The Road Not Taken." That remarkable poem that has been optimistically read at innumerable school graduations is named ironically not after the road traveled but by that unknown and unexplored road that for some undefined and indefinable reason was not engaged. What else might have been learned? The poem's narrator defines himself not by what he has learned but by what he has missed, the road less traveled and that has made all the difference. "Irony," I read, "is the simultaneous presence of two meanings between which it is not possible to decide." But a choice must ultimately be made and only one road traveled! One critic I have always enjoyed reading, Hayden White, says,

> What struck me in the reading of [Aristotle's] *Ethics* was the idea that it's impossible for us to perform adequately all the roles that we're given in a society without offending other roles. Any choice

---

14. Heller, *Catch-22*, 442.

> we make in our capacity, let's say, as teachers, is going to be detrimental to some other role that we are trying to play . . . One is put into situations of choice just by the nature of society. Society says we must perform all of our roles adequately, but the roles we are given are contradictory with one another. And so our lives are lived in contradiction . . . the attempt to live a consistent life is inauthentic.[15]

I am aware that the attempt to live in contradiction might drive us crazy, but the deeply sane accept and even enjoy such contradiction. Do I contradict myself? All right, I contradict myself. Hayden White says that the ironic stance will be the basis for living that is going to be contradictory "no matter what you do, unless you decide to do nothing, in which case that's hardly living, right?" It will be always true that another road could have been taken. My understanding of irony has taught me that meaning was not fixed and therefore, I am freed from the staid and conventional. I remember once choosing to teach Kafka's "Metamorphosis." I wanted to get it right and so I went to the library and began to study the critical commentary. No two critics seemed to agree as to the meaning of the work. I learned then and I taught subsequently that reading was to make meaning and not to find it.

### WHERE WOULD WISDOM BE FOUND?

I have long been concerned with wisdom and understand now that it is linked irrevocably to irony. Irony leads me forward. Once I thought that wisdom entailed being smart and that being smart was all about achieving high grades. For the most part mine were above average but perhaps below exceptional. I had then considered wisdom to be the accumulation of knowledge, but I have since realized that knowledge is both temporary and illimitable. I read a great deal. But the reading only taught me that there is no end to knowledge, and I will forever know only the smallest part of what can be known. Sometimes I go to my bookshelf and pull down a book, open it, and discover underlined passages and cryptic annotations that I had once entered on the page, and I would suddenly realize that I had read this book earlier. But where is its knowledge, I wondered? Where is the book's knowledge in my knowledge, or has it all passed into whatever I call my wisdom? Arnold Modell, in *The Private Self* says, "Aspects of one's

---

15. White, "The Aim of Interpretation, "65–66.

private self must penetrate the knowledge acquired from the other so that knowledge is translated into one's private knowledge."[16] I think that this private knowledge to which Modell refers is what I have come to know as wisdom, and that is eternally replenishable and renewable. Knowledge becomes wisdom when it transforms into private knowledge, and I think we can only know our wisdom when it sounds in our own language. Such private knowledge often requires a private language. As Dorothea Brooke in George Eliot's *Middlemarch* had stated when cautioned to avoid insanity and not forgo the accepted common meaning and knowledge, "I have never called things by the same name as others call them by."[17] Mrs. Cadwallader cautions Dorothea that others will think her insane, but Dorothea remains unconcerned. Of course, to speak that private language in public demands a bit of compromise because we must use a language the community will recognize. And so we rarely say exactly we mean and so we are rarely understood, but I think that perhaps to be understood should not concern me. It is madness to demand to be understood.

Perhaps it is that public knowledge must necessarily move through a filter—or through several filters—as it transforms into private knowledge. Those first filters might consist of what psychoanalyst Christopher Bollas refers to as psychic genera: our innate tastes, attractions, and interest. Why do I prefer oatmeal to cream of wheat, romantic comedies to horror movies, girls to boys, etc. Other filters are soon acquired and are the result of nurture, environment, and cultural priorities. Of course, there is a certain standard from which judgment for transmission must be made. Issues of social justice, concern for the widow, the orphan, and the stranger in our midst is one consistent measure and a firm foundation of ethics, as would be issues of personal safety. And education is a singular mode of such transmission. I have spent almost a half-century in the classroom offering filters. I have learned in the classroom that education can supply important filters only with this important caveat: I can teach but it is others who must learn. Winnicott writes, "In education you can hand on to the child the beliefs that have meaning for yourself and that belong to the small cultural or religious area that you happen to be born into or to choose an alternative to the one you were born into. But you will have success only in so far as the child has a capacity to believe in anything at all."[18] Perhaps this capacity is

---

16. Modell, *The Private Self*, 118.
17. Eliot, *Middlemarch*, 537.
18. Winnicott, *Home is Where We Start From*, 143.

like a door that should be kept open if education is to have any influence, but ironically any person's capacity to believe lies beyond the awareness of the teacher. The teacher ultimately works in ignorance and on faith. And it is also true that one will learn only what one wants to know.

Thoreau identifies insanity with his Genius, the latter a concept today replaced, perhaps, with that of Desire. I believe that Desire should be unextinguishable and yet unfillable, but the presence of Desire remains requisite for knowledge. A desire that can be fulfilled becomes merely appetite. Desire is rather, a central impelling force, like the pilot light on a gas stove: without that light the burners cannot be lit, but the pilot light itself cannot be found in the burner flame that cooks the food. I think the deeply sane are driven by Desire but accept with some grace that what they want finally is unattainable, thankfully so, but motivated by Desire they do not ever cease striving. The quest might appear insane and we often feel . . . well, unhinged. I think Dylan's "Red River Shore" is a song about Desire, a subject not unfamiliar in Dylan's corpus. In the narrative the girl from the Red River Shore epitomizes the persistent and powerful pull of Desire, and for his peace has sent him home to lead a quiet life. But the narrator has not been able to let go of this Desire for that girl, nor do I believe that he has lived a quiet life. But he wants to be certain that he had, indeed, once known the girl from the Red River Shore even if he could not finally possess her. He still wants to know his Desire was Real. But when he goes back to the bar to get some confirmation of his meeting with the girl from the Red River Shore, ironically no one there knew what he was talking about. They hadn't seen him or her! Only he can know his Desire. It was his Desire, I think, that created the girl from the Red River Shore. We pursue from Desire, but we never achieve our Desire. As Greg Brown sings, in my life I am looking for Rexroth's daughter and I guess that I always will be.

My psychoanalyst has referred to Desire as motivation, but for me that definition doesn't satisfy. I can be motivated by something other than Desire, by anxiety, for example, but perhaps anxiety is only frustrated Desire. And ultimately no one does really know what it is I am talking about, and sometimes even I am perplexed by attempts at clarity. And the last line of Dylan's song, "Sometimes I think, nobody ever saw me here at all, except the girl from the Red River Shore," always catches me up sharply. The narrator remains invisible to all except his Desire; it is a position of remarkable aloneness, even of loneliness, and yet, there is the comfort of the unreachable Desire that makes one present at least to one's self.

This creativity seems to me to be the essence of my life though I must acknowledge that the sense of angst and disquiet that this effort generates demands a strength and ironic acceptance I sometimes have lacked. I have been at times overwhelmed by anxiety and have taken to my bed or to drink or to drugs. I have hidden myself in a darkened movie theaters in the middle of the day rather than remain in the text or at the keyboard. Once following a Bruce Springsteen concert I hopped a train to Washington, D.C. to escape even my own home in New York City. Perhaps this anxiety troubles my hold on reality, but sometimes it offers me insight that too much sanity has obscured. Thoreau writes: "If one listens to the faintest but constant suggestions of his genius, which are certainly true, he sees not to what extremes, or even insanity, it may lead him; and yet that way, as he grows more resolute and faithful, his road lies." Following not our bliss but our Desire we march to a different drummer and seem out of step with others. Dylan says that "Some of us scare ourselves in the dark/To be where the angels fly."[19] As for myself, whenever I feel afraid, well, sometimes I whistle a happy tune, and sometimes turn to pen and papers (metaphorically speaking, since I write on the computer); I read and I write. And like Miss Reardon or Mr. Bojangles, sometimes I drinks a bit. Montaigne avers, "A man must be a little mad if he does not want to be even more stupid."[20] I have considered that insanity is a condition necessary in order to maintain one's creativity and sense of aliveness. Living creatively seems to me the essence of living; Winnicott says that by creative living means not getting killed or annihilated by a compliance that would obliterate my sense of self; or by reacting to the world that impinges and means to control. The reality principle, Winnicott says, is forever an insult. Sometimes I know I have insulted my daughters; I have stood too close behind them to keep them on a path I had already chosen; I did not trust that they could find their own way. But I hope I have done more and maybe even given them the strength to resist me and to learn to make their own lives. Maybe I have taught them that to live creatively is to see everything afresh all the time and then from their capacities do what they can with what they have seen. What Dylan wants remains always unattainable—that Red River Girl—and that impossible Desire becomes, I suspect, one source for his neurotic states. The song speaks of great loss but the song is itself beautiful. After all is done, I

19. Dylan, "Red River Shore"
20. Montaigne, *The Complete Works*, 925.

suppose all that remains are the visions of Johanna, Desire absolute, ironically, that makes it all seem so cruel.

## OF BUSINESS AND DESIRES

Having spoken to the Ghost and having received his charge, Hamlet dismisses the inquiry of his dear friend Horatio about what Hamlet has just seen and what he has heard.

> And so, without circumstance at all,
> I hold it fit that we shake hands and part;
> You as your business and desire shall point you,
> For every man hath business and desire,
> Such as it is . . . [21]

So that he might plot and plan, Hamlet demands immediate solitude from Horatio: Hamlet has, as do all men, business and desires. We have already seen a peek into his Desire: "I have that within that passes show . . ." he tells his mother who has chastised him for his persistent mourning over the death of his father.[22] But Hamlet has, nevertheless, been for some time torpid and withdrawn from business. Hamlet is often first seen seated amidst the standing and bustling court. In order to attend his father's funeral and as he says his mother's o'er hasty re-marriage he had come to Elsinore from residence in Wittenburg where he had lived the life of the student. Since his arrival at Elsinore Hamlet seems to have abandoned engagement in any type of business. His father's ghost's charge to his son to revenge his foul and most unnatural murder energizes Hamlet and demands that he attend to a business that might give some direction to his Desire. But the charge also raises Hamlet's already significant anxieties. My anxieties, too, often separate me from those I love. I have at times taken to my bed.

At Elsinore Hamlet had experienced Desire, but he cannot manage to effect business there. He refuses the objective world: in his obsessive focus on his Desire, Hamlet has neglected his business. I will not define the content of Hamlet's Desire, but I know that it burns in him. I know that he would revenge his father's murder, but until the play's end his Desire finds little material to use. When the ghost returns, he admonishes Hamlet not for his lack of Desire but for his failure to fulfill his business: "I come to

---

21. Shakespeare, *Hamlet*, I,5,127–130.
22. *Hamlet*, I, ii, 86.

whet thy almost blunted purpose." Ah, how much business have I avoided in my focus on my Desire.[23]

It is not that Hamlet cannot act effectively. When the players appeared Hamlet immediately planned a performance of The Mousetrap and written a speech to be inserted into it. When Hamlet acts from his Desire with an acknowledgment of an objective world he is remarkably effective, though his eagerness to expose the King almost destroys the set-up; Hamlet also steals the letter from Rosencrantz and Guildenstern pronouncing Hamlet's death at the hands of the English to whom he has been sent by the King, and then he rewrites the command effecting the execution of his so-called friends, whom he declares he would trust as he would two adders fanged! But Hamlet tends to ignore the objective world in the exercise of his Desire: he had stabbed through the arras killing Polonius hoping it were the king, even though a moment's reflection would have made known to him that it could not have been Claudius behind the curtain because Hamlet had just passed the King below in apparent prayer!

Neither I nor anyone else I have read can with absolute certainty define Hamlet's inability to effect his business, nor would I definitively attempt to define his Desire. It is enough to know that his Desire exists and his inability to realize his Desire in Reality immobilizes him. Observing the passion in the player's performance of Hecuba's lament, Hamlet berates himself: "Yet I,/A dull and muddy-mettled rascal, peak,/Like John-a-dreams unpregnant of my cause,/And can say nothing."[24] But Hamlet suffers not from a lethargy but from a solipsistic (narcissistic) fixation on his passion. He berates himself: "I am pigeon-liver'd and lack gall/To make oppression bitter, or ere this/I should have fatted all the region kites/With this slave's offal."[25] Consumed by Desire which would set the world right, Hamlet neglects his business in a distracted busy-ness.

I think thought often obtrudes on action. I have loved the life of thought and consider myself a capable, even respectable intellectual. About me always are books, academic and pseudo-academic journals, personal journals in which I deposit my thoughts and sometimes ideas gleaned from my reading and my genius. I have considered myself to be a careless scholar though I have been advised that my portrayal of myself ought not to be thought of as pejorative but merely descriptive. I have recognized

---

23. *Hamlet*, III, iv, 110.
24. *Hamlet*, II, ii, 593–596.
25. *Hamlet*, II, ii, 605–608.

with Thoreau that one can either live one's life or write about it, and I feel conflicted sometimes and even now as I work on this memoir that I neglect my life by writing about it. And too often I peak, like John-a-dreams, unpregnant of my cause and do not give agency to Desire. And I neglect my business.

Throughout their lives I have tried to provide my daughters objects to their Desire so that they might engage in their business. I pestered them with admonitions that they should read, read, read, and to study the materials in their fields and continue to grow into their chosen professions. I began to purchase books for them not long after they were born. By the time they were able to read they had libraries that many would envy, and when they no longer wanted books read to them, I joined them in silent reading before we both drifted off to sleep. Books and ideas were a primary connection to my daughters and has become part of my legacy to them. Conversation about texts has been an important subject when we have gathered. Often that conversation had led to other issues. And we continue yet to share our readings. We made belief possible. And now I hope that each knows how to realize their Desire even though the girl from the Red River Shore admonishes them to go home and live a quiet life.

One of my most influential critics, Terry Eagleton, says that "Whenever we stumble in literary works across a desire which starkly isolates a protagonist; renders him or her strange to themselves; expresses an ineluctable inner need; manifests an adamant refusal to compromise; invents itself in an object more precious than life itself; maroons a character between life and death, and finally leads him or her inexorably to the grave, we can be reasonably sure that we are in the presence of the Real."[26] That Real might be what I mean by Desire; it is the law of our Being that exists in spite of the forces of reality to which we all must make compromise. I think of Abraham sitting quietly before his tent, or out shepherding his flock, when suddenly he gets a command: Go to a land I will show you. The story says that it was God that spoke to Abraham, but I have long believed that it was Desire that addressed him: Desire was the fire of his being even as Desire sent both Ishmael and Bulkington continually out to sea. Abraham immediately obeyed this command and with his family and those who would follow him he heads out to a place he does not know though he will never arrive there. I think of the prophets. Each receives this call and either follows it or tries, like Jonah, to run from it. Desire need not be followed: Hamlet is called to

---

26. Eagleton, *Trouble with Strangers*, 190.

action by the Ghost but complains that he can "do nothing," though I think the presence of Desire cannot be denied. To ignore Desire would lead to a life of quiet desperation and to anxious feelings that follows from the frustration of suppressing it. The existence of Desire seems to enact a central ethic: Desire is the truth of ourselves. Sometimes it gets me in trouble, too.

Perhaps Desire and business may sometimes co-exist meaningfully. In "Not Dark Yet," Dylan sings from the depth of depression, "I can't even remember what it was I came here to get away from." The narrator appears to have lost all sense of business, though he does remember that his present situation in which he now finds himself resulted from some wish to get away from something. He has become oppressed by the world and his Desire has ebbed; his pilot light has dimmed and might even have seemed extinguished. Winnicott says that a False Self develops to protect the core True Self, and that the False Self seeks conditions that would allow the True Self to find some voice, to make appearance in the world. And if that False Self cannot create those conditions to protect that True Self, then suicide becomes the only option. In Act II Hamlet seemed to contemplate suicide: "To be or not to be, that is the question." Ironically, "Not Dark Yet" expresses just such a desperate stance, but I think that the creation of the song that speaks of this severe depression enacts a business that gives voice to Desire. The verses communicate an emotional weariness, but the song's creation relieves that depression. Dylan's narrator may not hear the murmur of a prayer, but in the song Dylan has created one. Desire has been realized in business. The creation of art derives in part from the meeting of Desire with the physical world; art engages business and desire even as the art itself describes the failures of business and desire. Shakespeare may have suffered much Desire, but in writing Hamlet he has done much business. I think that the separation of Desire from Business and Business from Desire does make cowards of us all. The rest is silence.

I wonder how my willing engagement in business fulfills my Desire, and to what extent I grow depressed when I try to disregard it. Dylan says his body is vacant and numb and he has lost all reason to even care! There have been moments when I have taken to my bed, to wines and liquors and pills to dampen Desire and I have despaired of purpose. But then it is a joy to find outlet in the materials of reality for the realization of Desire. I write and I read; I teach and I learn.

## ANXIOUS AM I?

### AN EXAMINING LIFE

The sources of our neurotic states are many and to examine them might take up a considerable effort in one's life as it certainly has done in mine and which practice now pervades this writing. Such study might be a life's project. Thoreau has always inspired me in this analytical project. He urges that to find oneself is the essential work of a life. In Walden he wonders about the quests of explorers: "Is [Lord] Franklin[27] the only one who is lost, that his wife should be so earnest to find him? Does Mr. Grinnel[28] know where he himself is?"[29] Thoreau argues that it is very easy to get lost in this world: one has only to close the eyes, turn the head up and spin around three or four times! Ironically, I have long believed that getting lost is a first step to finding oneself and I presumed that until I had found myself, I would remain absent to others. Lost objects, I argued, were called so not because they were those things that had been misplaced but instead were those that had not yet been found. A lost object, the rabbis said, was one whose purpose had not yet been discovered.

Lose yourself and you will be found. Find yourself and you would not be lost. Such study would be neither neat nor ordered and might often result in not a few embarrassing situations and disorders. "We shall never heap enough insults on the unruliness of our mind," Montaigne writes, and then admits, "I find—like a runaway horse, my mind in idleness gives itself a hundred times more trouble than it took for others, and gives birth to so many chimeras and fantastic monsters one after another, without order or purpose, that in order to contemplate their ineptitude and strangeness at my pleasure, I have begun to put them in writing, hoping in time to make my mind ashamed of itself."[30] Before the talking cure apparently there was the writing one; I am writing now.

A found memory: Once I almost went out on a blind date that had been choreographed by my mother and her general practitioner. I should have known from those origins that the tryst might not end well but I did, however, make the call required for the culturally bound male, and Melissa answered seemingly already aware that I was going to make overture by phone for what was to be a date. We were following protocol, I thought; so far, so good. And though I did start out on the date, the occasion did not

---

27. A British sea captain lost in 1847 in his voyage to find the Northwest Passage.
28. An American philanthropist who financed an expedition to search for Franklin.
29. Thoreau, *Walden*, 348.
30. Montaigne, *The Complete Works*, 31.

finish according to the normal trajectory of such events, first ones or otherwise. She suggested that perhaps we could go dancing at an uptown club that was then a popular spot for people our age and inclination but that was a venue, of course, unknown to me. I could identify with her designation of "our age" but not necessarily with her reference to our inclination. I do not remember being ever so inclined. Her proposal sparked an already heightened anxiety level. Dancing was an activity that was far down on my list of desired undertakings. Once, many years ago in preparation for the bar mitzvah season, several sets of parents enrolled us boys and girls in dancing class, first with Helga who came to our homes and then with Mrs. Saunders to whose studio we were carpooled by parents. The cha-cha, the fox trot, the lindy, the mambo, and the meringue comprised the totality of the standard curriculum. If the teachers had given grades, I think I would have earned a C.

As a teenager I had regularly watched American Bandstand but knew for sure that I would never look that adept and sophisticated on any dance floor. And as part of the curriculum in my high school gym classes we were subject to a unit of dance. I recall on the gym floor engaged in lessons on the waltz—one, two three, one two three—and somewhat incongruously also some sessions of square dancing: swing your partners, do-si-do, allemande right, allemande left, grab your partner and promenade home! It was all a terribly embarrassing situation: boys were lined up along the red line on one side of the gym and girls lined up on the opposite red line, and then at the signal the boys walked across the gym floor toward the girls' line to find their partner. We were expected to dance with whomever had been directly across from you and there were certainly some faces and bodies with which we and they didn't want to pair! Much jockeying for position took place. I never did have an opportunity to dance the waltz, but then such is the fate of much curriculum. Later, at college fraternity parties I had danced with whomever had agreed to attend with me, but I danced without any real conviction about what I was supposed to be doing on this (or any) dance floor, but then, we had all been drinking and besides, dancing then didn't require touching anyone. Indeed, you needn't even have looked at your dancing partner!

Melissa said that she worked until 7 p.m. but that she could be ready at about 10 p.m. I remember that I didn't recognize any enthusiasm in her voice, but then perhaps there wasn't much keenness in mine either. I agreed to the time arrangement, though usually at that hour I was not awake. I was a high school English teacher and I had to be in the classroom at 7:30 a.m., and my commute to Long Island on public transportation took over an hour and began at 6 a.m. with a subway ride to Penn Station and from there a journey on the Long Island Railroad to Great Neck. My anxiety level continued to rise but again I acceded to her plan more because I didn't know how not to do so than because I really wanted to continue with the appointment. I don't think I knew then that I could disagree and offer alternative plans because I had never really learned that I possessed any authority to make demands. And besides all of that, I was terrified of dating. My lord I had not the skill.

For the date I donned my best customary casual L.L. Bean catalog look, right down to the button-down oxford shirt, casual chinos, suede vest and blue-cream saddle shoes, and I headed out on the subway for the commute to her neighborhood. Manhattan is a large city divided parochially into very specifically defined neighborhoods: Washington Heights, Harlem, Morningside Heights, Upper West Side, Hell's Kitchen, Upper East Side, Lower East Side, Chelsea, Yorktown, Greenwich Village, Soho, Tribeca, the Bowery . . . all the way down to Manhattan's southern border and the South Street Seaport and what was once the fish markets. Melissa lived on the Upper East Side somewhere in the Sixties across town between Park and Lexington avenues. I resided on the Upper West Side and so I took the Broadway Express to 42$^{nd}$ Street, transferred to the shuttle to Grand Central and got on the uptown East Side lines. When I arrived at her apartment flat, I was alarmed to discover the presence of a young man occupying the only comfy chair in the living room. From the banter between them he was apparently someone with whom she shared some level of intimacy. She introduced us—I don't remember his name—I wondered (to myself, of course) why he was present in the first place. Perhaps he was meant to evaluate and pass some judgment on me, or maybe he was to chaperone our date. Was he going to accompany us to the dance club? I looked at my watch: it was 10:15 p.m.

As Melissa finished her dressing in an attire a lot more stylish than my conservative ensemble, she brought out some marijuana that she passed first to the other companion in the room who took his toke and then offered the joint to me. I pulled the sharp smoke into my lungs and passed the marijuana on to her. As I felt my head lighten, I took a very deep breath, and felt terribly uncomfortable. As Charlie Brown would note about his situations, my stomach hurt! I felt not lost but too glaringly found. How, I wondered, was I going to manage the next several hours. I was not only out of my security zone, but I felt uncomfortably without ballast. Sartorially I was certainly out of my element: the oxford button down shirt and saddle shoes had nothing to do with this crowd into which I was headed but was more symptomatic of my regularly chosen society. Here they seemed to me completely incongruous and slightly absurd. I felt absurd. It was time to abandon this ship or suffer a serious episode of seasickness that would embarrass me more than what I had suddenly decided to do. I placed my palms on my thighs and I stood up. I was going to take the road less traveled. I nervously smiled and with some internal sense of relief, surprised realization, and no little anxiety, announced that perhaps it were best that I just go on home. Melissa looked surprised, but in a tone that contained no spark of curiosity or disappointment wondered why I was leaving. I do not recall my response, and Melissa did not object to my going. Maybe it was the shoes! I slipped on my coat—we spoke of no plans to meet at any other time or place—and I closed the door behind me. At the click of the door latch I felt my heartbeat slow and my breath ease. I had been lost but now I was found. I reversed my commute on the subways reading the *Village Voice* that I always carried with me in my ManBag and fell asleep in my own bed about midnight. The evening had been a very awkward event and at the time seemed then and still now an embarrassing moment which I have shared with no one, and for years I have not recalled it to mind, and I think that it is only in the writing that I can remember it at all.

    Christopher Bollas has defined the self as the capacity to perceive the self. From this perspective—and one to which I ascribe—self becomes a mental activity, though it is an awareness that often begins in the body. I wonder now: what does that uncovered memory of Melissa now change about what I know about myself, how is my Self changed? I become aware at least and maybe again of the terrified man-boy who seemed to have had not an inkling how to negotiate a path through the social world, a skill I think I haven't even at this late date begun to master. I hadn't thought about the failed date with Melissa for so very many years, but clearly the memory waited to be uncovered, and these reflections that are here composed, in part based as they seem to be organized about my anxieties, made space for the memory. In the writing I place another piece of the puzzle in place. My Self is that which on reflection I come to know. Now who do I think I am? Or should the verb be always in the past tense?

## Anxious Am I?

This creates a paradox: to perceive the self in the present necessitates that the awareness occurs in retrospect, in a narration of the past. I have for some time wondered about the retelling of a life and have in the process come to question the truthfulness and accuracy of memoir and autobiography. Ironically, I am composing a memoir now, hoping in time to explain myself—well, to whom exactly other than to mostly myself? If the aim or impetus of the genre is reputedly the pursuit and narration of self-knowledge, then autobiography is problematic simply because the Self about whom the autobiographer would write is embedded in the past though the writer of the memoir exists in the present. The autobiographer, in this case *c'est moi*, can only see the past from his position in the present and therefore, can know the Self in the past only from that perspective. But the autobiographer cannot in the moment know the identity of that Self that exists in the present. Thus, in autobiography and memoir the self that constructs the Self does so from a position of partial ignorance since she has not reflected on, maybe does not even know, the present Self until that Self has slipped into the past. Our Selves might exist in the present, but they come into view only from an examination of the past. And since the memoirist writes for others, the life that is offered as self-portrait becomes less than the truth because that portrait, meant to be seen by those for whom it is intended, is therefore "revised" for that audience. The idea of the audience makes me anxious. How shall I portray myself and to whom? Once for a class in autobiography I gave students several self-portraits Vincent Van Gogh painted over the years and asked them to write an essay choosing one of the paintings and describe who and what Van Gogh had meant to portray. Was there a common thread than tied the paintings together? We compared the various iterations of Van Gogh by Van Gogh.

In the author's note to her novel *A Place of Greater Safety*, Hilary Mantel avows that "almost all the characters in it are real people and it is closely tied to historical facts—as far as those facts are agreed, which isn't really very far."[31] Facts, I think, are subject to interpretation and therefore, not really an expression of reality. Facts are reality with the life removed from it; to be meaningful facts demand context, though any context is neither readily available in toto nor universally agreed upon. Indeed, what might even be referred to as fact is already a value judgment! In Mantel's historical novel of the French Revolution, the array of characters is vast, and I had learned that each of them existed in roles much as Mantel had depicted

---

31. Mantel, *A Place of Greater Safety*, ix.

them, though I wonder whether any of them would accept her interpretations of their words and actions. How each individual defines their life and the way history has ultimately expressed those lives probably is neither consonant nor consistent. A life does not arrive whole and unalterable. We may write our lives, but others are left to read and interpret them. I wonder if Melissa recalls the aborted date-event at all? And does it matter as long as I do so?

Two-thirds of the way into the novel, Gabrielle Danton, George-Jacques' wife, dies in childbirth. Following her funeral, there comes a brief recounting of some of the effects found in her bedroom. We read: "The maid found a handkerchief under the bed where Gabrielle had died; a tradesman delivered fabric that she had ordered just weeks before her death." And her husband "found a novel, with her place marked." Of that novel author Mantel adds in a brief sentence: "And this is it."[32] When she died Gabrielle Danton had been reading exactly that novel in which she has played a significant role and that Mantel had written and I was now reading. Gabrielle Danton, reading *A Place of Greater Safety*, has been reading (in part) an interpretation of her life and of the events in which she has been both an observer and a participant. Mantel does not offer a hint as to which page Gabrielle had reached at the time of her death. Ironically, Gabrielle does not survive to the end of the novel she is reading. She does not learn how it all turns out. Well, I wonder, whoever does? No one reads to the end of the novel. I write it down but not all of it, nor compose to its end.

"I calls 'em as I sees 'em," asserted the umpire, but he and I "sees 'em" from limited and limiting perspectives. "Hey, Ump, are you blind?" someone calls from the stands. I define what I will call facts and create the Self who writes about that Self. As in a novel with or without fiction I read and write for plot and character, even of my own; I write and read for theme, and I have made choices and have interpreted them as I proceeded: I often learned something. Sometimes I have felt that I understood what was going on—the plot, the characters, events, atmosphere and theme—and at other times I felt somewhat baffled. Often, I discovered just the book I had required at the moment: I recognized who and where I was at the time. And sometimes at the end of the day I placed my bookmark on the pages where I had stopped reading, closed the book and hoped that I would rejoin it and my life tomorrow when I awakened. But who knows?

---

32. Mantel, *A Place of Greater Safety*, 524.

## Anxious Am I?

I am a character in the novel I am myself both writing and reading, but I do not know how or when it will end; I cannot write its conclusion though the book will definitely conclude. Events will continue even when I will not, and the future will change what was once to me a fact into something else that I cannot now or maybe ever know. I would like to know what comes next, to follow to its end this or that thread that has already begun, to add another piece to the puzzle, to remain immersed in the beauty and complexity of a woven textual environment, to know how the plot might conclude, but I admit finally that is not possible. At the end of the day and of a life I must close the book and go to sleep and leave for someone else to read to the end of this novel. To know for sure is to surely not to know. In Philip Roth's The Human Stain, Nathan Zuckerman furtively observes Faunia and Coleman at a rehearsal concert at Tanglewood in Massachusetts, and intuits that Coleman had told Faunia, his lover, the great secret he has trusted to no one else. Zuckerman writes: "How do I know she knew? I don't. I couldn't know that... I can't know. Now that they're dead, nobody can know. For better or worse, I can only do what everyone does who think they know. I imagine. I am forced to imagine. It happens to be what I do for a living. It is my job."[33] So is it with me: I am driven to the book by not knowing, for though I know I cannot know I can yet imagine.

In Jane Austen's Mansfield Park, Fanny Price says

> If any one faculty of our nature may be called more wonderful than the rest I do think it is memory. There seems something more speakingly incomprehensible in the powers, the failures, the inequalities of memory, than in any other of our intelligences. The memory is sometimes so retentive, so serviceable so obedient; at others, so bewildered and so weak; and at others again so tyrannic, so beyond control! We are, to be sure, a miracle every way—but our powers of recollecting and of forgetting do seem peculiarly past finding out.[34]

Of course, Freud did a great deal to explain the workings and misworkings of memory, as if memory were some mechanical device. Spinoza suggests that memory always starts in the body, and that the mind is, in fact, the idea of the body and neurophysiologist Antonio Damasio gave scientific credence to Spinoza's position. Memory often if not always does start in the body. Jeanette Winterson writes, "We bury things so deep we

---

33. Roth, *The Human Stain*, 213.
34. Austen, *Mansfield Park*, 180.

no longer remember there was anything to bury. Our bodies remember." I have learned something like this in yoga. As I move through the poses it is not my mind that directs my movement through the sequences but my body that knows the sequence: stand tall and look up; reverse swan dive down to standing fold; half way lift; right foot back left leg bent at the knee leaning forward and rise to standing crescent with arms framing the ears; right foot forward to meet left foot at the top of the mat; standing fold; reverse swan dive up; palms together through heart center, forward fold; halfway lift; left foot back and rise to standing crescent, arms surrounding the ears. Breathe!! Repeat. My mind is often astounded at what the body knows and what it remembers.

Once, I was driving home after an early morning run on the trail along the Red Cedar River. As I rounded a slight bend on Bongey Road and just to my east, rested the local elementary school. My two daughters had attended school there; I believe that both had enjoyed their work there and took some benefit from the education they had experienced. As on most mornings the school parking lot was filled with the cars of teachers, administrators, maintenance and custodial staff. And as I passed the school I experienced a pressure localized mostly throughout my stomach and chest, a pressure such as I might feel when I arrive too late at the station only to watch the train pull away, or when I watch my child go through the security gate at the airport. And I then recalled all of the early mornings that I had arrived to the parking lot at the high school at which I taught English.

I had worked joyfully at Great Neck North High School for fourteen years. I enjoyed pulling into the school parking lot each weekday morning to my assigned space and entering the quiet building to begin the day. I found a home in that high school as I think I had never felt since in any other educational institution in which I have spent time. And along with that memory I recalled that once at the end of the day I walked to my car in that same parking lot. I placed dozens of student papers atop my car as I unlocked the door and then unthinkingly proceeded to get into my car and drive directly to my apartment. I lived then not ten minutes from the school. The student papers must have fluttered up like butterflies, but somehow, I did not see them. When I got home and looked in my bag for the papers that I intended to begin reading, I couldn't find them. I remembered clearly that I had taken them with me when I left the building, and then . . . I cursed my forgetfulness, ran to my car, and drove not carefully enough back to the school. When I arrived at the parking lot, yes, there were the papers scattered about and littering the asphalt like fallen autumn leaves. I ran about collecting them and this time put them directly on the passenger seat of my car and drove home again and devoted the evening to those twice-collected papers.

And almost forty years later as I drove past the elementary school on Bongey Drive, first there were the visceral sensations for which I searched an origin—and then I remembered. And what had been emotion became feeling: love and regret; presence and absence. It wasn't the mind that remembered: it was the body. To have a good mind, Spinoza reminds me, we need a good body; the more complex the body, then the more complex the mind. So, it must be that memory demands an active life. That morning the memory started in the body and soon filled the mind.

Another instance: during the summers of my youth, I often drove to Jones Beach. Always summer represented freedom regardless of the necessity of employment. After all, even being gainfully employed was at the time a temporary situation. And during the summer of 1968 I did not work and instead enrolled at Hofstra University, taking classes in education. I learned to be a teacher to avoid the draft. I drove every morning on the Northern State Parkway that would take me to Meadowbrook State Parkway off which I would exit to Hempstead Turnpike and Hofstra University. During that summer I crammed in an entire semester of foundation classes so that when I returned to Roanoke College in the fall I could enroll in a student-teaching experience that would lead to a teaching license when I returned home after graduation. I don't remember reading very much for class that summer, though I do recall that for one final exam in Franklin Stein's class, Teaching Secondary High School English, a young man behind me pasted pretzels into his blue book. I never learned his assigned grade, but I expect it was at least equal to mine who had written for two hours on one hot summer morning planning a teaching unit about something or other.

But after class on many days at about noon or so, I left the school building and headed in my rambling red Nash Rambler convertible to Jones Beach. I longed for the healthy appearance a suntan would give to my white skin—in my now-advanced years I very much regret those hours baking in the sun as I worry about every developing skin growth and feel despair at the burgeoning liver spots which my dermatologist diplomatically refers to as "wisdom" spots. I wonder now if at the beach I found a certain freedom in the anonymity of the long stretches of sand and water, the insistent and steady sound of the waves, and the casual display of bodies, some of them that were even naked. That was a glorious summer during which I earned the sufficient education credits, and it was also the summer at the beach where I met the girl with whom I lost my virginity.

I would pay the fifty-cent toll and drive through the station and head toward the beaches. Through the booths the road ahead forked: the West beaches heading down one road, a road in the opposite direction to the East beaches. I almost always chose the West beaches because there (as I recall) the concession stands were less plentiful than they were on the East beaches and therefore, less amenable to families. And I wasn't then interested in physical nourishments . . .

And now it was so many years later . . . and I had opportunity to return to New York on a visit from my home in Wisconsin. I was driving to enjoy a social call on a long-ago friend with whom I had taught in Great Neck: I don't think our relationship had back then ended well, and we had not spoken in a good many year. But we were so much older then . . . And here I was again driving on the Northern State Parkway out to Centerport, Long Island, where Larry and Lily had settled in his retirement. And as I rounded the curve just past the exit for Shelter Rock Road, I experienced in my body a sensation that I had first felt during that summer when I had traveled so carelessly first to school and then to the beach and when I felt I was free. In that moment so many years later, I was transported back to that place and time on the Northern State Parkway, no less than was Proust by his madeleines transported to a former time, a former consciousness, a former youth. The event began in my body, and my mind recovered from the body's sensations the memory of those moments of my youth.

And our neurotic states remember. We keep repeating the past without really knowing that it is the past we are repeating. We believe that we are getting better, but really, we are just changing our clothes. Dylan writes, "It looks like I'm moving but I'm standing still." Sometimes I don't even think I look like I'm moving! I call my therapist. I have erred in so many ways. *Mea culpa.* I hope my daughters have been able to forgive me. I wonder now if memoirs and autobiographies are in some way pleas for forgiveness. Perhaps like all apologies, they are tools for learning. Or perhaps autobiographies are a last attempt to justify a life. In his writing Montaigne is looking for himself though that discovery will be more a creation than a revelation. I set out to write a memoir but maybe I am closer to composing a truthful novel fortified with fiction.

## Anxious Am I?

Montaigne writes in "Of Prompt and Slow Speech" (an essay that does not seem to be about either of these subjects, in fact) that because so much of his life occurs in casual and contingent circumstances it often happens that "I do not find myself in the place where I look . . . [but] I find myself more by chance encounter than by searching my judgment."[35] Montaigne admits that he often speaks with insouciance, throwing off a chance remark (which he acknowledges is often clever to himself but may not be so to his listener), but in the wake of that remark he soon loses the point he intended so "that I do not know what I meant; and sometimes a stranger has discovered it before I do."[36] His book of essays on subjects wide and random permits him to find himself as if by chance, and in the process of writing he might experience also great amusement. Montaigne writes, "This book was written in good faith, reader. It warns you from the outset that in it I have set myself no goal but a domestic and private one."[37] In the writing Montaigne would discover himself, thank you. Or can I say that in the writing he would create himself. I'm writing now.

John Berger's book, *Bento's Sketchbook: How Does the Impulse to Draw Something Begin?* links the impulse to draw to aspects of Spinoza's philosophy in the Ethics. For a number of years I devotedly studied the work of Baruch Spinoza. I was attracted by his rationalism, his advocacy of freedom and his apostasy. Spinoza talked about the ability to live fully in the present under the species of eternity. For him this would mean an acceptance that what exists does so by necessity and could be no other way. When we understand the essences of things, then we participate in eternity. Thus, Berger writes, "We who draw do so not only to make something observed visible to others, but also to accompany something invisible to its incalculable destination."[38] We draw to make something visible that demands to be visible—but what that something is we do not know until it is seen. And we bring that something to its proper destination, though we will know our accomplishment only when we arrive there. Then that object will exist where it must. When we make something visible, we make it be and bring it on.

I have for a time considered that we never do know for what we are looking until we actually find it. Thus it is in this writing here: I do not know what it will be until it is seen, and I will know what it is I sought only

---

35. Montaigne, *The Complete Works*, 31.
36. Montaigne, *The Complete Works*, 31-2.
37. Montaigne, *The Complete Works*, 2.
38. Berger, *Bento's Sketchbook*, 11.

when it appears. I must only be patient and vigilant. We, my family, at that time consisting of husband, wife and a one-year old daughter, moved in 1990 to Menomonie, Wisconsin, where I had accepted a position in the Department of Education at the University of Wisconsin-Stout. We dined out often at The Creamery, a lovely, upscale establishment frequented even by people from the Twin Cities, a location almost seventy-five miles distant. The Creamery was a family-owned establishment that had once served just as its name suggested, but it had long gone out of that service. The family patriarch was a Chicago architect, and he had designed the Menomonie space into a dining establishment and a small inn with a few comfortable sleeping rooms atop the restaurant. Dave Thomas took on the role of maître d'; Richard, his brother, had trained and then served as a chef; Katherine, the sister, became the bookkeeper; and John Thomas was a potter and ran a small studio where he displayed his work and that of other area artists. Adjoining the restaurant John had added a small gift shop where often when eating at The Creamery I would browse and where for sale were pieces of his work. Over the years I purchased various items from this shop, and one cherished acquisition was a square dish with eight-inch sides that had been glazed in his traditional styled colors of light cream and faded blue. On the inner lip of each side was a fish painted in a pale, yellow hue. In the middle of the dish was written, "Many men go fishing all their lives without knowing that it is not fish that they are after." The sentence was attributed to Henry David Thoreau, but I have never found the exact location of this citation.

However, in Volume 4 of his Journal, from January 26, 1853, Thoreau writes, "It is remarkable that many men will go with eagerness to Walden Pond in the winter to fish for pickerel and not seem to care for the landscape. Of course, it cannot be merely for the pickerel they may catch . . . They call it going a-fishing, and so indeed it is, though perchance, their natures know better. Now I go a-fishing and a-hunting every day, but omit the fish and the game, which are the least important part."[39] Thoreau's advocacy is for the search and not for the catch. He remains always in pursuit and reveals little interest in catching anything. In *Walden* he writes, "I long ago lost a hound, a bay horse, and a turtle-dove, and am still on their trail."[40] Thoreau acknowledges that some whom he has met have seen or heard of one or even two of these items and that they, too, were anxious to recover these things

---

39. Thoreau, *Journal*, IV, 480.
40. Thoreau, *Walden*, 16.

not merely for Thoreau but for themselves as well. We all, I think, seek the hound, the bay horse and the turtle dove—but not in those words. It is not fish we are after, finally, though often of this we are too much unaware; our Desire lies within us. I have owned that plate for thirty-two years now. It is not fish I am after.

John Berger suggested also that the impulse to draw might begin with the yearning to hold onto something when the present has passed. I call up again my belief that the Self exists in the past but is created in the present. Courage, Spinoza writes, is "the desire by which each endeavors to preserve what is his own according to the dictate of reason alone."[41] Winnicott has claimed that what is my own is not to be shared: it is a joy to be hidden but a tragedy not to be found, Winnicott suggested. What is kept hidden remains my own, ah, though what is hidden might cry out to be seen. To draw—to write—to create— requires courage. Berger's use of his mishearing of Woody Guthrie's "So Long It's Been Good to Know You" as "Hold on, hold on, it's been good to know you" explains the impulse to draw as the desire to hold onto something that insists be held onto, though what that something is may never be completely known until it is drawn. This explains the motive for which I write—to enact the idea attributed to E.M. Forster who is said to have claimed, "How can I know what I think until I see what I say." There is a dynamic expressed here: in the act of writing, Forster creates what he thinks because writing and speaking demand a linearity that gives material presence to thought. I write to think; if I didn't write, what would I know? Come Watson, the game's afoot.

### A PERSISTENCE OF MEMORY

In a Diary report in the 5 January 2017 issue of the *London Review of Books*, Alan Bennett comments on his discovery of the classification of hyperthymesia as a rare medical condition defined as an "unusual autobiographical remembering." I am intrigued by the idea that autobiographical remembering might be considered "a rare medical condition." Being myself inclined towards hypochondriasis, I suffer from several rare and not so rare medical conditions and am always interested in discovering a new potential malady from which I might now or in the near future suffer and subsequently make query about to my very patient primary care physician. I haven't found hyperthymesia listed in either Dictionary.com or my

---

41. Spinoza, *Ethics*, III, LIX, Note.

edition of the Oxford English Dictionary. Alphabetically the latter moves from hypersthenia—extreme or morbid excitement of the vital powers!—to hyperthesis—in philosophy the transposition or metathesis of a letter from a particular syllable to the preceding or following syllable (a definition I don't understand since the example offered appears in the Greek). There are numerous other hypers- listed in the dictionary but not hyperthymesia.

However, I have found that hyperthymesia exists on Wikipedia. There it is reported that American neurobiologists Elizabeth Parker, Larry Cahill, and James McGaugh identified two defining characteristics of hyperthymesia: spending an excessive amount of time thinking about one's past, and displaying an extraordinary ability to recall specific events from one's past. Why either of these characteristics might be considered a medical condition mystifies me. In any case, I find myself in the midst of writing a memoir and thinking excessively about my past, and I wonder if I have developed a case of hyperthymesia from which I am now suffering.

I want to consider for the moment my concern with the identification of hyperthymesia as a rare medical condition. I recognize that the loss of the ability to remember at some point becomes a medical condition: my mother suffered from dementia and didn't always remember who I was much less the events of her life. As I might expect, controversy surrounds the diagnosis of hyperthymesia, with some arguing against the reality of the condition and thereby ascribing the ability to remember so much to . . . well, to good memory skills. Those who define hyperthymesia as a rare medical condition claim that hyperthymesiacs seem to have little control over their stream of memories and hence, can't focus (nor function capably) in the present. This might suggest that the flow of memories occurs without provocation as an unbroken and interminable narration of past events occurring without any immediate stimulation.

But I find this latter belief too problematic. Outside of an isolation chamber a world always exists. Even within one of those contraptions a human being does not lose the world but only the physical sensation of it, and no one knows exactly what resides in the individual's body and exists in their world that might provoke any one thought from rising to the surface of an ever-moving stream. I think again here of the experiences of Proust and his madeleines, the peregrinations of Stephen Dedalus and Leonard Bloom through Dublin on June 16, 1904, or the preparations on the day of her party by Mrs. Dalloway. One can, I think, understand the source if not the motive for the appearance of any one particular thought—Proust redux. But then, as at least James Joyce, Virginia Woolf, William James and Sigmund Freud have taught us, thought occurs as a stream that flows continuously and without effort and is influenced by the complexities of the speed, location, and depths of the waters, by that which rests below the surface, by the conditions that exists in the environment, and by the events that occur that float above that subterranean stream. All of these factors and more influence the movement of the stream of thought, and who knows how the conscious terrain will subsequently appear and what will be known. Freud has even suggested that these surfaced memories are actually screens for more risky ones that must be kept suppressed.

I might suggest that hyperthymesia consists in the capacity to recognize some aspect of one's personal past in everything in the world, and as we move through the world it is no wonder that the memories appear to flood uncontrollably. Hamlet complained that all occasions do inform against him; perhaps the hyperthymesiacs also are constantly confronted by the world everywhere though they do not necessarily make complaint as a result of the torrent. Every object, internal and external, evokes a relation and use. Perhaps sometimes these memories might appear to be a burden, but I cannot imagine that the influx of images would represent a rare medical condition, though the feelings aroused might offer one some pause. Thoreau writes, "It is so hard to forget what it is worse than useless to remember! If I am to be a thoroughfare, I prefer that it be of the mountain-brooks, the Parnassian streams, and not the town-sewers."[42] But even Thoreau could not ensure that he could remain so sparkling and pure. Nor can I.

Sometimes my Broadways do run through the gutters, and there are memories I wish I could forget, but alas, have not been able to do so. Frank Kermode writes that learning one disgraceful thing about yourself is the beginning of self-knowledge. In this age of rampant moral hypocrisy, I appreciate this sentiment. I keep a shorter immediately present list and then a much longer catalog that I save for the psychotherapist. For instance: throughout my life I have been an habitué of musical concerts. Music has been from early on a stimulus, a support and comfort. In the late 1970s I believe it was, when I was yet a young and single man, I had purchased two tickets for a concert by good friends John Prine and Steve Goodman to be held at the Beacon Theater at 76th Street on Broadway in New York City. I had invited a lovely woman to join me. She was a relatively new

---

42. Thoreau, *Essays and Poems*, 361.

acquaintance whom I had met at Riverside Church when William Sloan Coffin was then the head minister. Riverside Church on the Upper West Side, and especially its minister, were associated with the left-leaning culture. Coffin was strongly opposed to the Vietnam War and counseled men who didn't want to be drafted. In 1968 Coffin, Benjamin Spock, Mitchell Goodman, Michael Ferber, and Marcus Raskin were arrested, tried, and convicted for this effort at counseling. On appeal their conviction was overturned. They had not given me advice, but I did somewhere receive draft counseling and then failed in my attempt to get assignment as a conscientious objector. Ironically, I won the first draft lottery with a very low draft number that assured I would be drafted, but I later happily failed my army physical exam. Perhaps that is another story for another time, but on this particular day at Riverside Church I think the event I attended was an anti-apartheid teach-in, and the woman I met was a freelance journalist.

It was acceptable at that time to smoke marijuana in concert halls, but I was wary of introducing drugs into what I thought might be a new relationship. As about most new relationships, I had some anxieties, and so like an alcoholic, I fortified myself prior to the concert by ingesting too many of the wrong drugs. At that moment of my life wine and drugs were my primary means of managing my anxieties: I smoked marijuana and drank regularly in order to get me through the dark nights of my soul even when those nights occurred during the day. Now I might recognize that I suffered from depression, and though I managed myself with sobriety during the week at school and in my classrooms, when away from these environments I needed artificial support. Hyperthymesia notwithstanding, of this particular concert by Steve Goodman and John Prine I regretfully remember very little, not even if I enjoyed it, but what I cannot forget and seem condemned to remember with mortifying ignominy was my behavior in the aftermath. When the concert was over, she and I walked outside the theater and stood under the marquee on Broadway. And as we stood outside the venue I turned nervously towards her. She looked at me expectantly. Now what? she seemed to ask; it was only about 10 p.m. But I really had no plans: I took her hand informally, mentioned something about my being tired, and suggested that with the concert over then the evening, too, had ended. I remember her puzzled expression. Maybe we might have gone at least for coffee or a drink or back to one of our apartments for an evening of sex. But I wished her a good night, turned away and abruptly sped uptown to my apartment. I soon arrived home, drank a large glass

## ANXIOUS AM I?

of wine and fell soundly asleep. I see still her alarmed visage as she stood there perplexed and I imagine not a little angry. I awoke the next day to deep shame and guilt, but I did not then possess the courage to call her with an apology and hope for a chance at another meeting: I never saw her again. My anxieties may have arisen from a sense of social incompetence with which I suffered throughout those angst-filled years, and I think that this was one of the rudest acts I can recall having committed, and I have no doubt accomplished my share of rude behaviors. I cringe still after so many years when I recall it. I wish I could forget it.

And as I recount that instance, I recognize yet another occasion I cannot forget. I had (again!) started a relationship with a woman whom I had met through mutual acquaintances. Well, our original introduction occurred at a gathering entitled The Bixsexual Forum. The group had been associated with my therapist at the time who had written a book called *The Bisexual Option*. Ironically, at the time both the woman and I were seeking a semblance of heterosexuality. I believe that this was my desired preference though I also had been prepared to experiment, and I recall that at the time she was interested in experimenting with heterosexuality because she had been up until then a lesbian. I was the test case, I suppose, as she was mine, and I am certain that we both failed the assay. I cannot now remember her name, but she was an attractive woman, thin and with silken blond hair cut close and carefully styled. She worked in a well-compensated administrative position for the Off-Track Betting Corporation in New York City. She and I established a somewhat hesitant relationship and we dated tentatively. I do recall one fraught sleepover where a terrified Me and an unfamiliar She attempted to have sex. I don't remember that we were very successful. We lay naked, kissed for several minutes and seemed to accept that it was time to sleep in the same bed but not together. The opportunity did not arise again because subsequently I acted like an ass.

In one of the early days of our connection she purchased for us tickets to the Broadway production of the one-woman show, *The Search for Signs of Intelligent Life in the Universe*, starring Lily Tomlin and written by her and her partner, Jane Wagner. Hyperthymesia notwithstanding, I do not remember much about the performance or in fact, anything else about the entire evening. It might even have been the same night we experimented with physical intimacy. But then, on another weekend several weeks later she called to say she had come upon tickets for a second Broadway performance, and though I immediately accepted her invitation, at the last minute I excused myself claiming to be deathly ill. This complaint was a falsehood, but as the evening approached, I began to experience heightened (though somewhat familiar) levels of anxiety. She commiserated over my illness and said she would invite someone else. I spent a quiet evening alone in my 400-square-foot apartment whose two windows looked into another apartment in the building behind and a courtyard filled with garbage cans in various stages of being overfilled. In the morning she called to see how I was feeling, and I thanked her for her well wishes. And then not too long after, perhaps a week or two, she called to say that through her work she had come to possess two tickets for the tennis tournament that was being held at Madison Square, and she asked me to join her. I again accepted her invitation almost aware that when the time for the evening came I would bow out of the event. And just so, on the day of the event I called her office to announce that again I had taken ill and could not join her. But this time I know (rightfully) she did not believe me and let me know that my behavior was unacceptable, which it was! She was angry and declared that she would not again invite me anywhere. And she hung up the phone. The relationship had ended . . . suddenly and badly. And this memory, too, will not leave me though it runs me through my sewers.

I think I know now what this behavior meant then; it represented more than just remaining ensconced within my well-fortified residence. Going out into the world meant engagement in relationships and the menace of intimacy. My lord, I had not the skill. This fear was so strong that I preferred isolation. My seclusion was not Thoreau's solitude, but rather, seemed more like the retreat of Fanny Price in Jane Austen's Mansfield Park. In the midst of that great mansion at Mansfield Park, there existed a room into which Fanny could retreat "after anything unpleasant below." In that room, she could "find immediate consolation in some pursuit, or some train of thought at hand. Her plant, her books, her writing desk, and her works of charity and ingenuity, were all within her reach."[43] In that room all became right and safe. My fear of intimacy was based on the experience of trauma in my childhood of unempathetic parents; of parents who were narcissistically disordered, who could not respond to and confirm "my sense of vigour, greatness and perfection." I remember as a child thinking that for my parents I was never good enough and never could be. Nor could I look up to them as sanctuaries of calm, infallibility, security, and omnipotence. From early on they were anxious, imperfect, and powerless.

---

43. Austen, *Mansfield Park*, 133.

## Anxious Am I?

I remember feeling always alone. I learned not to expect very much from intimate relationships even as I avoided intimacy with them for fear of re-experiencing the trauma of my childhood.

I remember that in my childhood I experienced the trauma from being unrecognized by nonresponsive parents. Today I appreciate that they were emotionally unavailable to me consumed as they must have been with their own troubled and even traumatic existences. I remember that my mother was the youngest of three girls. The eldest daughter, Millicent, was a skilled tennis player who actually played in tournaments and even once (at least) appeared in a match at Forest Hills against Helen Wills. Or so I was told. Phyllis, the middle daughter was a model, or so I was told. I have never seen any photographs of her in any advertisement. The youngest girl, my mother, had been born just prior to the onset of the Great Depression, and her father—my grandfather, a furrier—could sell no fur. Or so I was told. But for sixteen years, during most of my mother's early life, he visited Montefiore Hospital daily to feed his brother lunch. That brother, Abel Hirsh, suffered from the sleeping sickness—encephalitis. I cannot imagine how my mother experienced the abandonment she must have felt. I wonder what must have been her sense of inadequacy and loneliness.

My father spoke little of his childhood and there is little that I remember of our relationship outside of his silences and business failures. He and his twin brother were the youngest of five children. I remember that my father once told me that he had begun study at yeshiva but at the death of his father in 1942 he had dropped out and went to work unhappily in the family business. He had meant to become a rabbi like his older brother, and I think he had intended that I complete his plan. I was headed toward yeshiva myself when my mother put an end to my father's ambition for me. He never did talk very much about his family life, and much of what I think I remember may be mere speculation. Unhappy in the successful family business in which he felt constrained and underappreciated, he and his twin brother set out separately on their own to prove their unrealized capabilities. I do not recall what business Uncle Milton undertook, but neither brother was successful and in the end both separately suffered bankruptcy. I don't have many memories of my father's family: my mother didn't like them, and he . . . well, I guess he never made an issue of her aversion to them. I do recall that my parents had eloped and I have since suspected that his family didn't find my mother's family Jewish enough and so objected to their marriage plans.

Both my father and his twin had worked in the garment trade, my father first as a cutter and then as clothing manufacturer where his unending ambition and rapaciousness led to marginally illegal negotiations and deals and ended predictably in repeated business failures. At times I think my father just escaped being caught in his petty thefts and dubious transactions. I recall that at the time of the first of the bankruptcy auctions the fabric scraps on factory the floor from a shipment my father claimed had fallen off the back of a truck were recognized by the material's owner as part of his inventoried pieces. The suspicion led to an investigation to discover how these scraps had ended on the floor of my father's factory. Fortunately, but for reasons I never learned, this search did not proceed very far and my father escaped culpability but not guilt. For a brief time following a spell of unemployment I had joined his firm and became witness to his dubious achievements, and was mortified when I came to know some of his behaviors and his acquaintances. Sometimes when I looked at my father I remembered Meyer Wolfsheim, the man in Fitzgerald's *The Great Gatsby* who fixed the World Series. Eventually, I was freed from this familial commitment when again my father couldn't pay any of his bills and the factory went up a second time for auction and closed permanently.

Both of my parents suffered difficult childhoods and we three siblings were parented from within their own traumas and subsequent dysfunctions. They never did achieve any insight into themselves. I clung to my isolation to avoid repetition of the trauma. The world frightened me though I did so want to be a part of it. I think I became a wallflower. A wallflower hangs in the background while others step onto the floor and dance. From shyness, from fear, or from some other experience of anxiety, the wallflower keeps himself on the fringes of activity, sometimes as an astute observer of the scene but also one not prone to venture voluntarily into it. That the wallflower is present in the room at all speaks to her desire to dance, but something keeps her from moving to the floor. According to an online dictionary, the term "wallflower" refers to the fragrant flowers of *Cheiranthus cheiri* [that] came to be called wallflowers because they often grow on old walls, rocks, and quarries. The word originally described women at dances, but today I apply the word to men as well and to situations that are far removed from the dance floor. But I painfully remember myself at high school dances standing against the wall enviously watching the gymnasium floor at those boys who had already coupled or had been bold enough to make a request for a dancing partner. Some of those couples were actually having sex, an opportunity I could not imagine for myself. Wallflowers are not outsiders, but they are often found on the fringes of events; wallflowers are not antisocial though they may be socially averse. I believe that the wallflower could change the quality of the room and his life if only he would venture into it, yet the wallflower's wonderful fragrances have been lost to the crowded room because the flowers cling desperately, even longingly to the walls. And yet . . .

In Wendy Wall's "The Wallflower's Waltz" the grief of the wallflower is palpable and causes me to ache. The wallflower is ready to join the dance if only someone's welcoming hand would reach out an invitation:

> Won't you take up my hand
> Lift me off of my seat
> Spin me onto that floor
> Sweep me off of my feet
> A bloom withers on a vine
> Left alone left to chance
> And it's breaking my heart not to dance

I have wondered to whom the appeal is sung. The desire and loneliness expressed in the final line touches me. It is heartbreaking not to dance, not to join with others in joy and gaiety; that perhaps because of some private anxiety that paralyzes the will the wallflower sits alone against the wall and waits longingly and invitingly. It is painful to watch without a smile the smiles of the dancers. It does break one's heart to make the hand ready but have the invitation be unrecognized or spurned. Oh dear, *c'est moi*.

I wonder if one aetiology of wallflowers points to hyperthymesia: maybe wallflowers have become paralyzed by a traumatic memory. Hamlet's father's ghost demands "Remember me," and Hamlet declares he will remember nothing else. Memory can, indeed, incapacitate. The past would always remain somewhat present, and for some, wallflowers perhaps, this conflation might be a heavier burden than for others. They cling to the wall for support and protection, but it breaks their heart not to dance. Hyperthymesiacs might not be physically crushed by the influx of memory, but the hyperthymesiac might suffer from one or three particular memories. I have known such people. I have been such people.

Perhaps one "cure" then for this "rare medical condition" might be a learned ability to forget. But I wonder how the art of forgetting might be learned. In *Deuteronomy* the Torah says that when the people come to be settled in the land, they should blot out the memory of Amalek and what he did to them on their journey out of Egypt. But then Torah immediately cautions against the command to forget: "Remember what Amalek did to you on the way when you came out of Egypt, how he confronted you on the way and attacked among you all the stragglers at your rear when you were tired and weary; and he did not fear God. So it shall come about, when the Lord your God has given you rest from all your surrounding enemies in the land which the Lord your God is giving you as an inheritance to possess, that you shall wipe out the mention of the name Amalek from under heaven; you must not forget. Finally, never to forget..."[44] I have often wondered if Torah means do not forget to remember or do not forget to blot out the memory. The latter seems to me a paradox: the attempt to never forget suggests an ever-present memory. But perhaps hyperthymesia derives from those verses in *Deuteronomy*.

The processes of remembering and forgetting exist in a complex relationship. How to know what to remember and what to forget seems to me a regular irony which we all experience. I've been considering that memory embodies an essential sadness. In memory one recalls a past event that the present has somehow inspired. Sometimes in memory I recollect when things were better, and sometimes in memory one remembers the unhappiness that occurred in the past. At the bat mitzvah of my daughter, we remembered her grandfather who died of lung cancer three years prior. In the midst of happiness it might seem that there would be no call to remember a past unhappiness, but perhaps it is exactly in those moments that one remembers such circumstances exactly for the contrast that the memory offers to the events of the present. Maybe the memory of unhappiness drains just a drop or three of joy from the cup, not unlike the drops of wine spilled during the recitation of the plagues during the Passover Seder. In the act of dripping we diminish our joy by remembering the Egyptians drowned in the Red Sea. Memory changes the present even as it structures the past. Memory is a narrative construction and what it constructs is a life even when what is remembered is the experience of trauma—a breaking of the continuity of existence. At the core of memory resides a sadness that derives from an acknowledgment of a discrepancy between present and past.

Memory is not history. History purports to be facts, but as I have said facts are events with the life taken out of them. Historian Bernard Bailyn writes, "I am concerned with one of the central problems in the everyday practice of history that contemporary historians actually face none of

---

44. Deuteronomy, 25:17–19.

whom, as far as I know, believe naively that historians can attain perfect objectivity; none of whom dream that a historian can contemplate the past from some immaculate perch, free from the prejudices, assumptions, and biases of one's own time place, and personality; none of whom deny that facts are inert and meaningless until mobilized by an inquiring mind, and hence that all knowledge of the past is interpretive knowledge . . . "[45] History "sometimes an art,"[46] Bailyn asserts, attempts to offer a more accurate depiction of what might have occurred knowing well that such portrayal is always limited, incomplete, and heavily influenced by the present. Bailyn writes, "We cannot experience what they experienced in the way they experienced it."[47] We can only imagine. For example, as I viewed Kenneth Branagh's film *All is True*, I could not help thinking how dark life must have been without electricity. Even in Shakespeare's large and elegant Stratford home, the interiors, lit only by candles, fireplaces and windows in the daylight seemed perpetually gloomy. I kept wanting someone to turn on the light switch and illuminate the scene so that I could see it enhanced. How can I begin to imagine what our homes and our lives in them would be like in the absence of electric light when I have never known a moment without electricity save in the always short-lived emergencies. I can't quite know and remember now with any accuracy how life was then, but I can imagine and write the story.

Memory is hot and fertile, but facts are cold and sterile. This contrast accounts for the vitality of psychotherapy. In psychotherapy one creates a story-that-works from the facts that come available; psychotherapy offers life to the facts, though it must be acknowledged that those facts are inevitably changed by their placement into the story and are transformed from mere "facts" into elements of a constructed narrative. Yes, the Holocaust happened, and we have the facts—dates, names and numbers that confirm it. But the Holocaust possesses existential meaning in the stories that are its essence and that arise out of it: in the diary of Anne Frank, the memoirs of Elie Wiesel and Primo Levi and in the memories and stories of the many others who survived it and left records of their struggles, or like Allen and Helen Mastbaum who survived the horror and whom we drove each week to synagogue. To my children they told their stories. History as memory is sad; facts in the absence of story are not history. "But we must all still

---

45. Bailyn, *Sometimes and Art*, 21.
46. Bailyn, *Sometimes and Art*, 22.
47. Bailyn, *Sometimes and Art*, 23.

be storytellers, narrators—though of events lodged deep in their natural contexts,"[48] Bailyn writes. Those contexts may be remembered and named but they remain for the most part interpretable and resistant to any semblance of Truth even though they attempt to represent reality. History, like memory, embodies an essential sadness.

Writing this memoir I remember and capture reality by translating it into words. I continue to write; I wished I had written more.

## ON MEMOIRS, OR NOVELS WITHOUT FICTION

Over the past several years I have read many memoirs and autobiographies, and I have given considerable thought to the character of them and the writers who write them. Ironically, I am writing a memoir now! The main character in the memoir identifies as the author of it as well! The defendant claims he is innocent because he was at the scene of the crime and he observed that he didn't commit any wrongdoing, but if he seems now culpable then, he is very sorry and has since and certainly reformed. I think that the narrator of any memoir is, at best, unreliable. Memoirs have agendas and themes and the lives that are offered are heavily edited and often different from the lives that have been lived. For example, in *The Education of Henry Adams*, there is not a single mention of the suicide of his wife. This seems to me to be a significant omission. Philosopher Stanley Cavell titled his autobiography *Little Did I Know*. I think memoirs are historical—they do address actual lives—but they are not history. From lives lived, memoirs create a significance that the life didn't originally possess. The aim of the writing is not only discovery but creation. The memoirist reflects back in memory to create a character that moves forward. But as memory is fleeting then so too is the reality memory offers and thus, in the memoir the character who moves forward attains the status of fiction. Memoir writing as first person narrative becomes an original genre. David Vincent in *A History of Solitude* suggests that "the search for a narrative identity discoverable only through solitary self-analysis opened a path towards a new genre of literary autobiography."[49] I believe that memoirs have a close affinity to fiction and might be better classified as novels in disguise. Dickens' *David Copperfield* would be an example of such a genre as would the plethora of memoirs that today flood the bookstores. I think of Montaigne in his tower and Thoreau

---

48. Bailyn, *Sometimes and Art*, 52.
49. Vincent, *History of Solitude*, 6.

at Walden and myself in my writing spaces creating something for which we each have searched. I recognize that finally someone will read and interpret this one.

I have also lately wondered if one can live a memoir even before writing one, that is, to consciously create a character based not at all on an actual past but on an imagined one, a creation that would head toward some sought-after future. Such a memoir would actively portray a life different than the one that had actually been lived. These "memoirs" would be based on projection rather than reflection. For example: *The Imposter* by Javier Cercas narrates the story of Enrico Marco who at the age of fifty rewrote his life, ironically as did Don Quixote at that same age. Rather, Marco invented a wholly new existence based not at all on the one he had already lived. In this rewriting, Marco lived his memoir and, in that creation, became its hero. Cercas writes that Marco at fifty, "became deeply politicized, and completely reinvented himself, falsifying or embellishing or embroidering his past, gifting himself with a new name, a new wife, a new city, a new job, and a new life." Finally, Marco went so far as to claim to be a survivor of the Nazi concentration camp, Flossenbürg. Marco became the main character in the novel he chose to live, even as he was the main character of his memoir because he wrote the past that was needed for the character he had created.

Part II of Javier Cercas' book is titled "The Novelist of Himself," referring, of course, to Enrico Marco who through his imagination rewrote himself as a main character. The author of any memoir is the novelist of himself! I have for years not attempted the writing of fiction, but here in this memoir as I reflect and narrate, I think I may be engaged in writing a novel, perhaps one without fiction but a novel nonetheless. And the chapter title of *The Imposter* could ironically apply not only to Enrico Marco but to Javier Cercas, who is a published novelist as well as the author of *The Imposter*, the novel without fiction, and an author who in the writing comes to wonder about his affinity with his subject. Cercas acknowledges that the author of any book is not who he claims to be, that is, he is not "a good writer, a good citizen, a decent person and all that respectable drivel." The writer—Cercas—borrows and steals and appropriates without shame. And then, usurping his character Marcos's voice Cercas accuses himself: "And what did I do? I did exactly the same as you—no, I did it much better than you. I invented a guy like Miralles," a character in Cercas' novel *Soldiers of Salamis*, but I created a person who "was alive and . . . visited schools and talked to children about the horrors of the Nazi camps and about the Spanish inmates there, and about justice and freedom and solidarity; this man was leader of the Amical de Mauthausen, and thanks to him people began to talk about the Holocaust in Spanish schools, thanks to him people discovered that Flossenbürg camp existed and that fourteen Spaniards had died there."[50] What Cercas as Marco argues is that the fiction that Marco created had served a purpose—a truth-telling?—no different but more successful than Cercas' hope for his novels with fiction. An interesting admission, I think, for an author to have acknowledged. Marco has written himself as a hero. Am I writing myself the hero of this memoir? What am I claiming to have done?

The autobiographer, because s/he is writing, necessarily imposes pattern; in the creative act of writing s/he necessarily selects and adds those details that enhance interest in the work. Frank Kermode in his memoir *Not Entitled* admits that in the creation of memoir what ultimately results cannot be the truth! "It is a species of the good writing that cannot help eliminating truth from autobiography . . . [good writing] is a means of giving life the calm coherence of myth."[51] The nor'easters, those storms that disturbed, distorted, and disrupted the living of a life are tamed in the writing, but then, by that act of filtering and taming the substance of the autobiography becomes no longer exactly truthful. Kermode cautions, "If the honest truth is demanded, let it be remembered that few, and of them not many very honest, have been willing to claim that they told [the truth]; it is undeniable that its principal enemy, in autobiography, is, as I have suggested, not mendacity but good writing."[52] It is either style or truth and the wish for readership and some heroism gives priority to the former.

But the life that Marco presented as authentic and socially responsible was all a lie! I consider now, whose life told is truthful? *The Imposter* is a book about the deceptions Enrico Marco constructed in his rewriting of himself—his memoir— and of Cercas' journey to discover and to reveal those lies. In fact, Javier Cercas, the novelist, had considered writing a novel about Marco, but he felt he couldn't write a novel about Marco because Marco has already spoken so many lies that his life was already a fiction. But what is truth and what is lie in a memoir remains a question. Ironically Cercas notes, "The liar has no history," but then, what memoir is historically

50. Cercas, *The Imposter*, 299.
51. Kermode, *Not Entitled*, 154.
52. Kermode, *Not Entitled*, 155.

true? History, as historian Bernard Bailyn acknowledges, is sometimes an art, and Marco proved to be somewhat of a brilliant artist.

Reality kills, says Cercas, but literature saves. Marcos' memoir, fictive though it is, had saved him and gave him a new and useful life even though his narrated life was all a fiction. The truth of our being may actually consist of the knowledge of what we need to lie. T.S. Eliot writes that humankind cannot bear too much reality. And I somewhere had read and recorded this in my journals, "The truth is unbearable. It's not the lie that's terrifying, what's terrifying is the truth." I wonder now what it is from that which I am hiding in this memoir. I think my therapist might have some response to that question. We write what we can, but we fool ourselves when we imagine that our memoirs represent the truths of our lives. Jeanette Winterson says, "I wrote the story I could live with. The other one was too painful."[53] I wonder who I am writing here and what that other life might be.

Philip Roth says, "We are writing fictitious versions of our lives all the time, contradictory but mutually entangling stories that however subtle or grossly falsified, constitute our hold on reality and are the closest thing we have to the truth."[54] We are all fictions and that is our truth. In Kurt Vonnegut's *Mother Night*, Howard Campbell Jr.'s memoirs warns, "We are what we pretend to be, so we must be careful about what we pretend to be."[55] Marco lived the novel that he wrote. Did he know himself? And was he "himself" what he wrote? One version of the myth of Narcissus that Cercas narrates says that Narcissus was conceived from the rape of Liriope by Cephissus. Narcissus is born with incredible beauty and Liriope travels to the blind prophet, Tiresias, to ask if her son will live to an old age. Tiresias tells her that Narcissus will live to old age "if he does not know himself." Marco never does come to know himself, and the novel he had written kept him defensively ignorant. As I write now Marco is ninety-nine years old. I am writing now, and I believe that we never do know ourselves though perhaps the deeply sane do not cease looking.

I have spent a great many years in therapy discovering my ignorances, even as I continued to narrate and construct what I thought was my life story. One thing that I have learned is how much of my life was organized by what I did not know then. In Philip Roth's *I Married a Communist*, Murray Ringold, Zuckerman's high school English teacher, tells the grown Nathan

---

53. Winterson, *Why Be Happy When You Can Be Normal*, 6.
54. Roth, *Ready Myself*, 161.
55. Vonnegut, *Mother Night*, v.

Zuckerman that Murray's brother, Ira, had carried about with him the guilt "about what happened to you." Nathan responds, "Nothing happened to me. I was a kid," but Murray responds, "Oh, something happened to you."[56] Murray tells Zuckerman that as a boy he had not received a Fulbright award because of his association with Ira Ringold, a blacklisted Communist who the FBI erroneously and absurdly believed to be his uncle. Having not received the award and not knowing why he had been refused had changed the direction of Zuckerman's life. Nathan then considers: "Of course, it should not be too surprising to find out that your life story has included an event, something important, that you have known nothing about—your life story is in and of itself something that you know very little about."[57] The road not taken has indeed made all the difference. Of a life there is so much that is not known and this present memoir with which I am engaged is an attempt to know something even if it is not the truth. That the unexamined life is not worth living has served as my guiding principle. Thoreau argues, "Be rather the Mungo Park, the Lewis and Clark and Frobisher, of your own streams and oceans; explore your own higher latitudes—with shiploads of preserved meats to support you, if they be necessary; and pile the empty cans sky-high for a sign. Were preserved meats invented to preserve meat merely? Nay, be a Columbus to whole new continents and worlds within you, opening new channels, not of trade, but of thought."[58] I consider that I have consumed my share of cans of preserved meats, and my writings are some of the cans that I have piled sky-high. I am writing now the book with which I can live.

In fact, I can only know my life as a story, one that is organized by plot and theme, and one that I continually write and then revise. I think I started learning this with Jerome Bruner in *Actual Minds, Possible Worlds*, and reinforced even yesterday in a book by Robert Shiller entitled *Narrative Economics: How Stories Go Viral and Drive Major Economic Events*. In a review of the latter, Cass Sunstein writes that Shiller "is onto something important and often neglected. Many of our most significant decisions are made not by careful cost-benefit analysis but by stories that come into our minds."[59] But I am thinking that it is possible to know what event has had some importance in the development of my life only in the writing or

56. Roth, *I Married a Communist*, 15
57. Roth, *I Married a Communist*, 15.
58. Thoreau, *Walden*, 348.
59. Sunstein, "Once Upon a Time," 35.

telling of it. Whatever else a story is, it is a construction, and what is included in it has been assigned some significance by the writing of it. And since my life story is a construction, then of course, certain events will not enter into the plot I have constructed. Murray Ringold's narrative suggests to Zuckerman that whatever life story with which he had familiarity was at best incomplete and at worst just plain wrong! Zuckerman had not been lord of any realm but rather, has served perhaps as its jester. I am never all that I say I am, and thanks to Freud, et al., I acknowledge that I am always more than I could know and say. I will never know myself, really, though I can imagine. May I live a long life! In fact, the self that writes has to be different than the self about whom is written because the autobiographer sets an aim that is wholly different than had been the aims of the subject of the autobiography. The latter had no notion of ever being the subject of an autobiography, and the autobiographer in the present chooses those actions that coincide with the theme of the autobiography. My actions in the past cannot be considered coincident to the descriptions and motivations given now to them by me, the autobiographer. Even drawing upon journals and diaries, the autobiographer would have to choose those entries that seem in the present relevant to the narrative under construction.

However, if the Self in the past had already intended to become the subject of an autobiography—which was certainly not the case for me—then those actions in the past would have been governed by the necessity of their having to be written in the future. In this case, the life was always teleologically determined by the necessity of its autobiography, and the autobiography could not be considered a pursuit of self-knowledge: that future Self had been already organized in the past. The Self in the past could never have known where she might be in the future, but the Self writing in the present, in an ironic twist on the Hansel and Gretel story, had already dropped the white pebbles to orient the Self to "home." Philip Roth refers to autobiography as the most manipulative of genres: contained within every autobiography is always a countertext which the manifest text attempts to hide. When I write autobiographically there is always a latent material: why am I telling the story this way, I wonder. Who would I be if I told the story another way, I wonder.

In his memoir *Little Did I Know*, Stanley Cavell suggests that one problem in autobiography concerns the development of the narrative thread. This is no simple difficulty, Cavell notes, because at each step in the writing, "I seem to run up against a crowd of related matters that demand their expression."[60] Every occasion informs another, and each word suggests not only an alternative one but even remembers a different event. I think that these crowds of related matters inspired the digressions that Tristram Shandy claims to be the heart of his book. In order to disrupt the linearity that would corrupt whatever truth exists in the writing, Tristram keeps interrupting the narrative with digressions. "Digressions, incontestably, are the sunshine;—they are the life, the soul of reading;—take them out of this book for instance,-—you might as well take the book along with them."[61] Without digressions, Tristram says, there is no book! The center of the book is not the plot but the digressions from the narrative.

This appears to be the problem Cavell recognizes in the writing of his autobiography: there is no definitive end to the various paths he might take in the writing and to the life he would present. No one path would be his life but only a limited version of it: there are so many roads untaken. Of his own method Tristram says, "I set no small store . . . that my reader has never yet been able to guess at any thing. And in this, Sir, I am of so nice and singular a humour, that if I thought you was able to form the last judgment or probably conjecture to yourself, of what was to come in the next page,—I would tear it out of my book."[62] Digressions are necessary because no occurrence can be understood outside of the context in which the event occurred, and the digressions often directly and sometimes only vaguely engage that context. Reading *Tristram Shandy* is not about plot at all—though the book, ostensibly an autobiography that begins on the subject of Tristram's birth in fact doesn't narrate that event until eighty pages into the narrative! Tristram says, "I defy, not withstanding all that has been said upon straight lines in sundry pages of my book—I defy the best cabbage planter that ever existed, whether he plants backwards or forwards, it makes little difference in the account (except that he will have more to answer for in the one case than in the other)—I defy him to go on coolly, critically, and canonically, planting his cabbages one by one, in straight lines, and stoical distances, especially if slits in petticoats are unsew'd up—without ever and anon straddling out, or sidling into some bastardly digression."[63] Alas, take the digressions out of the book and you might as well not have a book at all! Thoreau had complained that education turns a meandering brook into a straight cut ditch! I

60. Cavell, *Little Did I Know*, 37.
61. Sterne, *Tristram Shandy*, 52.
62. Sterne, *Tristram Shandy*, 57.
63. Sterne, *Tristram Shandy*, 380.

have spent my life in the schools. I wonder sometimes if I am a meandering brook or a straight cut ditch?

In autobiography the teleology of the narrative arc maintains the tautness of the narrative, but there is so much else in which the event is embedded that maintaining an even thread seems honestly impossible. Since a whole life can't be narrated, then the life that is narrated is different than the life that was lived and the former depends very much on a memory that cannot be (thankfully) controlled. The autobiography is not the facts. Cavell admits, "I mean to speak from identities compacted in my existence, a matter of attaching significance to insignificance and vice versa."[64] Like shrapnel from a mine, these pieces fly out uncontrollably and some hit the consciousness of the autobiographer. But not all! The autobiography assumes the status of fiction: everything cannot be told. If what I say is not the whole truth then is it even a partial truth? Can anything be the whole truth? I think digressions obstruct the narrative thread and offers a more complex view of a life that remains always open to contingency and rewriting. Autobiography is an unfinished draft that will never be finished.

I act from an interminable number of decisions I make each day, though often, I think, I am not consciously aware that I have made a decision. In circumstances I have not wholly constructed I act, and though I have learned to assume responsibility, indeed, sometimes even take pride in that assumption, I also have understood that such pride derives from a very limited perspective. I acknowledge readily and regretfully that to assume complete knowledge is a fiction. But now I wonder if this acknowledgment is just an excuse for the many errors I have made. Marx said that the traditions of all past, dead generations weigh like a nightmare on the brain. Stephen Dedalus says that history is a nightmare from which he is attempting to awaken, and my dear friend, Bill, describes the present as a nightmare. What might be so frightening about nightmares is that in them I lack any semblance of control over my behavior; in my nightmares I am always threatened with dissolution. Perhaps nightmares derive from the fear of lack of control that the nightmares enact. Last night I dreamed that every time I stood up to assume my role in a social occasion there was someone already standing in my place. In my nightmare I was reduced to silence and helplessness. My nightmares arise out of my greatest fear: that I am out of control. But perhaps the whole belief that I am ever in control is the fiction. When Montaigne says that "I find myself more by chance

---

64. Cavell, *Little Did I Know*, 7.

encounter than by searching my judgment" I think I know what he means. I live a great deal in illusion.

My current situation is the result of a history of which I am not fully aware, and over which certainly I have had only marginal control. I go to therapy to narrate that history as I must and ascribe to my life some causality. In my sessions I offer up my history by writing a past, inscribing a self in that history. It is all a lovely fiction. Though actively imagining a past, it is really the future with which I am concerned. Perhaps I require a particular past so that I can change direction from it and move towards a future. I need a past so that I can keep on keeping on. But perhaps it is all a fiction: even my changes are partly a result of conditions not of my choosing. There are almost always pieces of the puzzle missing, and I don't even know what the final picture is supposed to look like. I think of Doris Day's question to her mother about what she might be when she grew up, and her mother answered what will be, will be. *Que sera, sera*. Well, that is one answer. Perhaps the sublime is a respite from history though what brings me to the sublime moment is always history.

## ON LORD JIM

Just before the catastrophic trauma of the election of Donald Trump in 2016, I had already intended to read Joseph Conrad's novel, *Lord Jim*. I have over my years read a significant selection of contemporary fiction with varying degrees of satisfaction, but I enjoy returning to old friends, to renew their acquaintance and catch up on our progresses. As have I, these friends have aged, and sometimes when I drew one out from its neighborhood and beg some companionship, its fragility becomes all too evident. The glue that binds has irrevocably dried; the covers slip off and the pages sometimes detach from the split spine. Too often when I pull a volume out to renew some familiarity or to enter into some new intimacy, the book comes undone in my hands and almost seems to be unreadable. I fear that my pens and pencils would further rend the lines and spaces; my own earlier voices engraved in the pages have, indeed, somewhat faded and too often seem in shadow. But I sit in my faux-Eames chair or at my desk and delicately embrace the volume and as I read gently turn through the pages and recover some of my past as I move with them into some future. As I read I see along the margins of the pages spectral words in a familiar handwriting addressing some once important and now recalled thoughts that draw me to my past. These books give me some access to that past and I hold onto these friends for my life.

Conrad is one of those acquaintances to whom I turn at various times and *Lord Jim* has remained one of those revered volumes. Recently I accompanied my daughter in her reading of *The Secret Agent* for an English class at university. I think we both learned something. Fifty-two years ago *Lord Jim* was an assigned text in a seminar course I was taking as an undergraduate at Roanoke College. My Norton Critical Edition of *Lord Jim* was purchased new for $2.95, and as I now read the novel some of the pages detached from the binding and floated down like autumn leaves, or perhaps they were more like drifting lost souls; but my writings and notes were thankfully still mostly visible in the borders and I would not abandon them. I determined to read this volume and not any other edition. I was then constrained to study *Lord Jim* not in any reclined position, not even sitting in the fifty-year-old Bentwood rocking chair or the newer Eames chair, but rather, seated at attention at my beautiful handmade desk with my journal alongside the text and a fountain pen in my hand.

The text of *Lord Jim* had sat quietly on my shelf since my college years because its presence connected me to some aspect of my academic and social past with which I would not part. It was 1969 and the world was changing. My fraternity, which was comprised of two Jews, some social misfits and outcasts, a strange assortment of eccentrics, and a physics major, had suddenly become popular. We owned the albums that defined the era—the Jefferson Airplane's *Surrealistic Pillow*, the Beatles *White Album*, Bob Dylan's *Highway 61 Revisited*, The Doors' *Strange Days*, Jimi Hendrix's *Are You Experienced*. I had deposited a great many quarters into the campus juke box playing Janis Joplin and Big Brother and the Holding Company and the Jefferson Airplane's "White Rabbit." Until that auspicious year, we fraternity brothers were the characters no one would speak to on campus and certainly not choose to date. We were obviously not Southern gentlemen! But then suddenly, in 1969, as the seismic shift in culture took place, we community of oddities and characters became sought after and dateable. I had returned to campus from the Thanksgiving holiday with a significant supply of marijuana, and when word leaked out to its presence a few almost kindred souls from other campus fraternities that had in the past avoided us suddenly beat paths to our door. Down in the basement of my fraternity house we strangers gathered in a storage room amidst bridge chairs and tables, put towels along the base of the door to keep the smoke from leaking into the social room, and became friends.

Conrad's *Lord Jim* was a text in the Senior Seminar, a required class for English majors that was held in Dr. Matthew Wise's upstairs office. It was in that relatively small room and during one significant class session and even before the eyes of Dr. Matthew Wise that Miss Roanoke College, who until that moment had always rendered me invisible, flirted with me and even at some point in the discussion actually rubbed her leg against mine! I took this unexpected occurrence as an astonished confirmation that the culture on campus had shifted, and I recall making a date with Miss Roanoke College for a dinner in a borrowed off-campus apartment that unfortunately but characteristically didn't end at all aligned with my fantasies. However, I have pleasurably identified *Lord Jim* with these particular and precious moments.

And why I had then chosen to reread *Lord Jim* I am not quite certain even as perhaps Marlowe is not sure why Jim chooses him to tell his story. I had known the story the novel told: it was on one level about cowardice. Back then I was an incipient draft dodger but perhaps not a coward. Sometimes a book settles me in my history even as my history rewrites the book. Maybe now I wanted to return to Roanoke College and to 1969, to Dr. Wise and Senior Seminar, to Miss Roanoke College and the comfort of the Blue Ridge Mountains; and I wanted to read *Lord Jim* with what I had since learned about reading from my experience and my study. I remembered then being enthralled by a critical essay by Tony Tanner, entitled "Butterflies and Beetles—Conrad's Two Truths," and felt drawn to the novel and Tanner's essay and to the memories both inspired. And then as I began the book the horror of the presidential election and the unthinkable ascension of Donald Trump to the highest office in not only the United States but perhaps in the world occurred. And suddenly this story of cowardice and moral strength, of beetles and butterflies took on new meaning and I read with renewed purpose.

I had been devastated by the election results and somewhat terrified of what the future (for generations) might hold for the nation and the world. My fears have been since realized. At our nation's helm was the captain of the Patna, the "incarnation of everything vile and base that lurks in the world we love,"[65] and whose actions had been criminal. The president, like the heinous captain in *Lord Jim* and like Cornelius, the Patusan trading

---

65. Conrad, *Lord Jim*, 14.

post's previous manager, was a bitter, deceitful, detestable man filled with hate and rage. Trump had been governed by a dangerous narcissism that bordered on the psychotic and led to actions that were most certainly criminal. Many of us would have liked to retreat without added terrors, quietly, into a sort of peaceful escape. But I felt that Lord Jim's cowardly desertion should not be our choice. Despite his high ideals and his glorious opinion of his character, at the moment of crisis Jim abandons those for whom he was responsible in order to save himself. This retreat could not be to what we could in the present resort.

My reading of *Lord Jim*, then, became focused by the despair I daily experienced during Donald Trump's term as president of the United States. Or perhaps I continued to read *Lord Jim* from within my despair and made the book speak to (or of) that anguish. I discovered that the novel suited my sense of gloom; its sensibility seemed apt to my own despondent sense of life in the wake of the election. At a minimum, *Lord Jim* is the story of human frailty and weakness, and how this weakness manifests itself not overtly but, as Marlowe says, rather like a snake hiding in the bush. That snake is all the more perilous because it remains concealed until it strikes. And Marlowe, to whom Jim tells his story, comments, "[Jim] was not afraid of death, perhaps, but I'll tell you what, he was afraid of the emergency. His confounded imagination had evoked for him all the horrors of panic, the trampling rush, the pitiful screams, boats swamped—all the appalling incidents of a disaster at sea he had ever heard of. He might have been resigned to die, but I suspect he wanted to die without added terrors, quietly, in a sort of peaceful trance."[66] Jim wanted to avoid the conflict, the messiness of the event, the futility of the attempt, the helplessness that he knew would be his in this occasion. Jim wanted to retire and lose himself in a fatal quietism. Despite his rather high opinion of himself, Jim cowardly abandoned the fatally wounded boat, the Patna, which was about to sink, and jumping ship in the crisis Jim had saved himself from the doomed vessel on board of which eight hundred sleeping pilgrims would perish. Jim had had the opportunity to awaken the sleeping passengers, but he had chosen rather to get himself to safety. I, too, often do what I can to avoid messiness and conflict.

But in my present reading of *Lord Jim* it was Stein, the German, to whom I was most drawn. He had escaped Europe as a result of his revolutionary activity that stemmed, I consider, from his own idealism and

---

66. Conrad, *Lord Jim*, 54.

romantic illusions. Unlike Jim, he had entered the messiness and conflict and paid dearly for his actions. During the years of his self-exile he had become a successful trader in the East Indies and had sent first Cornelius and then Jim to manage the local trading post at Patusan. As a hobby, Stein collected beetles and butterflies that the trader understood as exemplars of human types. In *Lord Jim* the characters of the captain of the Patna, Cornelius, Chester, and Brown represent the epitome of the former and Jim the exemplar of the latter. Cornelius, a beetle, "reminded one of everything that is unsavory." Jim, however, "is a romantic . . . romantic," Stein says, "And that is very bad . . . Very good, too."[67] Stein acknowledges that humans often aspire to be beautiful and delicate as are the butterflies, attempting to find "a little heap" of dirt on which to sit still upon the mud; but in fact, we are all beetles, crawling about slimily in that pile of filth. None of us are good enough. Stein says, "But man he will never on his heap of mud keep still. He wants to be so, and again he wants to be so . . . . He wants to be a saint, and he wants to be a devil—and every time he shuts his eyes he sees himself as a very fine fellow—so fine as he can never be . . . ."[68] Stein understands the futility of our romanticism and the reality of our baseness. He says to Marlowe, "It is not good to find you cannot make your dream come true, for the reason that you not strong enough are, or not clever enough . . . . And all the time you are such a fine fellow, too!"[69] Stein punctures the romanticism by which Jim will be eventually destroyed. Even Stein had so suffered. He says to Marlowe, "Do you know how many opportunities I let escape, how many dreams I had that come in my way?"[70] We are mortal and flawed. We are beetles aspiring too often to be butterflies in a world where that fragility dooms us.

I don't know . . . perhaps I am not such a fine fellow—a beetle perhaps like the rest, though I do maintain my illusions. I wanted to be a great teacher, but sometimes I wonder if my teaching wasn't more than a little self-serving: I wanted them to love what I loved. I wanted them to love and respect me! I am not sure I was listening to anyone crawling about as I was in the mud and slime. I wanted to write important work and to serve society as a public intellectual, but I lacked ambition and appropriate energies that might have made that opportunity feasible. I wanted to be a great

---

67. Conrad, *Lord Jim*, 32.
68. Conrad, *Lord Jim*, 130.
69. Conrad, *Lord Jim*, 130.
70. Conrad, *Lord Jim*, 132.

parent, but I too often got in my way: I had wanted the children to be me. And yet, sometimes I think that I was a good enough teacher and intellectual and parent. I once had many, many illusions, indeed, even yet hold on to some of them, though I acknowledge the current politics had cast a great pall over many of them. Stein maintained that one would drown by fighting to climb up out of the turbulence of this life, to be a butterfly and deny one's identity as a beetle; rather, Stein says, one must submit to the destructive element—to beetle-hood— and then use the hands and feet in the "deep, deep sea [to] keep you up"—to aspire to be a butterfly. Primo Levi had said that at Auschwitz the attempt to follow common morality and rules in the camp would lead to drowning. Survival depended on the ability to put aside the whole notion that humans were butterflies. In the camps, one only survived by crawling about in the mud . . . like a beetle. Thoreau had argued that "If within the sophisticated man there is not an unsophisticated one, then he is but one of the Devil's angels."[71] We must acknowledge there is more we should know about ourselves and always aspire to be better.

I consider that my life has been a constant vacillation between existence as a beetle and then as butterfly. I also think I can recall the opportunities that came my way, but I know how my dreams often kept me from acting. Thoreau cautions, "If we have thus desecrated ourselves,—as who has not?—the remedy will be by wariness and devotion to reconsecrate ourselves, and make once more a fane of the mind."[72] I know that I have often crawled about in the mud, but I remain committed to be better—oh, God, whatever that might mean. Jim doesn't end well: "forgotten, unforgiven, and excessively romantic."[73] I would not be murdered as was Jim for my romanticism, but I cannot abandon all hope for those who enter here. Like Stein, I will be sorry to leave all of this even as I marvel at the fragile beauty of the butterflies.

## ME THINKS I SEE A GHOST

I wonder how much past we are required to carry with us as we attempt to move forward. I have in the recent past several years reduced the space in which I now reside and have engaged in what is contemporaneously termed downsizing. Of necessity I have had the need to reduce the quantity

---

71. Thoreau, "Collected Essays and Poems, 357.
72. Thoreau, Collected Essay and Poems, 362.
73. Conrad, *Lord Jim*, 253.

of material possessions that over the years I have accumulated for sundry conscious and unconscious reasons. Things and memories... accumulate. I know what I remember. There lies about me always such a great quantity of my past and there exists inevitably an only imaginable but not actual future into which to carry some but not all of this past. The present remains only as an instant and becomes immediately the past about which I must make decision. Shall it stay or shall it go? All about there are photographs and artifacts: some extend back, well, almost eighty or ninety years.

Here is one of my maternal grandfather when he must have been in his thirties—but then, the standards of youthful appearances have changed so radically in the past century that really I don't know how old he might have been in this picture. He stands poised in long white pants and a short sleeve shirt, a wooden tennis racket held back in the form of a forward stroke. He is posed and not actually playing the game: I don't really know if he ever walked on the court as a player. He idolized the West Side Tennis Club that would not admit him or his family as members, though I am almost certain his eldest daughter did play there in tournaments she did not win—but the picture of him preserves an image of himself that he wished to send forward and that I responsibly have carried. But in fact, I never knew that man. By the time I met him things had changed. But I wonder should I now abandon the picture and him? And what shall I do with his shaving mug that now sits atop the mantelpiece? It bears his name, and probably it sat on the shelf at his barber's shop. It was in that mug that was mixed the soap that was brushed on his face. If I do not carry forward the mug then I leave behind not only my grandfather but the shop as well. But that mug gets so dusty... Recently I came into possession of my grandfather's naturalization papers and the loyalty oath my grandmother had to sign in 1936 because she had married an emigrant from Lithuania who might have been a Communist or worse, a Jewish Communist. I also have the Ketubah, or official marriage document, my mother kept in her possession throughout her life. I think this a bit odd because she certainly didn't pay heed voluntarily to any other Jewish practice.

My father's father died before I was born, and if there exists a picture of him I have never seen it (or I do not remember having ever seen it) and it might be in the possession of someone with whom I have long ago lost contact. In the album from my bar mitzvah I see a photo of my father's mother, Goldie, traditionally lighting a candle on the bar mitzvah cake, but this photo is all I retain of her. The only other memory I hold concerns her strong accent, but I don't really know from where she emigrated. I have no personal memories of her. My mother didn't like her, I think.

I possess a photo of my parents during one of their not too frequent European trips walking amidst some indistinguishable (to me) ruins. Had I been more attentive, I would recognize the hairstyles my mother then sported and be better able to pinpoint more precisely the year the picture was taken, but alas, my mother is frozen in my mind in a perpetual image and a single coiffure and I cannot recognize the location in the photograph. Toward the end of her life and suffering from dementia she cared very little about her appearance, much less the hairstyle she wore, though she continued until almost her death to direct my driving. From the depths of her almost incoherent senility she would look out the passenger side window and tell me when to turn into traffic and when to brake. My father's voice was silenced by his death years ago from lung cancer. He had smoked cigarettes since he was sixteen years old until they took away one his lungs at the age of seventy-seven. I might have been impoverished by the loss of my parents, but what is retained by the photograph?

And here is an image that I took forty-eight years ago in the dungeon at the castle in Elsinore, Denmark. The photo depicts a sleeping warrior who will awaken, legends say, when Denmark needs him again. I was then and may still be looking for Prince Hamlet, but neither of us are in the photo. I hung the photo over the toilet because it certainly looks like the warrior is sitting and contemplating on one as well.

There are photographs of me in my classroom when even I was young. I think I recognize the man . . . he once was me, and I admire that man his youth and even innocence (he is even, I think, quite good looking!), and with gratitude I look to him as my progenitor. In the photo he stands in the classroom confident and assured, an authority on something, I suppose. And alas, what shall I do with the picture of my friend, Steven, who died in the early days of the AIDS epidemic? Do I take his photo with me into the future? Without the picture, would I remember him? Or better, without this photo, how would I remember him? And I possess a more recent photograph of the Mastbaums, Holocaust survivors, who for years my daughters and I picked up every Shabbat morning for services. More than just them looks out from the photograph: It is the whole 20$^{th}$ century I see. Caring for them taught me a great deal about responsibility and freedom; sometimes when I look at their photograph I see my daughters.

## Before the Masts

I have traveled these many years with a poster of "Desiderata," the prose poem written in 1927 by Max Ehrmann, though when I bought the poster sometime during the 1960s the propaganda said that the piece had been discovered in St. Paul's Church in Baltimore, Maryland, and had been stored there since at least 1692. In fact, this erroneous dating of "Desiderata" stems from either a desire to embed its wisdom deep in American (and Protestant) cultural history, or a serious misreading of the devotional materials that were compiled by a Reverend Frederick Kates in 1956 and that included "Desiderata." St. Paul's Church was established in 1692, the year of the Salem witch trials. The prose poem reads to me now as cliché, but I think I remember that the poster was purchased originally in Greenwich Village in a poster store on West $8^{th}$ Street, and I might even have been in the company of my parents. There are many ghosts residing in that poster.

There are file cabinets containing articles I long ago read and even studied; I have long forgotten their contents though I suppose that I carry them with me daily as ghosts. If they were no longer physically present would I remember what I know and how it is that I have come to know it now? I cannot take it all forward, but what of my past should I carry on? And why? What shall be done with the master's thesis on the Syriac midrash from my Uncle Abel: a handwritten document turned in and approved by Columbia University in New York in December 1906! It was written on lined paper: there are no footnotes and no bibliographical entries! I am not interested in Syriac midrash, and I have never seen a photograph of Abel. But the thesis was discovered by a dear friend in the archives at Columbia and I cannot abandon either Abel or her. I own three books in which Abel's name is written in what can only be a fountain pen. The contents of the books do not interest me very much but trying to part with them rips at my soul the way I rip at the fading wallpaper I try to remove from the wall. I am named for Abel who died in 1935 from encephalitis after having spent eighteen years in the hospital sleeping.

Over the past several years, I have transitioned from living in a house that sat on four acres to an apartment comprising on a good day some 1,500 square feet. In the house my library approached organization on bookshelves arrayed about a large, finished basement, on bookshelves in the bedrooms of my two daughters, and bookshelves on the western wall of my cabin office that rested behind and away from the house. I owned many books. But they would not all find room along the walls of the apartment, and I began the process of triage: some books had to go.

## Anxious Am I?

Some books were easy recycled at the Half-Price Books store where one may purchase book at half-price but they certainly don't buy them at that rate! But I didn't mind because I was purging for the sake of living space. I would be able to continue to purchase new books. As I sorted through my library, I couldn't help but recall the tables of books listed in the wonderful first chapter of Italo Calvino's *If on a winter's night a traveler*. The narrator describes the adventure of entering a bookstore and passing by tables and tables on which were stacked so many categories of books for purchase for any number of reasons and reading strategies: books that you've always been planning to read; books that would deal with something I've been working on at the Moment; and books that I've always claimed to have read and now must really get round to it; books "That Fill me With Sudden, Inexplicable Curiosity, Not Easily Justified;" or books "That If I Had More Than One Life I Would Certainly Also Read But Unfortunately My Days Are Numbered."[74] And there are the books that had been purchased for a future reading in the days of retirement, a state I have of late achieved. These tomes and more rested on my overburdened shelves. And there were books on my shelf sometimes in duplicate, and books that I had tried to read but that I found incomprehensible, but maybe now if picked up again I might understand their contents. I would place these latter books back on the shelf like a gifted bottle of fine port wine I once purchased and tasted but whose subtle flavors have yet eluded me. The boxes of books I would sell also contained those that I once thought I should own given a particular image of myself I wanted to maintain but which books I think I really didn't have much intention of ever reading.

In the beginning the winnowing was easy and the stacks decreased. And yet there was no more wall space for bookshelves (and hence books), and I felt uncertain how to proceed. What should I do with Richardson's *Clarissa* which I had purchased and even read as a graduate student because Terry Eagleton, a favorite cultural critic of mine as I've mentioned, had done extensive work with the novel? Or what to do with the *Milagro Bean Field* trilogy of John Nichols that I had adored and written about in my dissertation on the American radical novel but which also I knew I would likely not ever read again? I was at a point where every book had to be examined with delicacy and concern. There were books up there that grounded me in my history: Tom Wolfe's *The Electric Kool-Aid Acid Test*, or Evelyn Waugh's *A Handful of Dust*, the work of a man whose politics I

---

74. Calvino, *if on a winter's night a traveler*, 5.

despised but at the time when I first read the book it epitomized a worldview that helped define the conflicts of the 20th century. And what to do with Addison and Steele: *Selections from The Tatler and the Spectator*. I thought that there was little chance I would need this text again, though I had read and marked it up almost fifty years ago in my undergraduate work at Roanoke College. I knew that The Tatler and The Spectator were essential documents for understanding the 18th century in Great Britain, and besides, I had purchased this Rinehart edition new for $2.35: today a pack of gum costs almost that much money. What should I do with Addison and Steele?

In such conflicted moments I would call Dan to help me with this final cut. Dan was a professor in the English Department and had earned his PhD from the University of North Carolina-Chapel Hill. Over the years our friendship deepened. With Dan I could talk about books, about "literature," about teaching and learning, and about our lives: children, money, sex, marriage and politics. We developed an intimacy that I shared with few others. Dan insisted that I keep D.H. Lawrence's *Lady Chatterley's Lover*, a book I first read under the stairs in the company of two female cousins. Dan argued that the book represented the cultural transition to modernism and should be retained to mark that change. However, he advised, most of Trollope could go. "Dan, how do you feel about Addison and Steele?" I queried. "A tough one," he said, "but I'd keep it." And I did. I needed no better recommendation. And most recently and remarkably, I find that for a book of my own that was published in 2020 selections from *The Tatler* and *The Spectator* had become well, somewhat central. Who would know? Who could know? Only Dan, I think.

Dan died April 29, 2017, at the age of seventy-three years. And I am inconsolable that I will not have those conversations that I so anticipated and enjoyed with him. With whom will I talk with such intimacy about literature and life the way once I sat with Dan? Who will advise me what books to sell and which I must keep?

How much of my past do I need to recall much less to carry physically forward with me so as to show some respect for that past and for my future? How many ghosts must I carry? How many ghosts follow me? To have the past do I need it somehow physically present? How much time do I need to devote observing the past in its several physical forms? Thoreau writes "We should be blessed if we lived in the present always and took advantage of every accident that befell us like the grass which confesses the influence of the slightest dew that falls on it; and did not spend our time in atoning for the neglect of the past opportunities, which we call doing our duty."[75] What do the authors of memoirs bring forward? And why do so? What ghosts are being materialized? Stanley Cavell called his memoir *Little Did I Know*. In *The Facts* Phillip Roth framed his autobiography with letters to and from his character, Nathan Zuckerman, who advised him not to publish the book: it was, Zuckerman claimed, untruthful! Henry Adams' memoir, *The Education of Henry Adams*, was an account of what Adams did not learn. Of course, we all have a tale to tell of our many selves, but what do we really know? Ironically, here I am writing a memoir concerning an anxious life about which I remain anxious.

Thoreau had said that a man is rich by what he can afford to leave behind. Ostensibly he was speaking specifically of physical objects: those things that could be carried out on his back in the event of a fire. But I know there is more to the past than the things we can physically carry out with us. In his discussion of the repetition compulsion, Freud provided substance to my claim: we never stop repeating the past even though we do not know what we are doing or even what past we reprise. I am aware that to repeat the past and expect a different outcome is madness, though it would be a different madness than either Emerson or Winnicott imagined. Santayana asserted that those who do not study the past are condemned to repeat it, but he was wrong. We study the past incessantly, but little is not repeated. Perhaps this is a result of what we have forgotten. I think this pattern is one source of much anxiety. But how shall I know what things I imagine can be abandoned? And how can these items really be forgotten? That which I remember defines who I am at any one moment, though it might also be true that what I have forgotten is not really gone and is equally formative. Freud suggested that the past I remember serves as a screen obscuring what really occurred and which I will never fully know. Forgetting and repressing are not unrelated. Perhaps it is equally suggestive to wonder what might be carried forward as it might be to consider what has accrued to that which has been carried. I wonder how my actions are inspired by visitations from my ghosts. Perhaps the ghost gave physical presence to Hamlet's unconscious. "My father, methinks I see my father," Hamlet says just before his encounter with the ghost. I look sometimes in the mirror and methinks I see my father.

---

75. Thoreau, *Walden*, 340.

What would it mean to consider that I am visited by ghosts who demand and direct my behavior. I think here of Andrew Marvell, pursued by his ghost: "But at my back I always hear, Time's wingèd chariot hurrying near." I remain ever mindful though too often remiss to the directive in the Hebrew Bible to care for the widow, orphan, and stranger in my midst. Aren't these, too, my ghosts? Emmanuel Levinas says that it is our responsibility to stand before the other and command them to command us. We may think of those others as ghosts "doom'd for a certain term to walk the night . . . " Indeed, what would it mean to say that everyone I meet everywhere is my ghost demanding I do something. "Art thou there, trupenny?" I am always amidst company. And there is as I have noted always time's wingèd chariot hurrying near. Once twelve years ago (or was it twenty years ago?) I received a call from one of my ghosts. Karen S. Karen was the first girl I ever took on a date, back when we were both in the ninth grade. From her wish to meet again I assume that she liked me and had then a good enough time to chance another such event! Then, my father had driven us in our gray Chevrolet station wagon; I guess he was the chaperone, though wherever we were going he left us alone and did not follow. On this more recent date Karen was being driven by her husband and brought stories of two grown children, though they are his and not theirs.

My past, as the ghosts of all others, pursues me. Dylan sings, "I can't even remember what it was I came here to get away from." I am aware but wary of my ghosts.

In his novel *I Heard the Mermaids Singing*, Christopher Bollas refers to the self as the "ghost in the machine." What he seems to mean by this description is that we possess knowledge that we do not know—the unthought known—"an inherited set of dispositions that constitutes the true self [and] is a form of knowledge, which has obviously not been thought, even though it is 'there' already at work in the life of neonate who brings this knowledge with him as he perceives, organizes, remembers, and uses his object world."[76] We all suffer from this gap between what we know but cannot yet think, much less speak, and the little we do know and can speak. Because we cannot speak this unconscious knowledge but from which we also cannot escape, we suffer from anxiety and depression! We know brief moments that for some reason become significant, but so much of what we know we cannot think and yet it remains a significant part of what we feel as self. We exist somewhat alienated from ourselves forever. It is no wonder

---

76. Bollas, *Forces of Destiny*, 10.

that we suffer depression. For example, sometimes I would run in the morning silences, and I sense I am not alone. I would hear things. Dylan speaks of this experience in "Every Grain of Sand;" when he sings, "I hear the ancient footsteps, like the motion of the sea. Sometimes I turn there's someone there, at other times its only me." He is in those latter moments utterly alone and without comfort. Sometimes when I ran I did so alone. But I delighted in those times when I sensed that there was someone there. It was then that I experienced a heightened awareness, the ghost spoke, and I felt a spiritual influx and pre (Balint, 1955)sence. Perhaps this still occurs when I feel most free. I feel that I can go on. But we cannot plan for those times, and in an instant that feeling is gone, and we are again alone and there is only me. There is so much that remains unthought, so much life I know but is not ever available to be spoken or pondered. Astrophysicists tell me that 85% of the total matter comprising the universe consists of dark matter and is not visible.

Interesting it is that the ghost cautions Hamlet that "howsoever thou pursues this act/Taint not thy mind." As if what the ghost demands could have any effect other than to taint Hamlet's mind. There is, indeed, something rotten in the state of Denmark: how could the ghost's charge to set the world right not taint Hamlet's mind? If I am visited always by ghosts, how could I not end up with a tainted mind? I think of Estragon's lament in *Waiting for Godot*: "Nothing to be done."[77]

## ON HOBBY-HORSES

Psychoanalyst Sandor Ferenczi notes that character traits are secret psychoses. The sum total of our traits and how we think of them are elements of our sense of Self, though we don't always know whence these traits might have derived. And some of these traits are made visible in what might be termed our peccadilloes. Tristram Shandy refers to these peccadilloes as **HOBBY-HORSES**, and as he says we ride them out when we will. Tristram avows a wonderful tolerance of others when he says, "But everyman to his own taste.—Nay . . . Sir, have not the wisest of men in all ages, not excepting Solomon himself,—have they not had their **HOBBY-HORSES**; their running horses,—their coins and their cockle shells, their drums and their trumpets, their fiddles, their pallets,—their maggots and their butterflies?—and so long as a man rides his Hobby-Horse peaceably and quietly along the King's

---

77. Beckett, *Waiting for Godot*, 1.

highway, and neither compels you or me to get up behind him,—pray Sir, what have either you or I to do with it?"[78] Atop our **Hobby-Horses** we appear to ourselves quite normal though to others we might seem not a little barmy. Since however wise we say we are, and since our wisdom does not override our **Hobby-Horses**, Montaigne cautions the sage to best remember his humanity "and moderate his inclinations; for to do away with them is not in him."[79] We will gallop atop our **Hobby-Horses** willy-nilly and we should accept that as we do so, so will others ride out the same. The sage ought to put a bit more wine in his cup, appreciate his inclinations and learn some humility.

There is no disputing against **Hobby-Horses**; and for my part I seldom do. I say with Tristram, "Be it known to you, that I keep a couple of pads myself, upon which, in their turns (nor do I care who knows it) I frequently ride out and take the air; tho' sometimes, to my shame be it spoken, I take somewhat longer journeys than what a wise man would think altogether right . . . "[80] *Mea culpa.* For example, I have for some time considered that I suffer (though I am certain that the verb, 'to suffer,' is too, too extreme) from agoraphobia: atop this **Hobby-Horse,** I experience discomfort when I am away from the confines of my home for any extended period of time, say, in excess of twenty-four or so hours, and I ride home at the first possible getaway. I am at present loath to travel any great distance.

I have considered the nature of my agoraphobia: of what it consists and how it becomes manifest. If agoraphobia is not about the particular space itself—it is not a specific space of which I am wary but of all spaces into which I might venture—then the agoraphobia must be about my relationship to space itself. Though I love looking up at the stars, I do not think I want to get any closer to them than I do at present as I view them through my window or even standing outside in the proximity of a back door. I do with some pleasure recall once standing on several consecutive and very cold, clear nights looking up at the stars and identifying the various constellations with my daughter for her school project. I do not "amuse" myself on roller coasters or Ferris wheels; I like my feet on solid ground and my stomach right side up. On an airplane (that I take infrequently) I always choose an aisle seat and do not glance out of the window. It is not from fear

---

78. Sterne, *Tristram Shandy*, 8.
79. Montaigne, *The Complete Works*, 303.
80. Sterne, *Tristram Shandy*, 8.

of heights—acrophobia—that I avert my view, but I experience mild panic by the extreme openness of the space out of the window.

I think that (part of) the problem with space lies exactly in my awareness of its vastness. Entrance into a wide-open space demands that choices be made in that space, and the choices (and possibilities) are, as seems the space, illimitable. I doubt my capabilities. As Guildenstern says to Hamlet when the Prince demands he play the recorder, "My lord, I have not the skill." I believe that this is why shopping in catalogs satisfies me: the choices there are limited by the number of pages! My agoraphobia represents my fear of making a wrong choice and stems from an ignorance of the rubrics I might follow in choosing. I recall once walking onto the floor of Macy's Department store on 34$^{th}$ Street in Manhattan in search of a dress shirt for a party to which I had been invited. Why I thought I needed a new shirt I do not remember. "Beware the enterprise that requires new clothes, and not a new man to wear those clothes," cautions Thoreau. I was certainly at the time not new. I climbed the stairs to exit the No. 2 Broadway subway line, strode confidently into the men's department that my memory seems to place on the first floor of Macy's, where I found arrayed before me table after table piled sky-high with many, many beautiful shirts. Each and all appealed to me, and I hadn't any idea how to choose from the vast array of fine-looking shirts. I would have them all!! In that space there existed too many beautiful objects from which to make a choice of any single one, and I did not think I possessed any material basis by which to choose only one. I looked about anxiously, turned around and went home. To the party I wore a black turtleneck and white shirt purchased, I suspect, from a catalog offering.

Adam Phillips says that we enter such a filled (Phillips refers to it as "cluttered") space as I had discovered on the floor of Macy's Department store in order to find something but that then in that cluttered space we discover something else for which we did not think to look. But for me that was exactly the problem, wasn't it? There was at that moment too much on that cluttered men's wear floor and I possessed no confidence in my capacity to choose any single one. "My lord, I have not the skill." Clutter makes me very nervous and up on one of my **Hobby-Horses** I spend an inordinate amount of time clearing away from table and counter any dish that requires washing; unload anything yet left in the dishwasher, clothes washer, or dryer. Dishes do not lie unwashed in my sink nor left for very long drying in the rack on the counter. Clothes are immediately folded back into drawers and hung in closets. I do pick up every scrap of everything that has wended its way to the floor, but not before I check to see if an important thought is scribbled on it. I do tend to live and work in somewhat cluttered spaces in which I often grow very anxious, but I am loath to throw away any random scrap of paper for fear that it might eventually hold the key to my thought. Freud says somewhere that we can tolerate the smell only of our own excrement. The agoraphobic prefers to stay close to his own familiar. The shower soap grows thin to transparency.

If I yet believe what I have elsewhere written, that home is what I must leave to go somewhere though never quite to arrive, I wonder if now riding on this agoraphobic **Hobby-Horse** I am attempting to never leave so that I can avoid ever not arriving. I stay home. I have been recently intrigued with a 1955 article by psychoanalyst Michael Balint entitled "Friendly Expanses—Horrid Empty Spaces." He describes two types of individuals: the ocnophil and the philobat, the former word a neologism derived from the Greek meaning "to shrink, to hesitate, to hang back," and the latter word a neologism stemming from the Greek word acrobat and meaning "one who walks on his toes," or someone who "walks away from the safe earth." Balint asserts that both personality types derive etiologically from the trauma experienced by the painful discovery of the existence of external independent objects and the loss of a primary narcissism: the original belief that the world and the self are one. The life stances of the ocnophil and philobat represent a strategy to deal with that trauma of separation: both the ocnophil and philobat want to return to that oceanic feeling when there existed in Balint's words, "a feeling of indissoluble connexion, of belonging inseparably to the external world as a whole."[81] Balint cites Freud's reference to Christian Grabbe's drama, *Hannibal*, to describe that feeling of connection: "Out of this world we cannot fall."[82] The ocnophil refuses the Reality principle (always an insult) that asserts that objects exist separate from the individual. The ocnophil clings desperately to objects to avoid those horrid, empty spaces that exist between objects. Holding the object the ocnophil feels that there has been no separation between her and the world. The ocnophil projects herself into the object and believes that as safely as the ocnophil can hold the object so safe in the world will be the ocnophil.

My tendency to hoard seems related to this characteristic, as also may be my practice to hold onto my books and papers. I want to be surrounded

---

81. Balint, "Friendly Expanses-Horrid Spaces," 231.
82. Balint, "Friendly Expanses-Horrid Spaces," 230.

by my books, to sleep in my bed, and to drink my coffee out of my coffee mug! Hugging these objects close to me I remain safe. Surrounded by my objects I feel secure. The ocnophil I may be holds the object close because the ocnophil inhabits the object. To leave behind the object would mean to lose oneself. Without objects held close, the ocnophile prefers not to function. I am fearful of those horrid empty spaces. And I am home with my objects.

But the philobat has a different relationship to objects and to space. She fully accepts the Reality principle (always an insult, nevertheless) and will not depend on objects that she knows have a separate existence from her. She will depend solely on herself; in the friendly spaces, then, she develops the skills to control the external objects. The philobat understands that the world is a place to enjoy her skills, and the friendly spaces are where the philobat experiences the greatest pleasure. From her experience of the original trauma, the philobat accepts that she exists alone and must depend on her own resources and not on the possession of objects. She develops her expertise and accepts that by using her own ability she can cope with any situation. In those friendly spaces the world as a whole will "click in" and by her skills she will be able to avoid any treacherous objects. The philobat, then, develops those skills to recreate the destroyed harmony between self and world that occurred in the original trauma. But the philobat must continuously leave the sense of safety so that she may continue to expose herself to hazards: then, with her developed skill, she exhibits control of herself and the objects! The philobat's main aim is to master the task so completely and with such ease (hence, the need for skill) that the skill should no longer require any effort. Thus, spaces for the philobat are for the most part friendly because she possesses the skills to sail (or fly or run) through them knowing that the friendly expanses of the world are there for her pleasure.

But it comforts me to me know that Balint acknowledges that in most people there exists a mixture of ocnophilia and philobatism. Up on one **Hobby-Horse** where I experience my insecurities, I am an ocnophile and I cling desperately to my objects. Though I am often made anxious by clutter, my ocnophilia tolerates its presence and atop this **Hobby-Horse** I let things accumulate. Even now on my desks (I possess three at present!) and all about on the floors of bedroom, office, and living room are books, journals, and papers; pens and pencils and journals in which to write; the coffee mug, and a glass of water. Though I could put any of these away, somewhere away, I rarely do so. And my desks are so carpeted with things that their surfaces are very often obscured. I don't even throw away my Stim-u-dents, those wooden dental implements that clean between my teeth, for I may continue to reuse them! My bookshelves are filled with volumes I know I will never read again, and I pile recently purchased books and editions of journals atop each other. I own too many worn corduroy pants and old shirts with frayed collars. A man may be considered rich by what he could afford to leave behind, but I am not rich and remain uncomfortable with leaving anything behind. I now do not leave. I can't always find what I am looking for, but I am comforted to know that somewhere what I want is there and when I find it, I can hold it close to me. I am not a good extemporaneous speaker: I require the printed text before me. Balint notes that it is not accidental, that philia, love, is joined to the grasping of objects. As I age my ocnophilism intensifies.

My philobatic nature, however, has led me to develop an array of skills. I read and I write, sometimes with not a little acumen and proficiency. Roth says, "This is what happens when you write books. There's not just something that drives you to find out everything—something begins putting everything in your path. There is suddenly no such thing as a back road that doesn't lead headlong into your obsession." I write books, and with them I travel extensively even though often I do not actually leave my homeless home. I maintain several comfortable chairs for reading and beside each I keep various accessories to accompany and facilitate that endeavor. I do have this habit of dreaming and often I am not to be so easily found. I am content to be lost. And my lord, I do have that skill! In the obsessive pursuit of something, I gallop freely, happily and with great abandon. I purchase yet a great many more books which only increases the physical library and exacerbates the clutter but alas, Dan is not here to help me winnow.

I also have in the past traveled into what became the friendly spaces as I have described, though now I rarely leave home and when I do it is in short spurts and often fraught with anxiety. The Freudian in me recognizes that the restricted spaces which secure the ocnophil suggests both the womb and the tomb, the wish for either represents the ultimate denial of living my life. I do, as I have said, suffer from hyperchondria, another one of the Hobby-Horses in my stable, but I neither want to reenter the womb or slip into the grave. I hope there is more day to dawn. I do not sense that my agoraphobia stems from this desire for dissolution, though it is also true that our phobias (how we defend ourselves) tell us a great deal about what we desire.

There is no disputing against **Hobby-Horses**; and for my part I seldom do. I acquire a great many things all of which are intended to make my life richer and easier. In the moment the purchase seems like a great notion but often it doesn't end that way. Regularly, I gather foodstuffs for meals. During my long-term residence in New York City, I learned to buy my vegetables daily from the green grocers and carry home only what was necessary for that day's meals. I maintained in my home a small selection of snack food, the latter a miscellany that grew apace with my neurotic states, that during the pandemic increased precipitately, and were purchased by what seemed to be on sale. I try to buy only what I immediately require, and as I grow older I do indeed require less. I enjoy the daily and limited shopping though there are certain aisles I have never traversed—and I relish cooking and consuming what I have purchased as some evidence that I remain alive!

I continue to buy many, many things: with the UPS/USPS and the Amazon delivery persons I remain somewhat familiar; they make polite inquiry about my health and I return the concern. When I lived in Wisconsin the thawing dirt driveway in the Spring returned to Nature, and I especially enjoyed when the UPS man would leave my deliveries at the bottom of the driveway where I had parked my unlocked car, because it could not navigate up the drive in the mud. I buy gadgets, items I consider might make my life more organized and less rigorous but that never work out quite as I had expected even when I have successfully assembled them; and there are small furniture items that I believe will relieve the accumulation of clutter but somehow only serve to increase it, alas! My agoraphobia and the pandemic has made entering stores aversive, and now much that I purchase outside of my daily provisions comes from a catalog or via Amazon; the pandemic only exacerbated my anxiety of venturing out and continuing aversion to entering any store other than the food market.

Oh, and I buy clothes. Ironically when the clothes arrive I put them in my closet and refuse to wear them. These new products accumulate, entombed for some time, as it were, in their plastic wrappings. When I go to dress myself and survey the collection, I inevitably choose an older garment rather than the newer one. I purchase a new sweater, and I note that the moths have been enjoying the old, and then I nevertheless put on this older and hole-spotted one. I have of late been considering what motivates this obsessive compulsion not to wear the clothes I have purchased for the express purpose of wearing. Sir, have not the wisest of men in all ages, not excepting Solomon himself,—have they not had their **Hobby-Horses**?

Perhaps this particular gallop is not unconnected to the rest of my stable: if I open the package and put on the new item, it immediately begins to become worn, and soon, alas, will wear out. But if I don't put the garment on, then the article of clothing remains inviolable and will last forever. Of course, the assumption here is that I, too, will last forever and will one day actually wear the new garment, but, of course, that notion is obviously problematic. The refusal to open the package serves as the charm that wards off Death. Cultural anthropologist Ernest Becker says that "reality and fear go hand in hand." That is, to be alive is always to be threatened by Death. Becker argues that we pass this fear on to our offspring and this transmission has actually led to the survival of the species. They are trying to kill us, Yossarian cries! Who? Everyone!! Becker suggests, "The result was the emergence of man (sic) as we know him: a hyperanxiety animal who constantly invents reasons for anxiety even when there are none."[83] As we repress our fear of death so that we can actually function productively in the world, we project that internalized fear out of us and create danger everywhere, even when there might be no reason to fear. Ah, welcome home, Alan!

Freud addresses this particular **Hobby-Horse** of mine. He notes that as long as the Pompeian artifact lay buried under the volcanic ash it remained preserved, but once it was recovered in the archaeological dig it became subject to decay. So is it with memories: when I do not think upon them, they remain untouched, but as soon as they are uncovered, these memories are subject to the natural effects of the present, and then they become, if not inaccurate, then certainly unreliable.

When I do not wear the new shirt, it remains useless, but it does maintain its purity. Its lines stay smooth, sharp, and straight. Unworn trouser seams continue uncreased and their colors do not fade. The new shoes bear not a trace of the ground on which they were meant to walk: they will last forever. I often imagine how good I might look if only I would step outside in my new shoes. I sigh and put on the older, worn pair, and save the new shoes for a brighter, sunlit day. Ah, but the feet for which I purchased them will continue to scuff and bruise regardless of the shoe, and soon the new

---

83. Becker, *The Denial of Death*, 17.

shoes will seem no longer appropriate. Nor might they any longer fit my feet that change shape and size as I age.

And I am thinking now that it might be also true that I fear that having used and then used up the new item, no others will be forthcoming, and when the garments with which I presently adorn myself wear out, I will stand naked and hungry out in the world but for lack of reserve. We are all in the spell of something demented!


## MUSIC, MUSIC, MUSIC

Albert Einstein remarked, "If I were not a physicist, I would probably be a musician. I often think in music. I live my daydreams in music. I see my life in terms of music." Einstein was a physicist and he did play the violin. I suppose as the former he heard and studied the music of the spheres, and as the latter he accompanied his scientific imaginings with heavenly sound. I think in both mediums he made wonderful music. I appreciate Einstein's acknowledgment of his relationship to music because I think that I have understood my life in terms of and informed by the music to which I have listened. I have lived always accompanied by a musical soundtrack! I cannot exactly remember when music became central to my daily life, but I also cannot remember a time when music was not a constant and integral element. Music informed and commented upon my life in ways that seemed immediate and significant, and music served me as the beat of that different drummer to which I cared to march. I have always resented Muzak in the elevator the way I begrudged the white bread in the family's breadbox: both products lacked flavor and character. It was the seeded rye sliced thin from the local bakery that I wanted.

My parents had purchased a spinet piano that for some reason was painted a spackled orange, and for several years I took lessons from Mr. Arthur Poppe, who arrived hopeful to our home every week. But I lacked talent and determination. Mr. Poppe never scowled or scolded, but as I executed (a word carefully chosen here) the various pieces—for some reason I remember playing poorly Hungarian Dance #5 by Franz Liszt and the first movement of Beethoven's Moonlight Sonata—I would sense a series of mournful, frustrated sighs from a patient but perhaps not very well paid Mr. Poppe. Chuck Berry may have demanded that Beethoven roll out of the way in anticipation of the arrival of rock 'n' roll, but I believe my piano playing turned dear Ludwig over in his grave. I just didn't care to practice.

These piano lessons did not enamor me to performance, but ironically, they helped to establish some foundation for my lifelong devotion to music.

Later, in my twenties, I took up the guitar hoping that I could join in a rock n' roll band, or else become a progressive and famous folk artist like Pete Seeger, but my continued aversion to practice and my love affair with other texts precluded both possibilities and I abandoned the instrument. When in my early forties I became a father, I returned again with some dedication to the guitar because I believed the instrument would somehow offer me entrance into my daughters' school classes where my minimal skills would not be noticed or were at least not a matter of concern to kindergartners. I did manage to teach both my daughters' classmates the verses to "This Land is Your Land" that do not often find expression in the school, and around the winter holiday season and round of school concerts I and a colleague on mandolin taught for performance alternative songs to the clichéd Christmas airs that were the program in most schools. To both of my daughters' dismay, I played and sang my way through their middle school years and then at some point I was by them officially banned from their classrooms. As the girls had risen in grade, my marginally competent skill playing became more evident—there were students in their classes whose ability far exceeded mine—and I retired—or was retired—from performing in that venue. For a brief time, I played somewhat clumsily in a band made up of academics that we called The Scholarly Notes. I consider that we may have been scholars, but our notes often were off-key and certainly not in the book.

Music had been a required class in the curriculum at Jericho Junior-Senior High School on Long Island. From Mr. Schweitzer I was introduced to forms and styles of music that later I would come to adore. From the perspective of this fourteen-year-old, Mr. Schweitzer seemed wizened and wise, but I suspect he was hardly into his thirties at the time. I recall him as a tall, thin man who wore a relatively shiny gray suit the jacket of which flapped like wings as he danced about the room. He gamboled about at the front of the room as if to a music that played in his head; the room in which we met had been constructed as a rehearsal-performance space with tiered rows of seats sufficient for a practicing chorus or an audience. Mr. Schweitzer also sponsored and supervised the school chorus.

Until this class much of my music had emanated from a radio unit that rested on the headboard of my bed or that played on a transistor radio held tightly to my ear. From both of these devices flowed rock 'n' roll music.

## Anxious Am I?

Before 1964 and the arrival of the Beatles and what was termed "the British invasion," most of what came over the airwaves was referred to as bubblegum music, a pejorative reference I believe to the age and maturity of the listeners. I did love Bazooka bubblegum and those pink, stiff slabs of gum that accompanied packs of baseball cards. And there also was the music from 45 rpm discs that played at parties where close dancing and experimental sexual play occurred. I recall parties that were explicitly referred to as make out parties at which Johnny Mathis records were played as prelude to and inspiration for make out sessions. I sometimes brought my 45 rpm records with the red inserts in the centers to those parties but did not enjoy the consequences of their having been played.

I remember enjoying music class, and I am certain that it had an influence on me equal to but perhaps more subtly than that of my English classes. And it wasn't only the technical aspect of the forms about which I learned and to which I was drawn in school, though this was certainly an important element of the curriculum. But I learned with Mr. Schweitzer the beauty of melody and the earthiness of song. On vinyl discs that were played on a Victrola to which was attached no external speakers, we listened to a wide range of what is now called classical music. It was for me a revelation. I heard Dvorak's Symphony #9: From the New World, a composition I have returned to often when a certain feeling of anxiety overtakes me. In Mr. Schweitzer's class we also sang songs from the Gilbert and Sullivan corpus, and now into my seventies I can still remember lines from Gilbert and Sullivan's operetta, *H.M.S. Pinafore*. We were also introduced to opera with the one-act piece, Amahl and the Night Visitors by Gian Carlo Menotti. That I recall this production suggests to me that this was a significant event though I could not explain why it might have been so. Hallmark sponsored a TV performance of the opera that I did not watch. Today I am still not at all fond of opera.

In music class we also were taught and performed a repertoire of American folk songs accompanied by Mr. Schweitzer on the piano. Before there was the folk song compendium *Rise Up Singing* to which I have long been devoted, there was Mr. Schweitzer's selections. I remember specifically learning about my gal Sal pulling the barge on the Erie Canal. Now, more than fifty years later, I listen joyfully to Bruce Springsteen's wonderful version of that song on the album, *We Shall Overcome: The Seeger Sessions*. For me that song has a long history and it is given greater meaning by the existence of that history. Indeed, I learned some American history and geography from Mr. Schweitzer's music class, and later, much later, I taught an American history class through the medium of folk song. I heard tales from one student who years later informed me that in a high school history class he had passed an exam from having been taught and having learned Nancy Schimmel's song, "1492."

Among so many other aspects of music that I have enjoyed, music also encouraged the possibilities and joys of community. Bruce Springsteen's version of "Pay Me My Money Down" on We Shall Overcome: The Seeger Sessions exemplifies some of this. This work song of anonymous authorship (as should be all true folk music, Dylan would say) is attributed to African American stevedores in the Georgia Sea Islands. The song begins with Springsteen playing alone on his guitar and singing almost plaintively—"Pay me my money down"—and then the musicians who have been gathered in his home begin to join in the song first singly and then all together: the entire ensemble plays and creates a raucous and joyful sound. And then the real fun begins as Springsteen starts calling out direction: he calls for the violin to take the solo, then he calls to the accordion, then to the trumpet, and then he makes a request to everyone for a change of key: "Then let's bring it up to $B^b$." That verse ends and Springsteen calls out "All right, someone," and someone cheerfully, gladly enters improvisationally and picks up the conversation. "Back down to D," Springsteen calls, and then he says, "Everyone solo," and at that moment everyone is playing alone together, and the sound is magnificent and glorious and fun. I thought that our lives might be lived as the music in this song was performed. Ensemble and solo; solo and ensemble.

Music taught me that community was possible even as the music created the community to which I wanted very much to belong. Such was the invitation in the Grateful Dead's "Scarlet Begonias:" There, in Grosvenor's Square "Strangers stopped strangers/just to shake their hand/Everybody's playing/in the Heart of Gold Band."[84] Ah, if our lives could only be like that! But even in our frustrating defeats, the community could take comfort in our solidarities. Dylan sang in "Honest With Me," "I'm not sorry for nothin' I've done/I'm glad I fought—I only wish we'd won." Me too. Solo and ensemble. Ensemble and solo. The Grateful Dead invited: "Come hear Uncle John's Band playing to the tide/Come on along, or go alone, he's come to take his children home,"[85] and I wanted to go along, and often I made the

---

84. https://genius.com/The-grateful-dead-scarlet-begonias-lyrics.
85. https://genius.com/The-grateful-dead-uncle-johns-band-lyrics.

journey. I learned from Pete Seeger that in singing together there is no such thing as a wrong note. I hope I have lived and taught a little of this truth.

### NOTES FROM MY CATALOG

Music has drawn me to community and I am secured and nurtured there. Music plays even now as I write, and though I am by myself in this room, I am not really alone. In the coffee houses of Greenwich Village and the solitude of my spaces, I have taken some respite from my troubles in the music. For example, there is a Scottish drinking song written by Walter Watson (1780–1854) that I have now heard sung by Gordon Bok, Ed Trickett, and Anna Mayo Muir originally entitled (in the Scottish) "Sae Will We Yet." As a drinking song I suppose the lyrics would have varied from tavern to tavern and from drinker to drinker, and so the liberties that Bok, Trickett, and Muir took in their interpretation remains in the tradition. Actually, I think not a few drinking songs would seem an appropriate accompaniment to our troubling times. I have read the news today, oh boy! In the version of the song by these three folk artists I don't have the sense that "So Will We Yet" is so much a drinking song as it is one of comfort and hope, but perhaps that is what drinking songs are all about anyway! I have turned to this particular drinking song in these very difficult times for some shelter from the storm. I have often felt calmed by the voices of Bok, Muir, and Trickett.

We live in dangerous times. The presidency of Donald Trump had become the horror we expected, and the clouds of fascism have moved swiftly across our horizons. Each morning during the four years of his reign I awakened with a sense of dread and horror—some call my obsession with Trump and his reign displacement and projection—but me, I called what I saw to be fascism, and I knew that my fears didn't arise from my own demons; they were actually out there in the White House and in the domains of justice and the institutions of government that were supposed to protect democracy but which he and his horde of Republicans have done what they could to tear down. The pandemic worsened the condition, turning us veritably housebound and paranoically isolated. Poverty levels across the globe have increased and too many children went hungry. Climate change threatens the survival of the planet even as wars decimate its populations. The list of dangers could fill pages . . . and yet despite the darkness at the break of days I have taken some comfort in Bok, Muir, and, Trickett's version of that old Scottish drinking song. In these dangerous times I have accepted the invitation in the refrain.

> Come sit down beside us and give us your chat
> Let the wind take the cares of this life off your back
> For our hearts to despondency we never will submit
> We've always been provided for and so will we yet.

Some of us have been lucky. We've always been provided for and had warm fire-lit rooms in which to sit and to sing during the harsh winters. Some of us have even helped provide for others. We have marched and sung together. We sang:

> Come lift up your voices so hardy or frail
> Enlighten up your hearts and enliven the tale
> We will always be the merrier the longer that we sit
> We've sung together many a' time and so will we yet . . .

I have during the recent past years often wondered if, indeed, so will we yet. I suppose that I do not think I or my friends will ever become homeless or even poor, but I am concerned about the integrity of our freedoms; I am anxious about the nation's future and that of my children—and not only the future for my own daughters. I have felt despair. And yet . . . in the song I hear the voices of hope and I am comforted.

> And a song for you singers who keep your voices clear
> Good health to you and happiness to all that you hold dear
> For the world as you would have it be, you sing with all your wit
> And ease the work of providence and so will we yet . . .

From the song I recognize that there are others like me out there; for most of my life we have sat and drank because we have had to always struggle and even sometimes laugh. We have accepted that we would struggle to effect change and even sometimes quarrel with our idealism. Trump and his gang have stolen our birthright and made a cruel mockery of our lives, our culture, our history, and our ethical grounding in the Constitution and civil sense. But in the face of that Trumpian outrage, the song urged:

> So lift up your noble hearts with laughter and song
> And may your days be brighter and your nights not so long
> For your joys were welcome here as woes you would forget
> And when you wept we wept with you and so will we yet.

## Anxious Am I?

This no-longer drinking song calls me to community. It reminds me that the comfort of others can be—should be—offered and enjoyed without qualification.

The music to which I listened brought me to a community in which I felt welcome and in which I was nurtured. I have often taken comfort and experienced joy in the music and frequently, I have found some wisdom and strength there. I believe that I still do. There has not been a time in my life when music did not assume a formative and supportive role to my daily meanderings. I was early drawn to folk music—it seemed somehow to be an expression of my idiom. A first song I played on a juke box—I am old enough not to remember if I put in a nickel, a dime or a quarter into the machine—was "This Train," a song from Peter Paul and Mary's first album. That was in about 1962, but I am also old enough not to remember exactly what year it actually was—I imagine I must have been about fifteen. I had already spent some time considering the fate of Tom Dooley and had anguished over the horrible lot of a man named Charlie who for lack of an extra nickel for the fare increase couldn't get off of the train on an increasingly expensive Boston subway. But in their music and their presence, Peter Paul and Mary helped open my consciousness to the responsibilities of social activism and social justice. It was on that piece of vinyl that I heard for the first time the anthemic songs "If I had a Hammer" and "Where Have All the Flowers Gone." In that era of bubblegum music, of "Yummy, yummy, yummy I've got love in my tummy," Peter Paul and Mary stood on the cover of that first album against a red brick wall that I knew to be in Greenwich Village and sang of Sorrow and Justice and of repairing the world if we only had our way. They drew me and others like me into the cause, much energy proselytizing, even sometimes marching and always singing the songs. Peter, Paul and Mary allowed me to listen in the company of my parents to Bob Dylan's notice that it was their responsibility to get out of our way because they didn't understand us, even as later Peter's song, "Day Is Done," comforted us that our parents could if they would join in the struggle. I learned from Peter, Paul and Mary more about metaphor than I did from Ms. Bueschel, my ninth-grade English teacher. When they sang the traditional folk ballad, 'The Cruel War," I knew what war they were talking about; later, when they sang the Weavers' spirited folk song, "Wasn't That a Time" I knew to which Revolution they were referring. Even poor Puff the Magic Dragon was dragged in unwittingly and unwillingly as an element in the secret code of our burgeoning drug culture. Peter, Paul and

Mary taught me about the struggle, and they stayed with me through it. Once I heard them sing, there was no turning back.

Peter, Paul and Mary were an element in my developing social consciousness, and it did not hurt that Mary's long blond hair flew seductively about with the passion of her singing. Ah yes, I fell in love with her with all the passion that a virginal adolescent could muster. I remember once traveling to some venue in New Hampshire to sit quite literally on the floor at her feet at what was for me a very early incidence of a folk music concert. My sensibility drew Peter, Paul and Mary to me and I to them and to all folk music, in fact. They led me to good trouble. Indistinguishable then was the zeitgeist and my own personal demons. The world was about to explode—I was about to explode—and I discovered in the folk music an articulation of my personal and political angst.

As I have said (too often) I had spent not a few weekends in the coffee houses of Greenwich Village visiting the Gaslight (now a central location in the popular series The Marvelous Mrs. Maisel), the Village Vanguard and the Village Gate, the Bitter End, the Café Wha? and The Café Wha Not? Eric Andersen, Tom Paxton, Joan Baez, Dave Van Ronk, the Chad Mitchell Trio, Carolyn Hester, Patrick Sky, Bob Gibson, The Fugs . . . there were more. I listened to Judy Collins and became keenly aware of the personal, political, even philosophical direction I had chosen and that Judy Collins represented. She sang "Anathea" on an early album, a ballad that addressed the venality and corruption at the center of the public order and that resonated then with my adolescent rage and rebellion. Along with Dylan's version of "Seven Curses," Judy Collins' performance of "Anathea" condemned the American system of justice without having to explicitly name it. The civil rights movement highlighted the violent racism that permeated our society, and Judy Collins sang Shel Silverstein's "Hey, Nelly Nelly," and Malvina Reynolds's "It Isn't Nice," songs that promised that the long road to freedom that we had to trod would eventually turn our dreams into a reality. Eric Anderson's "Thirsty Boots," written in tribute to those who participated in Freedom Summer, has played in my life for over sixty years. For me this was a song of struggle and solidarity though not at all one of triumph. Anderson offered respite to his weary friend from the tensions he had experienced on the road and inviting him to rest for just awhile. But implicit in that offer is the acknowledgment that soon the friend must and would be going out again. For some reason I have associated this song with the failed candidacy of George McGovern to whom I then looked for a way out of hell, and when

## Anxious Am I?

I hear the song I am reminded of the struggle and my too-uncertain place in it. Actually, the theme song of the McGovern campaign was Paul Simon's "Bridge Over Troubled Water." Such is memory. If they had asked me, I might have suggested that they choose Simon's song "America." I, too, had gone off into America, and even before that song was written I, too, on the Greyhound bus from Roanoke College counted the cars on the New Jersey Turnpike on my way to my parents' home In Queens, New York. The war in Vietnam, still in its earlier stages, was a vague threat that had begun to rise in consciousness and to trouble me and us. And these folk songs spoke to my sense of disquiet, unease, and outrage. I knew that the folk music to which I yet remained committed represented the generation's attack on the system it condemned in language and influence no less powerfully than did the Port Huron Statement in 1962.

Bob Dylan was then and has been since one of my master teachers. For better than sixty years my consciousness—my conscious self—has been influenced by Dylan's work—by his very presence in my culture. I remember once sitting in the back seat of my parents' gray Chevrolet station wagon on our way to one of the Catskill Resorts for some economically ill-advised family outing. I believe that it must have been 1965, and we were in a somewhat aged vehicle when from the radio station came Dylan's voice singing (it might have been) "Like a Rolling Stone" or "Positively Fourth Street." It had to be one or the other because FM radio did not exist then and only those two songs were AM acceptable, and the station had to be either WABC (Cousin Brucie!) or WINS (Murray the K!). My parents had condescended to listen to rock 'n' roll radio in the car when we children were passengers. And from the front seat my mother, without turning her head toward us in the back, spat out mockingly, "He sounds like he's in pain." I responded, "He is!" I was.

Dylan has consistently articulated my angst and my rage. His was a community I was drawn to join and meant to keep. I remember: in 1965 Dylan's composition "The Lonesome Death of Hattie Carroll" excoriated the corruption that lay at the heart of the South, the justice system that had made slavery legal and Jim Crow the law of the land, even as the song condemned those who philosophized about injustice and did nothing to end it. *Mea culpa*. The song made me anxious: was I one who had now to bury the rag deep in my face. Ironically, I remember one afternoon during my freshman year. I lay on my bed listening on my portable stereo record player (it was brown with detachable speakers!) to "The Lonesome Death of Hattie

Carroll" on Dylan's album The Times They Are a' Changing. He sang about William Zanzinger a man of privilege and disdain, who callously killed the maid, Hattie Carroll. Suddenly. my roommate at the time, Peter Bucheister, an avowed racist and anti-Semite, sat straight up on his bed and cried out indignantly, "Hey, that guy is my neighbor. That song is a goddamn lie!" To defend the song or Bob Dylan at that point seemed an absurd endeavor. I was in the South, and Bucheister was a Southern bigot. Having discovered I was Jewish, as a vicious prank Bucheister had sent the American Nazi Party a letter in my name requesting membership materials. Receiving them I remember my panic. I immediately sent off a letter to the FBI declaring that the letter to the Nazi party had been sent by a practical joker and that I would like my name and reputation cleared immediately. The FBI, still then under the directorship of J. Edgar Hoover, himself not known for his tolerance of differences except his own, wrote back that they did not keep a list of members of such organizations (Ha!), and that there was nothing further that they could do in my case. Thus far my record remains clear—at least in terms of Nazi affiliation.

Music, no less than my books, has accompanied me in my life and provided me with the strength and resolve to persist. In the late 1970s, during a time when I was seeking desperately to break out of my family orbit, at the end of each school day where I worked as an English teacher I would return home on public transportation and arrive finally at my studio apartment in New York City, a home that was no bigger than was Thoreau's cabin at Walden Pond. I understood this apartment to be my cabin on the shores of my Walden Pond where I was trying to learn to live a life that was not foundering on the shores of quiet desperation. I had even placed between the only two windows in that apartment, both of which overlooked not the pond but the alleyway filled with garbage cans and the windows of the apartment of another building, a framed sepia-toned photograph of a replica of Thoreau's cabin I had taken several years prior during my first pilgrimage to the shores of Walden pond and where I illegally spent the night. The photo became my altar. I retain it still.

Each day as I entered my apartment I would head to the turntable (then I owned a turntable, large floor speakers and vinyl records) and cued up Bruce Springsteen's "Independence Day."

> Well say goodbye it's Independence Day
> It's Independence Day all boys must run away
> So say goodbye it's Independence Day

## Anxious Am I?

*All men must make their way come Independence Day*[86]

As I threw off my school clothes and changed into my running gear for my six-mile circuit of Central Park, I would turn the volume on the amplifier up very loud. I lived in an apartment building occupied mostly by young people of whom I was one, and some of my neighbors were music students at Mannes College on the Upper West Side, and no one ever seemed to mind the excessive volume emanating from my apartment. I played that song again and again until I was completely ready to again confront the world. As I struggled for what I thought was my freedom, whether that struggle was right or wrong, legitimate or illegitimate, Springsteen's "Independence Day" gave me strength to persevere. That song is forever linked to those months of struggle and anguish.

And then again, the music often held me up from sinking down. At an extremely low moment in my life, after attending the funeral of a friend who died a violent self-inflicted death, I flew to Canada for a long-planned weekend with a dearest friend. This was a yearly expedition that has now continued for at least thirty years and in three different locations. But wherever and whenever I arrived, directly from the airport we would go straight away to a bar-restaurant where we would unwind the immediate events of our lives and our relationships. That evening I talked about the suicide and the funeral and drank two single-malt Scotch whiskies and a beer all the while consuming from a straw bowl a portion of steamed edamame beans. I think we arrived home finally at about 11 p.m., which would be 1 a.m. at my point of origin, and Bill led me to the guest room. After carelessly emptying my luggage, I changed into my nightclothes and exhaustedly went to bed.

And in the morning I awoke too early—5 a.m.—with the previous day's events still too fresh and raw. I carried my reading book (probably something by Philip Roth and by him probably *The Human Stain*), my journal and fountain pen down the stairs into the living room, turned the dial that lit the gas fireplace, switched on a small reading lamp, and sat in the corner barrel chair. I read and wrote for an hour or so before anyone else had awakened. And then, when it became just light enough to ensure I would not get lost or hit by a car, I put on the running clothes that I had brought with me, strapped on my runner's watch and my iPod and headed out on the roads. I remembered all too well the funeral and understood that I was grieving. The iPod control was on shuffle: the songs would play

---

86. https://genius.com/Bruce-springsteen-independence-day-lyrics

randomly, and there were hundreds of songs loaded up from which the algorithm might choose. I was not in any sense in control of the playlist. But as I stepped out onto the road and switched on the device, the first thing I heard that morning following the burial of my friend was Carrie Newcomer's composition, "The Gathering of Spirits." And she sang,

> Let it go my love, my truest
> Let it sail on silver wings
> Life's a twinkling and that's for certain
> But it's such a fine thing
> There's a gathering of spirits
> There's a festival of friends
> And we'll take up where we left off
> When we all meet again.

Surprised and comforted at the serendipitous yet fortuitous choice from the playlist, I listened as I ran, and I felt the ache in my chest start to ease and myself to breathe a bit more evenly, and I thought that, no, we probably would not meet again but yes, perhaps we all would be well again. Newcomer's song is forever linked to that moment of difficult comfort and hard-wrung joy. Every time I hear it, I am solaced.

Winter is difficult here in the Upper Midwest. There are weeks where the temperature does not reach to zero degrees Fahrenheit. And here it snows early and late. From late October until early May there exists the possibility not only of a snowfall but of a real winter storm. In late November, always around Thanksgiving, the sky turns a dull shade of gray, and I stare despondently out of the window and acknowledge that today is as good as it is going to get until the advent of spring. And in that moment I hear Gordon Bok singing "Turning Toward the Morning." He cautions,

> When the darkness falls around you
> And the Northwind come to blow,
> And you hear him call your name out
> As he walks the brittle snow:
> That old wind don't mean you trouble,
> He don't care or even know,
> He's just walking down the darkness
> Toward the morning.

This song speaks about winter's advent and the effect its coming has on the human spirit: When I lived in the house at that time of the year, I would take a deep breath and gather in my things from out there and carry them in here. I stocked the cupboard and made certain that those things that would bring me comfort were stored close by: flour for my bread and muffins, beans and rice, cereals and grains; a bottle of scotch and a case each of beer and wine. I brought out the snow shovels, and I sighed for the coming of spring that would not arrive for too many months. In St. Paul where now I live, the winter is too, very, very cold, but here in the city the snow gets dirty and ugly, and I am loath to venture anywhere. Like the bears I would hibernate. Bok's song acknowledges the dolorous effect of winter on the human spirit but offers hope from within the frigid air and beneath the snows. Bok says, "One of the things that provoked this song was a letter last November from a friend who had had a very difficult year and was looking for the courage to keep on plowing into it . . . " Winter here demands respect and resignation, strength and acceptance. Winter is not an easy season here in the Midwest: the frozen air, the hard, cold, cold ground, and on so many days, the steady, pervasive grayish hue can depress the spirit. Even the sky appears changed during these winter months: the clearness of the evening and the canopy of stars appear colder next to the stark nakedness of the trees, their branches like skinny, craggy stiff fingers pointing upward. I suppose that is why our first response to winter is to light the candles and bring the green inside. With the advent of winter I come into the house, light a fire, and know there will be flowers tomorrow. I get no urge for going. The music offers me strength.

 Music has helped to situate me in time and place. For example: when I lived in New York City, on the morning of the first frost on WNEW-FM, Dave Herman would play Joni Mitchell's song, "Urge for Going." She would sing: "I woke up today and found, frost perched on the ground/It hovered in a frozen sky, then it gobbled summer down."[87] This was a song that was then unavailable on her vinyl albums though Tom Rush included it delicately as part of his early work. But I would hear Joni's version only when Dave Herman would spin it, and he played it only on the morn of the year's first frost. When I would hear the notes of Joni Mitchell's lone guitar on my radio, I would know that not only was summer over but that fall had passed as well and that the cold, stark winter was upon me. It was time to take out my heavy, wool coat and my flannel-lined dungarees, and to make sure I had at least two pairs of gloves and a set of mittens. My body would contract just a bit to gather and hold in its warmth. The music led me forward into winter.

87. https://jonimitchell.com/music/song.cfm?id=71

## Before the Masts

Now, for the past thirty and odd years I have lived in the Midwest, and WNEW-FM is no longer a viable radio station and Dave Herman no longer plays the music. But when the frost first appears on the ground I think of Joni and Dave and New York. The winters here in the Midwest are bitter and the first frost comes early on. I love them nonetheless and I get no urge for going.

In 1970, on WNEW the then early morning disc jockey, Michael Harrison, played as his opening theme song Gordon Lightfoot's "Minstrel of the Dawn." It was the first cut of Gordon Lightfoot's album, *Sit Down Young Stranger*. And each morning with the music I would arise out of the bed and prepare for the workday. Hearing that song, and especially in the early sunless wintry mornings, calmed me.

> The minstrel of the dawn is here
> To make you laugh and bend your ear
> Up the steps you'll hear him climb
> All full of thoughts, all full of rhymes
> Listen to the pictures flow
> Across the room into your mind they go
> Listen to the strings
> They jangle and dangle
> While the old guitar rings.[88]

The invitation arrived profound and warm. I would arise and ready myself for the day's work: I was a high school English teacher in Sayville, New York, but I lived in my parent's home and the drive to school took well over an hour. But the minstrel's invitation promised me a day of thought and language; I felt then that the music played just for me. During the winter months the driving was often treacherous and always a bit lonely. But Lightfoot's music had calmed and prepared me for the day. I could be a minstrel of the dawn.

And sometimes I learned from the music just what I needed at the moment to know. I had taken too many drugs that day and just the right kind. I had spent part of the late afternoon at the movie theater watching a remastered print of Disney's *Fantasia*, and then, it was suddenly the end of the day, and I returned home. Even from my meager windows I knew it was a dark night. I was alone in my Walden cabin, and for some reason that I cannot now know I put on Bob Dylan's Blood on the Tracks, an album I had owned since it was first released in 1975. Now, I was standing singly and

---

88. https://genius.com/Gordon-lightfoot-minstrel-of-the-dawn-lyrics

alone in the middle of my studio apartment probably with a glass of wine in my hand, and I heard:

> Purple clover, Queen Anne's Lace
> Crimson hair across your face
> You could make me cry if you don't know
> Can't remember what I was thinkin' of
> You might be spoilin' me too much, love
> You're gonna make me lonesome when you go,

And I understood even for just that single moment a relief from my existential dread. Everything does inevitably end, but in the meantime and in this moment, I could enjoy being spoiled. That song is forever linked to that instance of insight, and whenever I hear that song, I experience some relief from my anxiety and I can sense for my life direction and hope. I can go on.

She had asked if I had anxiety. Oh God, yes, I do, I answered. Sometimes it just comes upon me and wraps itself around me like a coarse, harsh woolen blanket. There was a time when I was younger and these hypos would come upon me, that I would take myself out on the roads and give myself a good talking to, but today I am so much older now and sometimes even a good walk doesn't offer me calm. I think that the rhythms of the walk don't satisfy my angst or jog my thoughts or calm my anxious disquiet as did once the running. In the walk I got no relief to help shake off the anxieties. Sometimes when the hypos hit, I would withdraw into some room accompanied by a book or journal, fill a mug with coffee or tea, or a tumbler with scotch. Sometimes then I would sit in a comfortable chair and for awhile listen to music and sketch out my thoughts. One such day I heard the song "1000 Lovers" by Lynn Miles, and I have returned regularly over the past several years to it when I am overcome with my angst for which I know no immediate source and from which I would seek some relief. Her words offer me some comfort. She sings:

> A thousand lovers could put their arms around me,
> A thousand wishes could fall like summer rain,
> A thousand mothers could sing hush now don't you cry,
> There's nothing in the world tonight that's gonna take away my pain.

You see, this song is not about the saving power of love or even the painful loss of it: a thousand lovers couldn't help. Neither is this song about getting what you want: a thousand wishes could fall and yet tender no pleasure. Nor is this song about nurture and unqualified love: a thousand mothers could sing comfort and still one would not be soothed. No, none of these solaces are going to take away the pain. And I think, what is this pain but the anxieties that I suffer in my daily living in this world and in no other, and from which pain there is no relief. Seneca cautions me, "Night does not remove our worries; it brings them to the surface. All it gives us is a change of anxieties."[89] The night might offer different troubles than those of the daytime, but the anxieties remain. However, perhaps in the hearing of the song it was enough to know that there are pains from which there could be no relief. It is a consolation, finally, to know that it is not pathology from which I sometimes suffer but the inevitable experience of living. I remain anxious but I learn that I am neither alone nor crazy.

Seneca says, "A slight feverishness may deceive a person, but when it has developed to the point where a genuine fever is raging it will extract an admission that something is wrong from even a tough and hardened individual."[90] Sometimes a song articulates an ever-present anxiety and ironically joins me to a community. Such occurred when I first heard Harvey Reid's song, "Show Me the Road." Reid sings, "Show me a sign, tell me a reason/Cold winds have scattered these seeds I've sown." In these lines spoken to the universe I hear not a demand but a plea. The petitioner seeks some sense of hope, some sign, that all his effort has not been in vain and that the seeds he has sown, like those of Johnny Appleseed, have grown roots. As for me: of all my students over the almost fifty years I have been in the classroom, only two remain connected to me. Should there be more? I have loved the classroom both as student and teacher, often at the same time. Explicit in Reid's words is the reality of the cold, harsh winds that blow furiously and anonymously, and the despairing suspicion that all his works will not bear fruit. Despite our work and honest intent, our seeds are blown about by those cold winds; they do not land on fertile soil, and they will not grow roots. In these lines I hear resignation and despondency, yet in these lines as well I hear an acknowledgment of the struggle and its cost. "Lord, let me live to see another morning/Show me the road that leads to my home!" I take some comfort that somewhere there is a home to which I can retreat. Somewhere, I would not be alone. And the song reminds me that there is community out there even in my moments of

---

89. Seneca, *Letters from a Stoic*, 111.
90. Seneca, *Letters from a Stoic*, 101.

## Anxious Am I?

downheartedness and depression. Even as I write now and cast these seeds, I wonder into what ground they may grow.

I think, though, that for me the idea of home is conflicted. I have long found the McGarrigle Sisters song "Talk to Me of Mendocino," a heartbreakingly beautiful expression of longing and of home. I have been consumed for a long while concerning issues of home. These thoughts have long made me anxious. The song's narrator means to head West back to Mendocino from the state of old New York where she has been residing contentedly since first she started roaming. Suddenly, however, she had become homesick and wants to head back home. But I wondered: Why now? And why does she ask her companion to talk to her of Mendocino. Does she need to be convinced to undertake the journey by spoken images of the place? But she must already possess such images, I think. Or do the images require speech to have some actuality? Is it talk that is necessary to inspire her journeying? Or will the talk substitute for the travel? In her mind she seems to have made the journey as she imagines moving through South Bend and onto the Western plain. And why does she make query, "Must I wait, must I follow?" The song had suggested that she has been the initiator of the travel and so I wonder why does she wonder if she must follow? Or is it the other who wants to wait but she is anxious to set out for Mendocino? Perhaps in her talk she hopes to inspire her other to join in the return. The paradoxical nature of her questions, whether she must wait or follow suggests to me a kind of emotional paralysis. Does she want to go back to Mendocino or just to be talked to about it? If I punctuate the line "Won't you say come with me?" with a comma after "say," then she asks a question; but if there is no comma then she makes a statement and requests that her companion invite her to join the journey back to Mendocino. And who is it, then, who wants to return?

Perhaps longing exists in the tension between going and staying. Dylan despairs about being stuck in Mobile with the Memphis blues again . . . longing to be somewhere else but being for some reason incapable of moving. And this travel need not be merely a physical journeying but can be embedded in feeling as well. She desires to go but must be convinced; she wishes to stay but feels compelled to go. The images of home (and not the home away from home!) draw her to Mendocino, but there is an underlying lethargy despite her Desire. I wonder: if she had come of age in New York, then does she head back to Mendocino to enter an adulthood or does she imagine a return to childhood. Her return to Mendocino will be permanent: she anticipates the sun rising over the redwoods and asserts that she will not rise to leave Mendocino again. Ironically, it would seem that it is she who talks of Mendocino. I wonder what she really wants to hear.

And then, sometimes in the music I experience simple joys and light-hearted freedom. Such occurs for me in Joni Mitchell's "Carey," a song I've enjoyed for almost fifty years and of which I never seem to tire. The lively jauntiness of the song cheers me regardless of my mood. Just yesterday on my walk I replayed the song three times. Maybe I needed to do so then! As does so much of my music, "Carey" leads me to muse and reflect on my life. The song concerns levels of comfort, represented here by the physical comforts she in her present experience lacks. Mitchell longs for her clean, white linen, fancy French cologne, and a rented fine piano, but in the present she suffers from dirty fingernails and sticky beach tar on her feet. There exists somewhere—maybe Amsterdam or Rome—the ease and even security to be enjoyed from the layers of adorned sweetness and fancy French colognes with which we may anoint ourselves and that serve to raise us, I suppose, above the malodorous and offensive smell, grit and dirt of the street. What the narrator of "Carey" misses far from home are the trappings of her culture that are part and parcel of her familiar civilization.

Culture is the practices and beliefs which a particular civilization deems acceptable and to which it attaches significance. Terry Eagleton says that culture is the product of a civilization that requires some "spiritual foundation" that the culture would offer. I appreciate Eagleton's characterization of culture as the social unconscious, "the vast repository of instincts, prejudices, pieties, sentiments, half-formed opinions and spontaneous assumptions which underpin our everyday activity, and which we rarely call into question."[91] Culture in Western civilization is the practice of eating with utensils except when we dine at an Ethiopian restaurant or when we indulge in a slice of pizza from our local pizzeria or a hot dog with all the fixings and a slew of napkins from the local food truck! Culture is farting when alone, even while walking down the street, but not under the covers when accompanied there. This social unconscious, not dissimilar I think from Raymond Williams' structure of feeling, is prelinguistic: it exists as the sense of reality of the everyday life that we hold without linguistic articulation or even thought.

---

91. Eagleton, *Culture*, 49.

## Anxious Am I?

Carey's narrator misses her civilization and the culture it supports. Her comfort would derive from the relationship she has to the culture of her civilization. Comfort is about becoming acclimated to the luxuries that we can take for granted. And she has every intention to return to her civilization, but before she does so, well, she invites Carey to get out his cane! For the moment with her beach-tarred feet and unwashed body smells, she urges Carey to "laugh and toast to nothing" with the freaks, soldiers and friends. Sometimes the appeal of the grunge feels comfortable as long, I suppose, as one understands that it is a choice and that leaving it is an option. But tonight, Carey, we'll celebrate the immersion into the carefree, even untroubled and uncultured life. For now, the night is a starry dome, and there is the Matala Moon and some scratchy rock 'n' roll playing somewhere, and let's celebrate whoever is here—even that bright red devil that fixes me here now. It is sometimes good for just awhile to forget culture and enjoy dirty fingernails and suffer the beach tar on the feet as long as I know that there is some clean white linen to which I can return. Every time I hear "Carey" I consider how I have become acclimated to the comforts I have accepted in my life and I recall a time when I experienced with joy the beach tar on my feet and my dirty fingernails. Sometimes I determine not to shower.

Memory is a wonderful thing: though it does come heavily enclosed in context. I sip my coffee in my own mug, and I am remembering through the music. The music leads me sometimes out of the world and sometimes it leads me right back to it.

I am not at all a man of constant sorrow, and I haven't had trouble all my days though I've experienced my share of anxiety. And I am a man not free of defeats and anxieties that often keep me awake all through the night and sometimes trouble my days. I have suffered some difficulties, disappointments and setbacks. I married early and not for life and eventually divorced. In my public and private dealings I've often been referred to as vinegar, son of wine. Sometime in my early twenties while working for my father in his factory, he fell into financial difficulties and requested that I, rather than he, sign something—I didn't understand then what that document had meant—and besides, my father said I shouldn't worry. But when his business again failed that document made me culpable for $50,000 and I declared financial bankruptcy. Since then, I have lived in some terror that I would one day run out of money and be forced to live on the street. I tell my daughters that from them I want only a basement apartment. I married and divorced. I have remained wary about most relationships, alas, and have failed in more than my share. I maintain a wide berth and do not venture out very far. I lived through the presidencies of Ronald Reagan and George W. Bush, and for four years (not counting the primaries and campaign vituperative garbage that spewed from the candidate's mouth) suffered the slanders, smears and lies of the liar in chief, Donald Trump. I survived. There are a great many very bad people out there. And I recognize that I speak from a position of some privilege: I am white, middle class and have enjoyed the opportunities those positions assume. As Housman writes in his poem "As I Gird for Fighting," "'Tis sure much finer fellows/Have fared much worse before."[92] I remain thankful with some qualifications.

But in my more difficult times, I would think of the Mary Ellen Carter. In Stan Rogers' song the "Mary Ellen Carter," the craft that had been piloted by a drunken captain and a smashed first mate ran aground in a gale and sank. (I am reminded here of Conrad's *Lord Jim* and the captain of the Patna.) The owners of the Mary Ellen Carter announced that they are done with the wreck, have already collected their insurance monies, and now laugh derisively at those for whom the Mary Ellen Carter had served as a shelter from the storm. They pleaded with the owners to raise and recover the ship, but the owners refused to do so and cast the supplicants out of the office. But the friends loved that boat that had seen them through the gale, and they vowed to raise the Mary Ellen Carter again.

Well, the Mary Ellen Carter might be a sunken boat, but it served also as a vital and potent symbol of resistance to power and a call to loyalty to the community. Refusing to accept her defeat, the friends of the Mary Ellen Carter spent the spring months preparing the submerged boat to surface again despite the difficulties that confronted them in that task. It is spring now, as I write. The work required was arduous, dangerous, and often painful, but the Mary Ellen Carter had been their strength over the years and now they were committed to saving the ship ever aware that though they raised it the Mary Ellen Carter would no longer head out onto the seas but would instead do service floating at the dock: perhaps as a restaurant, a coffee house, a place of community, of quiet and refuge. They would not allow her to crumble into scale and be forgotten! The Mary Ellen Carter, abandoned as useless junk by "the laughing, drunken rats who left her to a sorry grave" had to be recovered not for its future service on the seas but for her places in the hearts and minds of those who loved her. They could

---

92. Housman, 94-I

not let the ship or themselves suffer ignominious defeat. In my moments of despair and loss of hope, I think of the Mary Ellen Carter. Rogers sings:

> And you, to whom adversity has dealt the final blow
> With smiling bastards lying to you everywhere you go
> Turn to, and put out all your strength of arm and heart and brain
> And like the Mary Ellen Carter, rise again.

I gain courage every time I hear that song, and for more than thirty years I have listened to Stan Rogers sing it. What is to be done?

> Rise again, rise again - though your heart it be broken
> And life about to end.
> No matter what you've lost, be it a home, a love, a friend.
> Like the Mary Ellen Carter, rise again.

I don't know to what extent I have the strength still to go below and patch her rents and stop her vents . . . I wonder what strength I have yet to raise either the Mary Ellen Carter or myself. I have concern what those efforts might finally mean. Oh, I read the news today. But like the Mary Ellen Carter, I mean to rise again.

And finally, I think often about "Bob Dylan's Dream," another song to which I have been listening for more than fifty years. Dylan had written the song when he was yet in his early twenties from a melody called "Lady Franklin's Lament." Lord John Franklin was the British sea captain who was lost with his entire crew attempting to navigate the Northwest Passage, and the song's narrator, his Lady, bemoans his disappearance and regrets her loss.[93] Dylan's song, too, is about an irrevocable loss not of a body but of a naiveté that could not hold. Dylan's lyrics speak presciently of the romantic innocence of youth that really has no viability in the future; he laments its loss that is sad, even tragic, but that is also inevitable and even necessary. Dylan sings of that room where he and his friends sit "forever in fun," yet acknowledges that their chances to remain there "really were a million to one!" The wish is priceless—"Ten thousand dollars at the drop of a hat, I'd give it all gladly if our lives could be like that—" but the reality is that that innocence cannot be long held at the expense of a life to be lived. I wonder now what rooms I would return to now. I think that to begin to live one must leave those rooms and enter the very messy world. The loss of innocence can be painful and even devastating. Hawthorne's Young Goodman

---

93. This is the same Lord Franklin of whom Thoreau wrote, "Is [Lord] Franklin the only one who is lost, that his wife should be so earnest to find him?"

Brown traveled into the forest to meet the black man, and on his way he passed all of the townspeople including the minister also heading into the forest center and to the meeting with the black man. There, Young Goodman Brown saw even his wife, Faith. Brown returned to town having lost all hope and promise and from that moment lived a lonely, embittered life. The shattering experience ruined Young Goodman Brown as the innocent faith in which he had believed vanished. Brown couldn't survive the loss of his ideal.

I wonder what could prepare someone like Young Goodman Brown or my children to the awareness of the Devil in the forest but a sense of irony. I don't even think that it is evil that is to be confronted in the dark forest, though certainly that might exist as a component of what might be found there. What might be confronted in the forest is doubt and uncertainty, and it would require strength to survive the awareness that innocent faith is neither pure, absolute, inviolable—or sometimes even effective. Faith is a hope that exists in the midst of the muck and mire; it does not remain unsullied. Montaigne writes, "The elements that we enjoy are corrupted, and the metals likewise; and gold must be debased by some other material to fit it for our service."[94] Hope is the belief that there will be a future though the content of that future or even the path to it remains unknown. I maintain belief that our early innocences and ideals, like first loves, are never forgotten, but to be of use they must be made into alloys by our experiences before they can become viable. I think irony might serve as that instrument to create the mixture because irony acknowledges that nothing is all that it seems and irony attests that everything might be something else. Irony reminds us that there is always the road not taken.

As I age, I have recognized surprisingly that the purity of the ideals that once I held on to so fervently and innocently in the turbulent days of my youth have actually become strengthened because they have been mixed with other elements and have since become alloys. Reality might be an insult, as Winnicott has said, but it must be accepted if we are to get along. Whatever wisdom I have come to possess and that even I have created exists as a result of that amalgam I assemble from my Desire and the materials of the objective world. I think that the innocence of my youthful ideals has developed into something else through its contact with that world outside of that Edenic room in which it was so easy to tell black from white and wrong from right. I remember loud impassioned discussions around

---

94. Montaigne, *The Complete Works*, 619.

dinner tables, wine bottles and pints of beer; about brilliant opportunities I held to be achievable: we anticipated the revolution at any moment. I recollect with some affection the illusions I maintained about myself as I became a partner and a parent, even as I recall the ideal children that I invented and with whom I would have lived. I remember every vote I cast that I believed would turn the world to paradise, forgetting that the world was out there in the land of Nod east of Eden. Nod is where Cain with whom I have long felt some sympathy settled and built cities that were always in need of repair. How much in the illusion has vanished and what was gained by that loss! The ideals of youth are lovely to hold and difficult to abandon, but only by doing so does the work begin. I still want a better world, a better life, a perfect family, an ideal relationship, but I've abandoned belief that my visions are other than mine alone and ultimately are unrealizable. Montaigne observes: "I speak my mind freely on all things, even on those which perhaps exceed my capacity and which I by no means hold to be within my jurisdiction. And so the opinion I give of them is to declare the measure of my sight, not the measure of things."[95] I concur.

I think that I began this learning with Dylan when I realized that the absolutism that I held as a youth finally would have to be abandoned. Age, rather than solidifying beliefs, often demanded review and revision. I learned that I could plan only so much but even those ends would remain in doubt as the means changed. I couldn't see into the future. Tolstoy addresses this uncertainty in War and Peace. In Volume III, Part Three, Chapter 2, Tolstoy addresses the Battle of Borodino during Napoleon's invasion of Russia in 1812. The narrator disputes the notion that battle plans are drawn up by commanders in the quiet of their tents and then executed according to plan. He writes, "A commander in chief always finds himself in the middle of a shifting series of events, and in such a way that he is never able at any moment to ponder all the meaning of the ongoing event. Imperceptibly, moment by moment, an event is carved into its meaning, and at every moment of this consistent, ceaseless carving of the event, a commander in chief finds himself in the center of a most complex play of intrigues, cares, dependency, power, projects, advice, threats, deceptions, finds himself constantly in the necessity of responding to the countless number of questions put to him, which always contradict each other."[96] One of Tolstoy's points is that armchair generals and historians construct their

---

95. Montaigne, *The Complete Works*, 361.
96. Tolstoy, *War and Peace*, 825.

analyses in the absence of any of this complexity and therefore, inevitably err in their oversimplified conclusions. There is too much complexity to conclude anything with any great degree of sureness.

As in battle, so in life. Interestingly, in Tolstoy's novel almost nothing turns out the way it had originally been intended. In our crude and uncivil modern times we refer to this phenomenon as "Shit happens," but in fact for Tolstoy and Dylan this shit is in fact life and life only. Life is too complex to ascribe a single effect to any specific cause: in hindsight a pattern can be attributed to events, but that pattern cannot begin to approximate the complexity and ambiguity of life. Pierre recognizes this in Volume II, Part V, Chapter 1. Seeking answers to his questions, he searches in books: "He read, he read everything that came to hand . . . " But regardless of what he had read at night, when Pierre awoke in the morning, "all the old questions seemed as insoluble and frightening as ever."[97] In such a state he would grab for another book. Pierre comes to understand that his reading—all activity finally—is an attempt to avoid the realization that "Nothing is trivial or important, it's all the same." Often, I behave so as to avoid this realization.

---

97. Tolstoy, *War and Peace*, 538.

# PATHS IN

## ON BEAUTY AND TENSION

I APPRECIATE beauty but have been often confused by the politics of aesthetics. I know what is beautiful to me, but often disagree with others who have different standards. The concept of beauty has been contentious to aestheticians, critics, and philosophers each of whom have argued for their particular definition of the beautiful and the products that accorded with it. I was often confused by how and why disagreements concerning the occurrences of beauty occurred. I wondered how the critics could have dismissed the beauty of *Moby-Dick* that is by some now considered a great and classic American novel; how was it that Bob Dylan's *Self Portrait,* infamously excoriated by Greil Marcus in 1970 when he wondered, "What is this shit?", had become today the object of serious reevaluation and sincere appreciation. Why couldn't art critics who interminably dispute the skills and products of their subjects agree: paintings that were haughtily dismissed as incompetent in the 19th century today sell for millions of dollars; why did Van Gogh die impoverished and without selling a single painting when now his works sell for tens of millions of dollars; why did the first audience of Igor Stravinsky's now canonical *Rites of Spring* jeer the composer and his composition; why over the years has the reputation of Nobel Prize winner Ernest Hemingway (for one) suffered, even as recent scholarship on non-prize winner F. Scott Fitzgerald has discovered in his corpus a deep irony that characterized the hollowness and corruption of the twenties for which until now he had been considered its emblem. In the beginning I had thought that there ought to have been a defined standard for the beautiful and that this measure should be universally accepted and consistently taught. I had been trained as a New Critic and had learned that beauty was inherent in the structures of a poem: Archibald MacLeish wrote that "a poem must not mean, but be."[1] Beauty just is, and it became for me an intellectual quest to discover it. I searched my books to learn its qualities so that I could know and enjoy it.

1. Macleish, in Sanders, *Chief Modern Poets of England and America,* II-333.

But things changed. I came to discover that such universal standard did not exist and that therefore, my quest to know and grasp the beautiful led me often on fruitless paths and I ended up seeing only what they told me to see. I was confused. And I began to realize that beauty was not an inherent quality but something that occurred in relationship. Beauty, I understood, was an activity, an event and not an immanence; beauty was an experience and not a quality intrinsic to the work itself. I hadn't always liked the books about which the critics praised, and sometimes I admired those they disparaged. I have never appreciated the beauty of the soprano voice or saw beauty in a Rothko painting, but I do remember standing entranced at the Metropolitan Museum in New York before Jackson Pollock's "Autumn Rhythm." I came to understand that an awareness of beauty required a dynamic engagement between the participant and any canvas-type which she approached and earnestly addressed and that such engagement would be steeped in a complex individual and cultural history. Beauty was not a category but a description of a feeling that arose in a relationship between an audience and a work, and that one important source for the occasion of beauty seemed to me to occur from the perception of an apparent tension that the work exhibited in its elements and the subsequent release of that tension that the work effected.

The event of beauty occurred when a perceived tension found a means for some constructive release. The sources of the tension could be personal, cultural, physical or psychological, visual or aural, might even be real or imagined. I have known the unpleasant experience of anxious tension, and when I work toward its release I feel so much better: I may even at times feel beautiful. And I have more recently appreciated how tension plays an important role in the senses of beauty I have enjoyed not only in music but other areas of my life, like the glory of pink and orange tints in the darkening blue sky at sunset or the painted vibrant leaves in the fall against the clear blue sun-filled sky. I have come to believe that the beautiful world as I know it is held together as the result of balanced physical and emotional tensions and paths for its release.

Tension exists in the pull of opposing forces that keep things stable and in place. But tension demands a means of some relief and release, and so mechanisms to effect that release must be available. If there is no possible means established for a release of the tension, then the structure will finally collapse, and this event will not be pretty. I think of the bridge collapse in Minneapolis in 2007; of the building collapse in Miami in 2021;

and of various psychic episodes when I have taken to my bed for a spell. But when tension resolves without collapse there happens a sense of release that can be known as beauty. I think that the very production of art and other forms of creative work arise from the tension experienced between a wholly subjective feeling and the awareness of an external and objective Reality. The artist requires the latter to express the former; there must be materials out there with which to create and give release to the tensions.

 A source of the beauty that I have experienced in music derives from the transition of a created tension into harmony. The transition from a state of tension to one of concord, often difficult but always meaningful, results in beauty just as the transition between poses in yoga practice elicits and reflects a beautiful harmony. In yoga the body holds a pose in tension and the bones and muscles absorb much of the body weight. In the absence of release the body wobbles and eventually collapses. During the transitions out of tension to a new pose, my muscles move my body with some hoped-for grace and elegance from one place and plane to another. Moving through transitions is mentally and physically demanding and when it successfully occurs it is beautiful. Tristram Shandy argues that what is critical in life is exactly this movement from one moment or attitude to another. He says "Attitudes are nothing ma'am—'tis the transition from one attitude to another—like the preparation and resolution of the discord into harmony, which is all in all." In the yoga practice each moment exists in a tension that demands movement and that movement resolves that immanent tension and produces concord. Perhaps this is what Mozart meant when he said, "The music is not in the notes, but in the silence between." I think here of John Cage's piece, 4'33." In that sometimes excruciating silence exists the tension that begs for resolution with sound, but in Cage's piece there is no release of that tension because there are no notes. James Pritchett writes of the performance of this work, "That tensions will arise, with controversy and notoriety following, is only natural. Confronted with the silence, in a setting we cannot control, and where we do not expect this kind of event, we might have any of a number of responses: we might desire for it to be over, or desire for more interesting sounds to listen to, or we might feel frightened, insulted, pensive, cultured, baffled, doubtful, bored, agitated, tickled, sleepy, attentive, philosophical, or, because we 'get it,' a bit smug." The resolution of tension produces beautiful music. Cage's piece offers no resolution and I experience no beauty when it is not heard, but I can hear the resolution of Mozart's silence in the timbres of expressed notes.

## Anxious Am I?

As an example of this tension and resolution and the experience of beauty, I would offer the closing bars of the first movement of Beethoven's Seventh Symphony. The coda to the movement begins not with sound but with silence. For two whole measures, Nos. 387–88, Beethoven composes a rest. It is as if the entire symphony has come to an abrupt halt. Then, in measure 389, the flutes, clarinets, violins, violas, cellos and basses sing a single note, but this note is not in the key of A major that is the dominant key of the symphony; rather, it sounds in $A^b$, a step down from the original key signature, as if to suggest that the whole foundation is falling apart, even crumbling. Tension between the entire first movement and its coda is prepared. Next, Beethoven writes another two full measures of silence. These measures represent for me a halting beginning, a hesitancy to speak. The silence itself represents a tension. It does not know what to say. The silence exists in no key. The music of the coda has begun, ironically, in silence. And if the key of A in which the symphony is written represents a bright sound, then the $A^b$ key which musically begins the coda moves away from that brightness. Indeed, in measure 391, the bass and cello begin a line which musician and critic Michael Steinberg refers to as "obsessive," and these voices, too, are written in the key of A minor, a mournful and even tragic sound. And this line of basses and cellos descend in half-step notes which again do not belong to the A major key signature. Beethoven has created a multiplicity of tensions here: there is the halting willingness to speak, the descending notes out of key, until finally in measure 399 the bass and cellos finally arrive at notes in the A major key. The music aspires to resolution and arrival but is continually frustrated by the orchestration. In measure 399 the basses and cellos briefly arrive home, only to quickly leave it again, singing notes which again do not belong to the key signature, circling home, sometimes voicing notes in the A major key but somehow unable to sustain it; they hover about home without the ability to attain it, singing notes that do not belong. There seems to be the desire to arrive home, but none of the comfort of arrival.

The tension continues as the basses and cellos play notes not in the key signature while the upper voices, the flutes, and clarinets, begin to sing in key. Furthermore, the rhythms remain unbalanced, with the notes in unequal time, producing on the whole a driving, relentless movement. The rhythms continue unbalanced through the next several measures; the whole sequence reflects a tension and unsettledness as the basses and cellos struggle to join the upper voices. Nor is this conventional: traditionally, it would be the lower voices, the basses and violincellos that would serve as foundation and the upper voices which would seek their security. Here, it is as if the foundation, which should be strong and solid, was itself trying to find the structure which it should undergird; it is as if the foundation itself sought some grounding. And then, in the upper voices at measure 400, the rhythms become regular, and the basses and cellos begin to ascend to the Tonic, finally arriving at notes belonging to the A major signature. Then, at measure 423, the rising bass and cello and all of the orchestral voices return home and the symphony explodes in a sound that is magisterial, resplendent, and glorious. The rhythms which until now were unbalanced become regular and all the tensions are resolved in jubilancy. And so, Beethoven closes his coda and this first movement of the symphony: all the instruments are now in the major key, grounded in the Tonic; there are no uneven rhythms, and the sound is bold, ecstatic, and heartening. This joyfulness and expectancy derive from the resolution of a created tension. I find it beautiful. Musical tensions resolved into an exclamation of triumph, the flutes and piccolos fly above the basses—I would not define my emotion here. Words would only reduce the sublime to the mundane.

Another example of this experience of tension and its release occurs in the Byrds' recording of "Wasn't Born to Follow." Immediately after the lines, "And if you think I'm ready/You may lead me to the chasm where the rivers of our vision/Flow into one another," two guitars play against one another, and slowly, inexorably a tension builds.[2] It is a difficult tension that I have experienced in this break; it is about struggle and growth, hurt and pain. This was what I experienced during the 1960s that extended into the 1970s. I loved them, and I hated them. I love them yet. And then, suddenly, during this musical break, when the tension seems to me almost unbearable, there occurs a resolution, and the disquiet between the guitars resolves into a harmony and a flow and a sense of ease. Like the rivers of our vision, the guitars flow into one another, and there is calm. This, too, was what I experienced during the 1960s that extended into the 1970's. I loved them and I hated them. I love them yet. The transition from tension and discord to release and concord creates a sense of the beautiful.

Take away the tensions and there is no music. Without the release of tension there is no beauty but only continual argument and pain. Laughter and weeping are instruments of tension release. Sometimes even too much joy creates a tension that necessitates release leading at times to tears or

2. https://genius.com/The-byrds-wasnt-born-to-follow-lyrics

laughter. I think that the cacophonous scream is symptomatic of the presence of tension. The scream is not itself beautiful, but it makes possible the experience of beauty. I have known in my life some very distinguishing screams. Of course, there is the horror contained in Edvard Munch's painting, "The Scream." Within the painting itself the tension the scream arouses remains unresolved, but a reading of that image by a viewer attempts to resolve the tension in the image of the figure's cry and allows for an experience of beauty. I have been enamored of that painting for much of my life. Fay Wray's uncontrolled and terrified screaming in *King Kong* certainly sets a high standard for the genre: that particular scream evokes a tense danger, and the film's edited sequences offer some release from the tension and for many creates an experience of cinematic beauty. High on my list of notable screams is the terrified cry that emanated from this quaking eleven-year-old as I sat frozen in my seat holding my banana-flavored Turkish taffy (Smack it and crack it!) watching the Japanese horror film, *Rodan*, at the Plainview Movie Theater on Long Island. The first sight of those giant ants upon which the great monster fed touched something deep in my unconscious and triggered an involuntary cry from my terrified soul. (The candy also served as relief and provided sufficient work to my dentist.) I have returned to that scream with affection over the years, and though I cannot now say the film was beautiful I can say that at the time the film enthralled and the scream broke the felt tension. And another scream that I recall with great pleasure is that which occurred when Butch Cassidy and the Sundance Kid leap off the cliff into the waters below to escape the posse which inexorably closes in on them. The expletive they scream as they leap offers release from the tension as the two manage here to escape capture. It is for this viewer a beautiful moment.

There are other screams significant to me: perhaps Janet Leigh's horrifying cries in Hitchcock's Psycho remain high on my list, as does Stanley Kowalski's animal evocation "Stella!" in *A Streetcar Named Desire*. I do not experience Stanley as beautiful in any way, but his scream embodies the play's tension and makes space for an experience of its beauty. And again, once driving home from school I became stuck in a superb traffic jam on the Triborough Bridge. I wanted passionately to be home, to throw off the day's clothes, and head out for my run. It must have been a spring day because I remember sitting dead and deadly still on the bridge with no place or means to move. I remember rolling up the car window and in frustration beginning to scream. My sound moved nothing but for a moment the scream relieved my frustration, my tension, and offered me the patience to sit still just a little longer.

But sometimes the scream itself is just beautiful. I am drawn to Ronnie Hawkins's scream during his performance of the classic song, "Who Do You Love?", at the Thanksgiving event celebrating the final performance of The Band that was filmed and thus, memorialized in the film, *The Last Waltz*. In four escalating shouts, Hawkins displays neither fear nor terror nor frustration but a sheer and uncontainable joy that the scream relieves. On that stage at that time, the world is just too much fun. "Big time, Bill, big time," he speaks from the stage to the event's producer, Bill Graham. And what was big about the time is the irrepressible pleasure of the moment that could only be expressed in the tension-reducing scream. It was beautiful.

A scream articulates something that is ineffable by anything other than the scream; maybe the scream might at times be an expression of the sublime. I have understood the sublime as an awareness of inexpressible beauty. On a morning run, I listened four times to the second movement of Beethoven's Seventh Symphony because the tones of it uplifted my spirits and relieved my tensions. I consider it a sublime creation. It inspires an emotional response that is inexpressible and therefore, even unintelligible, not unlike the scream. And the experience of the sublime ennobles and is a realization of beauty. I am raised up by the experience of the sublime. I can experience the sublime and I can even respond to it though I cannot exactly describe it. The idea of the sublime reminds me of Robert Heinlein's *Stranger in a Strange Land* where the experience of understanding something completely is referred to as to grok. There was no word in the English language, I suppose, for the concept for which Heinlein grasped, and so he invented one. The word has since passed out of currency, but some of us still recall its usefulness. I had originally studied the sublime as an undergraduate English major when it was associated with Byron's Manfred, and more recently, the sublime came up in conversation with my daughter, Anna Rose, who asked what the sublime meant. Maybe she had heard Hannah Montana use the word. I told her that the sublime was a word that could be applied to an occurrence that was inexpressible. She asked if the Holocaust was sublime. It was a great question, I think. But I answered that for me the sublime raises our lives to a level of some ineffable exaltation and glory. Inexpressible as the Holocaust is, thoughts of it only drag me through the muck and the grime. But, I suggested to her, the response of the fighters in the Warsaw Ghetto, the courage with which they fought against the

Nazis might be considered an incident of the sublime. Perhaps the sublime is a respite from history, a relief from the tension that history embodies, though ironically, that which brings me to the experience of the sublime is always history!

## ON DRINKING

I no longer drink to any excess these days, imbibe mostly a single drink and sometimes add a second, and there have even been moments when I have found it essential to pour for myself just one more. I begin the evening with such cocktails, the onset of which occasion in my retirement has inexorably crept to an earlier hour. I might serve hors d'oeuvres as an accompaniment to the cocktail, and though the carrots and celery are usually enjoyed they are not essential. In retirement there is not much necessity to wind down the day, but I have long established a daily structure with a cocktail hour as an end to the day and I have continued that practice. For years, when I spent my days in study and the classroom, and until the children left home for college and other things, the ritual of an alcoholic beverage while cooking served as cocktail hour ritual and gave me comfort and helped me transition into a new space. I relished the aesthetics of the contents of a crystal tumbler of scotch, a beer mug or wineglass nestled happily amidst the vegetables. I cooked up some lovely thoughts having a drink while preparing dinner. For some time now I have purchased microbrewed and not inexpensive beer: I can spend anywhere from $6 to $10 for a six-pack; recently I treated myself to a new double-hop India Pale Ale that was priced at $11.99 for six bottles! My purchases are a small luxury that I can afford, bourgeois though the indulgence may be. Compared to a case of Budweiser Light (24 cans) that might cost $16.00, my immoderation might seem excessive, but I have learned the difference in character between crafted beers and mass-produced ones even as I know the difference between coffee beans roasted at J&S Beanery and the coffee served at most local diners and restaurants in the United States; or from the Maxwell House coffee in blue cans that my mother purchased and brewed in a tin percolator. But my motive for drinking is sensory satisfaction and not drunkenness. I love the taste of a well-brewed beer and especially so on a steamy summer day. My scotch comes with a higher price tag, sometimes as much as $85 a bottle, and the wine (of any and all countries) at $15.00 a bottle.

Montaigne writes that drinking is one pleasure that age does not take from us. I am thankful of that as I stumble through my eighth decade. Ever the pragmatist, Montaigne suggests that as we age some individuals search for better-quality bottles, but he cautions that if we attempt to drink only the finest wines—if we keep trying to find the most perfect and finest wines and liquors—then it must be that we will have to drink a lot of bad wine in order to find the really good ones. This seems to Montaigne to be antithetical to the pleasure one ought to derive from drinking in the first place. Therefore, Montaigne advises, "to be a good drinker, one must not have so delicate a palate."[3] Montaigne says that a coarser palate in fact intensifies the potential for pleasure. We should increase our pleasure as we age, he writes, and not look for occasions that might disappoint us by drinking a bad bottle of either an expensive or cheap wine, scotch, or beer.

I like to have my drink during dinner preparation but, when possible, I like to share my drinking as well. A very perfect evening involves friends, good food, and an assortment of bottles of wine. I appreciate the sentiment of Henry David Thoreau: "I think that I love society as much as most, and am ready enough to fasten myself like a bloodsucker for the time to any full-blooded man that comes in my way. I am naturally no hermit, but might possibly sit out the sturdiest frequenter of the bar-room if my business called me thither."[4] I think what dear Henry suggests here is that with the right companion he would be prepared to remain seated at the table until the bar closes. This is not the usual portrait one has of Thoreau, but I relish it. As for myself, I have never closed any bars, and I do not get drunk—it is better than fifty years since I overindulged—though at times at occasional soirées I have sometimes imbibed more than usual and have had in those moments some interesting ideas. Well, at least to my mind they appeared so! Indeed, I have found that in relative moderation drinking lubricates and stimulates the moving parts of my mind and that of the friends who sit about the table. Drinking is a practice of realizing pleasure, and as sitting about the table with friends is pleasurable, drinking all the more increases the pleasure. Montaigne urges, "To drink French style, at two meals and moderately, for fear of your health, is to restrain the god's favor too much. You need more time and persistence . . . And so we should make our daily drinking habits more expansive and vigorous."[5] I think that

---

3. Montaigne, *The Complete Works*, 299.
4. Thoreau, *Walden*, 151.
5. Montaigne, *The Complete Works*, 300.

Montaigne advocates not drunkenness but conviviality; I think Montaigne would soon be found at Thoreau's table in the barroom.

Like so many of Montaigne's essays (at least as I read them), "On Drunkenness" has a tendency to saunter about: digressions are, after all, the life of the book! In the midst of his thoughts on drinking liquor and its effects, he suddenly digresses into a lovely encomium about his father for whom Montaigne seems to have had great respect. He admired his father's zest for life which somehow Montaigne aligns with the joy of drinking, but then, realizing he has drifted somewhat from his topic he concludes this section with a resounding command: "Let's get back to our bottles!" I like that.

Montaigne declares that drunkenness has a tendency to push to the top all that is at the bottom: I hear in Montaigne an early form of psychology's recognition that wine loosens the inhibitory reflex, uncovers contents from the unconscious, and ironically, aids in memory, though he acknowledges that while somewhat inebriated we say (and do) things we wouldn't normally do while sober. In drink what has been repressed may be released. Alas, many of those acts undertaken in drunkenness are not necessarily exemplary, and I am certain that of these deeds Montaigne would disapprove. Nevertheless, though Montaigne finds drunkenness a "loose and stupid vice," it is less malicious and harmful than the other vices that he charges frequently clash more directly with society in general. But what Montaigne prefigures here in his advocacy for drunkenness is our contemporary concept of the victimless crime, such as recreational drug use, or the employment of call girls and gigolos (the employment of the latter not at all as frequently reported as is the former). Montaigne seems not to encourage public drunkenness so much as private inebriations. Montaigne also defends drinking by suggesting that since "we cannot give ourselves pleasure without its costing us something,"[6] then drinking is something that has minimum cost. Montaigne here precedes some words of contemporary philosophers: Bob Dylan declares that "every pleasure has an edge of pain/Pay for your ticket and don't complain." Montaigne acknowledges that though inebriation has its cost, it is the price one pays for its pleasure.

Quoting respectable authorities, Montaigne even encourages drinking—even sometimes drunkenness—because such indulgence makes possible pleasure where pleasure seems not imaginable. Montaigne writes, "For drunkenness to Plato is a good and certain test of each and every man's

---

6. Montaigne, *The Complete Works*, 299.

nature, and at the same time suited to give older people the courage to make merry in dances and music, useful pastimes that they shy away from in a sober mood."⁷ Drinking increases our capacity for pleasure as we age, though it certainly has the potential to do so even in our youth. Physical aging presents so many disappointments. Receding hair and gums. Failing eyesight. Rising blood pressure and dwindling erections. Weakened urine streams that often dampen and stain undergarments and trousers. But, as Montaigne reminds me, a drunkenness in moderation (yes, a wonderful contradiction) rather than one that disables is to be appreciated. No less a man than Ralph Waldo Emerson would aver that, "As insane persons are indifferent to their dress, diet and other accommodations, and as we do in dreams, with equanimity, the most absurd acts, so a drop more wine in our cup of life will reconcile us to stranger company and work." Emerson had averred that a bit more regular insanity in our lives would offer a reasonable way to work our way to reality. A bit more wine in our cup of life might offer succor.

Lastly (though perhaps not finally), Montaigne avows that poets and artists often are carried outside themselves in their creative processes: in the heat of artistic and courageous activity, people "lose" themselves and cannot answer for their extraordinary accomplishments. Assuming that a reliance on too-much-reason often constrains us from such fanciful flights that enable creative activity, Montaigne, after Plato, states that such accomplishments do not happen unless our wisdom is "obscured by sleep or by some illness, or lifted from its place by celestial rapture." The poetic frenzy and madness of artistic creation or prophecy Montaigne ascribes to a certain madness "that transcends our own judgment and reason." Drunkenness facilitates such a state. Tolstoy had written, "If we allow that human life can be governed by reason, the possibility of life is annihilated." And D.W. Winnicott has cautioned that "we are poor indeed if we are only sane!"⁸

Of drunkenness Thoreau suggests in "Higher Laws" that the world is enough to intoxicate the minds of men and women and that water suffices as the only necessary liquor. But not always: Thoreau admits, "But to tell the truth, I find myself at present somewhat less particular in these respects. I carry less religion to the table, ask no blessing; not because I am wiser than I was, but, I am obliged to confess, because, however much it is to be

---

7. Montaigne, *The Complete Works*, 302.
8. Tolstoy, *War and Peace*, 1131.

regretted, with years I have grown more coarse and indifferent."[9] I suspect he has taken the advice of his friend Emerson and taken to imbibing greater quantities of alcohol . . . and perhaps even coffee.

## A PARABLE

I had never thought of myself as a cat person: my mother despised cats, in fact, for some vague and undisclosed reason. When I was a child and the family lived briefly in a house, we owned a Shetland sheep dog named Laddie, but we moved back to Queens and to an apartment in Rego Park which prohibited pets, and my parents put Laddie down, an interesting euphemism for having him killed. But as I matured into adulthood[10] for over thirty years I became a keeper of cats. This is how that relationship began: while on a bicycle trip with two friends, we passed a barn that advertised on a cardboard sign the availability for adoption of kittens. Now, kittens (unlike newborn humans) are alarmingly adorable, and the four of us were all charmed. One of our traveling companions was a veterinarian and he and his wife adopted one of the litter. He promised that if we adopted one of those yet unchosen kittens he would care for it even without remuneration. Their cuteness and his offer seduced my ex-wife and myself. The next day we returned in our car and adopted two kittens. Perhaps it would have been more judicious to settle for only one cat, as did the veterinarian and his wife, but I thought that it would be unfair to separate the selected one from the companionship of siblings. I had known something about separation. Crouched there in the barn with one kitten cradled in my hands, I had visions of myself sitting in a comfy chair before a fireplace reading the great American novel and with a cat purring contentedly on my lap. At the time we chose a male and a female, named the first Henry David and the second Emily. The kittens, soon to be cats, joined our living arrangements in our Washington Heights apartment in New York City. I never did own that comfy chair nor have I definitively found the great American novel, though sometimes I did come close to the latter and have purchased not a few in search of the former. Over the next few years, Henry David gained enough weight to suffer the bane of obesity that now plagues American society. He became too heavy to jump onto my lap or chase mice and I became too old

---

9. Thoreau, *Walden*, 237.

10. I have long subscribed to Kurt Vonnetgut's counsel, "Maturity is a bitter disappointment for which no remedy exists, unless laughter could be said to remedy anything."

to raise him up. And if I did manage to lift heavy Henry David onto my lap there was nothing of the appeal or charm that I had imagined might accompany the experience back there when I crouched with the endearing kittens in the barn.

Henry David and Emily came with us when we moved from a five-room 11th floor apartment to a house on four acres in a semirural environment in Wisconsin, but they were already indoor cats and at first would not run free in the great outdoors. At times they would look longingly out of a window admiring the size of what they might have imagined was that lovely room out there! Eventually, Henry David did slowly waddle out of doors though not to any good end. He was too fat to catch moles and too slow to avoid traffic. I buried Henry David in our backyard after a fatal run-in (or run over) with a car. Emily had been cruelly shot with a BB gun and was saved by our local veterinarian, but she never after that ventured very far and died in the house after eighteen years. But over the years we somehow had attracted other cats and often to my regret we adopted not a few. Well, actually we didn't really adopt them so much as accept them: we seemed to be living in some feline version of *101 Dalmatians* and there was not a Cruella de Ville about the premises. Concerning the cats, at various times there was Alcott, CLR James, Thunder, Matilda, and of course, Henry David and Emily. I think at one time we numbered, fed, and cared for a regular brood of four or five cats of various ages and personalities and names living under our roof. Some of the cats were somewhat independent and demanded only a regular diet and a clean litter box, but not a few were needy and it was rare that I could sit in any chair, comfy or otherwise, without one of them leaping into my lap demanding attention and concern, save, of course, for overly plump Henry David. (When the cats weren't present, my daughters sometimes might choose my lap over a couch or chair.) And for the most part, the cats lived peacefully in the house with occasional (and too often tragic) forays of a few of them into the great outdoors. Most of the cats ran out of their nine lives early and met a violent end; I think only Emily lived out her full and natural life.

The romantic perspective I early held concerning cats did not blossom into any sort of reality; under Henry David's weight and the necessities of feeding them and cleaning the malodorous litter boxes the idyll soon ended though the cats remained. Once we even hired an animal psychologist to deal with Henry David's acquired custom of urinating on my pregnant wife's clothes: I think he had become jealous. Since Henry David couldn't get up on the couch the psychologist talked with us; he resolved none of our issues, not even those concerning Henry David. As I have often noted, reality rarely rises to the level of fantasy and I suppose that that disappointment is not only accurate but helpful. Reality is always an insult. And so I suffered in relative silence at the intrusion of the cats into my solitude: for years I worked in a basement office amidst the stench of their seemingly ever-full litter boxes and the odor of their cat food. Eventually, I had built for myself an office-cabin about fifty yards behind the house a bit to the east and nestled into a bit of wooded area. I had moved my writing and study out of the rank basement and thereby relieved myself of the constant presence of cats. The peace out there came dropping slow, and I think that out there I possessed a quiet solitude. Out there in the cabin I found refuge from human and feline company. And through the years back there in the house one by one the cats passed on to another world in one fashion or another. I vowed that when the last of the cats died, we would then be cat-free and would in the future remain so.

And so, I was dismayed when one day I observed sitting patiently outside the door of my office cabin a black cat. I possessed a vague sense that I had for several weeks prior observed the creature stalking the perimeter of the backyard, but I did all I could to avoid any contact or serious notice of the animal. Certainly I made no social overture to it, but I believe that it suspected the presence of some well-fed cats living within the house, and so the black cat had decided to survey the territory and hope for the best. At the beginning whenever I entered the backyard either on my way to or from the cabin the black cat would scurry into the brush from where it rested. I would apologize to the cat, *sotto voce*, for my intimidating presence and would do my best to move about my businesses oblivious to it. I was firmly opposed to a relationship with yet another cat that would require food and shelter and veterinary care. Whenever possible I tried as best I could to avoid the black cat who seemed to lurk in the environs.

Sometimes in the early afternoon I would carry my lunch out to the cabin where I would enjoy my meal in quiet solitude. Lunch might consist of a grilled cheese sandwich (with potato chips accompaniment, of course); or a store-bought salad; or even some dreaded (but not dreadful) left-overs from the previous evening's dinner. And in a moment of absent-mindedness I carelessly (and thoughtlessly) tossed an unfinished plate of uneaten food into the brush outside the cabin. Better there than in the garbage can, I thought, though we tended no garden and had little need for compost. And very soon the black cat appeared and lapped up the tossed-out fare.

The next day at lunchtime the cat returned to the brush under the bare tree and looked about for the discarded leftovers as its next meal. Through the cabin windows I could see it sitting out where it had earlier eaten the discarded remains and wondering (I imagined) when its meal might be served. And so, I looked down at my plate and stepped outside and intentionally fed the black cat the leftovers of my leftovers. This became some custom, and soon, while I ate the black cat rather than wait for me to toss the leftovers into the brush, chose to sit outside my cabin door staring in, the reverse of the housebound cats sitting at the windows looking out. They, however, were warm and well fed, and winter was icumen in. I couldn't bear what I imagined would be the suffering of the black cat in that brutal season. And so, I brought some of our house cats' food out to the cabin and began a daily feeding of the animal knowing well that this act would condemn me to a regular practice. And then I purchased a dedicated supply of cat food from a local Walmart for the black cat and the routine had commenced.

I know they say that nature is red in tooth and claw, but I think that if there is sin, then what we humans have done to the animals of the earth enacts our great sinfulness. Perhaps this particular black cat was, in fact, a feral cat, but there yet were too many mistreated animals roaming about the outdoors that had been abandoned by people who had grown weary of caring for them or had become too poor to feed them. There is a long, sordid history of our cruel massacre and exploitation of the animals of the earth, not to mention the wholesale dispossession and slaughter of our fellow humans. I supposed I was part of that crime and maybe in feeding the cat I attempted to enact some penance. In the beginning, I fed the black cat because it was there to be fed, and in the house at the time there lived several domesticated, healthy, and well-fed cats. The black cat had arrived at my cabin door, albeit unbidden, and I supposed it was hungry.

Having eaten what I served it the cat would often continue on its tour of the neighborhood. I think it belonged to no one and yet to everyone; I do not know if anyone else gave it sustenance, but when I put food out for the cat, I felt magnanimous, ethical, kind, like a mensch, if you will. And the cat ate and it was fed. I believe that not soon after the start of this relationship the black cat took up regular residence on the property sleeping in the brush about the house and cabin.

## Anxious Am I?

The routine became thus: at 5:30 a.m. each day, as I would exit the back door of the house, the black cat would meet me and wail its early greeting: "I'm hungry. It's about time!" Sometimes in the dark mornings the cat's eyes were all I would see. I wished the cat a good morning and headed out toward my Walden cabin. The cat walked forward before me, turning occasionally to safeguard that I was still following behind. We together walked the short distance to the cabin; I stepped carefully to avoid tripping over the cat that measured my steps with watchful attention and too-close proximity. I feared falling over the cat and breaking something that I still required. I arrived not without concern to the cabin door, too oftensometimes inadvertently knocking against the cat as we trod the short path. The motion light would turn on (I do not know at whose motion the light responded) as we approached the cabin. I would enter the room and turn on the switch to illuminate the inside.

On most mornings, while I would orient myself within the cabin and settle into my daily occupancy, the cat would sit immediately in front of the door staring into the now-lit room, declaring its hunger with some urgency and even complaint. And on each morning I put my coffee mug on the reading desk and headed to the bookshelves under which I had stored the cat's store-bought supplies. I grabbed a bag or can of soft food and also now the bag of hard Purina Cat Chow and headed back out into the dark. I preferred to prepare his breakfast outside the cabin because the odor of the cat food was foul. As I exited the door of the cabin with the morning meal the motion light turned on again and the hungry cat moved out of the way, but turned soon back toward my busy, crouching figure and made steady exclamation as I filled its bowls with food. It paced close to me now seemingly unafraid of my presence. On one morning the black cat must have been especially hungry (the weather has turned blustery and it probably needed to build up its levels of fat) because even while I still squatted serving breakfast, it began to taste from the bowl of soft food. On another morning as the cat ate, I reached out to scratch its neck and it did not pause in its feasting. But soon it grew again suspicious and moved back behind the corner of the cabin, disguised behind the single burning bush planted there; for its comfort I arose and re-entered the cabin and the cat returned to the bowls and finished its breakfast. Then, as had become accustomed, it sat down before my door to bathe itself and took a cat nap.

The black cat adamantly refused to enter the cabin. It would from outside look inside through the glass-windowed door, watch me gather its breakfast stuff; and as I exited with the food the cat would move back from the door and voice what I liked to assume was an expression of thankfulness, though, it might also have been a complaint about my tardiness and/or the food selection. But into the cabin the black cat would not venture. Once, and only once, the black cat crossed the threshold, and he immediately panicked and began racing frantically about the interior searching for a way out. I alarmedly opened the entrance door and the cat leapt relievedly outside never to enter in again. But this alarming episode did not deter the black cat from our regular morning routine: it just meant that it would forever stop at the front door and wait for service. As I became more familiar and less threatening to him, as I filled the bowls that sat under the canopied dining area, the cat not only paced by my side but began to insist before it sat down to its meal that I scratch its neck, rub its head, and offer it some physical, voluble morning greeting. It pushed its head and neck into my hand and caressed my leg with its body. It was more than food that it had come to expect.

An hour or so later, having finished my coffee and engaged in some early morning writing, and having fed the black cat, I would head out for an early morning run. Upon returning I would shower and prepare breakfast for my daughters before they headed to school and for myself before I headed back to the cabin. But now, when I returned the black cat would still be sitting before the door. As I approached the cat rose and began to cry as it had done in that earlier morning hour. I supposed the cat seemed to believe that every time I opened the door to Walden I would give it food. Or maybe the cat was simply greeting me and I didn't understand! Nonetheless, clearly the black cat had begun to set up semipermanent residence in the environs of Walden. During the day it slept in the woods that surrounded the cabin, probably he would prowl the environment about the house, or sit somewhere close by the cabin door enjoying the warmth of the sun on those days when it shone. One morning in the fall the sky was full of clouds and there was frost perched on the ground, and I thought that the black cat might consider that one day when the weather turned cold it would have to cross the cabin threshold after its morning meal. But as I said, that occurrence did not happen save for that one unfortunate visit. And as the black cat sat in front of the door or outside in the brush across from a window, it still looked inside with some wonder and curiosity. I wondered if it would ever again throw caution to the wintry winds and venture in. And then

## Anxious Am I?

I considered: were this event to occur, would the black cat then consider itself a resident or a transient visitor?

In the winter the black cat took up steady dwelling underneath the deck at the rear of the house where I believed that it slept at night; during the day the cat continued to lay in the tall grass outside the cabin, sometimes napping in the tentative warmth of a late fall or a brilliant winter sun; sometimes it lay deep on the hill to the north of the cabin where it could be protected from the chilling wintry winds. And whenever I went in or out of a door (of either that of the cabin or the house) the animal approached the bowls and addressed me. Over the winter months I think that the black cat ceased to travel very far.

At long last it became spring and then summer, and the black cat didn't require housing the way it had during the bitter, snowy winters. Whereas during the cold months I think that the cat lived sheltered under the back deck, now the cat didn't need protection from the elements and wintry cold. The weather was now warm enough so that it could come out from under the deck and sleep atop the table I had placed outside my cabin door to protect its food bowls from any inclement weather. The black cat had now taken up seemingly permanent residence immediately outside of the door of my cabin! And whereas in winter the black cat would eat and then head back to shelter, now it finished its meal and laid down directly outside the door on the welcome mat. In effect, he was actually blocking the entrance: ingress or egress dislocated him and he was not pleased when he was disturbed. Having been forced to move from the door he seemed to be safeguarding, the black cat would return to the doormat with a look of exasperation and displeasure on its visage at the displacement and lay down again to its rest. In the heat of a summer's day he sequestered himself in the cool brush outside the cabin and came out only at my comings and goings, and, as usual, expecting some feeding at each. And what intrigued me was the fact that he no longer left the environs of the cabin. As if he were a guardian of the premises he didn't move from the cabin's perimeter. But I thought that what he was guarding was the expectation of the next meal: his presence guaranteed my return!

Sometimes the black cat demanded attention, and I would sit down on the deck steps or on the walkway to the cabin and scratch his head or under his neck; he would roll over onto his back and insist that I rub his stomach, and if I stopped attending to him he slapped me with his front paw. He looked at me with half-closed eyes and I think he was happy. And if from my desk I turned about in my chair and looked out of my door, I could see the black cat asleep guarding the entrance but also preventing my leaving this home. And so, what had begun, I thought, as a somewhat spontaneous gesture had now become a relationship and a responsibility. I had assumed some obligation for the black cat. And I understood that my once-casual, even gratuitous gesture had become something more than I might have originally intended.

    I remember a time in New York when I too casually and even cavalierly gave dollar bills to a homeless man sitting outside the Red Apple grocery store around the corner from my apartment; after a few daily passes he developed some expectation of my presence, and when he would see me coming he would eagerly approach and offer me greeting as I reached into my pocket for a dollar bill. "Hello, my friend," he would call, though the words were slurred because he lacked most of his teeth. "Thank you kindly," he said as I went on my way and he returned to his place before the store. At first, I handed him money only when I walked north on Broadway, but soon I began to give him a dollar bill when I passed on my return. Sometimes when he greeted me I stopped and engaged in conversation. I learned his name— Freddie—and there developed between us some vague social ease. He told me his story: he obviously suffered either from some cognitive disability or drug addiction, and he lived on some disability allotment. I came to understand that his disability check was collected by someone else who was in charge of his care and with whom he lived, and I don't know that he ever saw any monies himself from the social services check, nor am I certain what truth his story actually contained.

    In one of our conversations Freddie informed me with an excitement that was childlike that his birthday was imminent. It was November, I recall, and I went out and purchased for him a rag wool sweater from a shop on 72nd Street between Broadway and Columbus Avenue, and on his birthday I gave him the sweater. Sporting a great grin he put it on and stood proudly before the entrance to the Red Apple grocery again begging handouts, a little warmer, I hoped, and certainly more fashionably attired.

    But what else could I do? Once I had established some relationship, I was not free to abandon it at my whim. An almost automatic, even casual, act of some generosity had become an ethical obligation. Random acts of kindness transformed into acts of commitment. I saw Freddie a few times after his birthday, but despite the cold he did not wear the sweater. I didn't ask where it had gone, but in both directions that I walked I gave him the customary dollar bills and went about my business. Then one day I didn't see Freddie ever again.

As was inevitable, I think, it happened. One day the black cat did not appear for breakfasts, lunches, or dinners. There had occurred a change in the customary pattern: though the black cat did not greet me in the dark mornings, nevertheless I would serve out the meal in the morning though it would remain uneaten during the day. Interestingly, in the morning the food would be gone. I wondered who had been dining in the just big enough bowl, and I grew somewhat anxious that a raccoon had discovered the full bowl and was frequenting the environs. Raccoons scare me. Of course, I acknowledged somewhat regretfully that it was I who had occupied the environment where once raccoons and others once roamed freely. I ultimately was the intruder, l supposed. And I continued to wonder about the black cat. Perhaps, I considered, it had found a better place for repast and residence.

A week passed and I began to think that the cat had, as it is said, moved on. And then, late one afternoon, when I came out to Walden, he was lying beside the cabin looking, I thought, rather peaceful. I was glad to see it. But there was about the cat's demeanor an air that suggested to me that something was amiss, and as I drew nearer the cat didn't scamper up as had been its habit over these past several months. I considered that after its roamings the black cat had come home again, so to speak, and now lay at the cabin warming itself in the sun. The bowl was empty and so I went inside the cabin where I stored the food and grabbed a can from the floor, brought it outside, opened it and spooned the gooey mixture of salmon and cod bits all over my hand and filled the bowl. And as soon as I put the food down, the cat stood up and . . . and limped to the dish. The cat kept its right rear leg—now hanging lifelessly—off of the ground. It had obviously been injured in either a confrontation with another animal or in an accident with a passing vehicle that sped along the road carelessly oblivious of the wildlife that shared these spaces. It disturbed me to recognize the animal in pain . . . and yet, the black cat did not whine or complain or rail at the gods. It hobbled with grace and stoic purpose to the bowl, ate, groomed itself, and headed off to wherever it would sleep for the evening. I was glad that it had been so warm these days; at least the black cat had not to also contend with the weather that usually oppresses us in March and early April.

I have resisted adding a moral to this story, but I do love aphorisms. My ethics rests in my relationship to the Other, be it the homeless Freddie or the nameless black cat. And once I had accepted this responsibility, I was obliged to it. A bane and a blessing. For over a year I fed the black cat with some pleasure but mostly with a sense of responsibility and obligation. Then one early morning I walked out to the cabin and there, sitting next to the black cat was a little white kitten. My black cat had adopted a child and brought it to the source of sustenance. Ah, yes, the little cat was scruffy, disheveled, motherless, and hungry, and I suddenly imagined my black cat roaming the neighborhood looking for strays and bringing them home. I suddenly had visions of a long row of hungry cats lined up outside the cabin and I had alarming visions of replacing my cabin's shelves of books with cans of cat food, and I then envisioned a life that consisted of filling empty bowls with cartons of malodorous cat food. I imagined that somewhere in town existed a sign (I had first mistakenly written "a sigh") that advertised my cabin as the local soup kitchen and invited all of the stray cats to make their way there.

What had begun as a singular and hopefully isolated feeding with a single cat turned into a regular obligation and open invitation to strays. And now I found myself obliged to two individuals; and one of them for the time being had seemed to have opened my doors to the needs of others. When does the ethical commitment I had once accepted stop exponentially growing? Perhaps it is that once the gates open there is no closing them.

## ON CONVERSATION AND SILENCE

Over the years I have thought about Gregory Bateson's observation in *Steps to an Ecology of Mind* that most conversation consists in an attempt to avoid a fight. What he precisely says is that "Most conversations are only about whether people are angry or something. They are busy telling each other that they are friendly—which is sometimes a lie."[11] Much conversation, Bateson suggests, avoids honest engagement in the effort to prevent disquiet, embarrassment, or anger. As a consequence, much conversation intentionally becomes anodyne. It is polite, innocuous, inoffensive, and not meant to communicate very much at all. Conversation enacts a carefully defended presence and this conversation does not constitute a substance. It is not meant to communicate anything so much as it is designed to alleviate or even avoid personal anxiety and social tension. There is much that one doesn't want to know or say. We step about in our colloquies with caution

11. Bateson, *Steps to An Ecology of Mind*, 12.

and restraint as a means to protect some willed ignorance. Much conversation insists on the answer and eschews the question: whatever resulting interchange occurs is declarative, definitive, and spoken in cool, detached tones. There may in conversation occur a polite exchange of pleasantries that would serve to maintain the calm though offer little opportunity for empathy—by which I would mean a careful listening—or for a caring, which might be understood as sympathy. Thoreau says "Speech is for the convenience of those who are hard of hearing." I think that what Thoreau meant is that too much conversation, or what might be referred to as talk, means to avoid communication and intimacy. Arguments erupt from conversation when alternative versions of events are presented as fact rather than as vision; or when statements are offered as conclusive rather than as perspectival; or when the fault, dear Brutus, is asserted to be never in ourselves but in our stars.

In the attempt to avoid a quarrel, a great many topics are customarily avoided, and much of what is said encourages a continued invisibility. Bateson suggests to me that much conversation becomes defensively perfunctory, and too often only communicates the reality that sincere interest in others is in short supply. Politics and religion except among those who already agree in these matters are hazardous topics, and therefore, much prohibited, as are issues concerning money, excretion, sex, and death. I find that I enter much conversation apprehensively, tentatively and with caution, and I frequently try to slip out of danger with dutiful expressions that are mostly void of substance and empty of meaning. People pass each other daily with a mechanical "How are you?" but remain in motion without waiting for reply. Actually, for the most part no sincere reply is proffered because none is expected. The response to "How are you?" when one is expressed is often "Good," but I note that rarely do people wait for details, and at a hint that more is forthcoming they speed away like the White Rabbit: "I'm late, I'm late, for a very important date!" And I have of late come to wonder, what exactly does good in that context mean, anyway? Sometimes in response to our query the reply offered is "Don't Ask," and perhaps we feel relieved of responsibility, and we proceed in conversation no further, or in some sort of bizarre competition we respond in passing, "Ugh, me too!"

To consider that conversation may be founded upon the lie, however, does set me thinking. Lying, says Colin Burrow, is a social act that depends on the beliefs of him or her to whom the lie is told. Lies seem to be claims that we are willing to accept because we would want to believe what the lie says about ourselves, others, and the world. I imagine that is why stories about death and the afterlife are so powerful: I would prefer to think that even when I had died I am not really dead—or at least am not gone. The liar in the lie addresses those beliefs and ideas that the "lie-ee" holds, and the betrayal that the lie-ee experiences occurs not only by the lie itself but from the appalling realization that one can be a person who can be lied to and who is therefore, manipulable, and credulous. The lie-ee discovers herself as deceivable, and that realization can lead to shame, humiliation, and self-hatred. The betrayal derives not only from what the liar says to be true but from what the lie-ee believes to be true only to discover that she had been a fool to so believe. Sometimes the lie-ee will work to maintain the lie as a means of maintaining a semblance of self-respect. If as Bateson suggests that most conversation is based on lies, then I think that most conversation takes place between very fragile selves.

Maybe what Bateson referred to is the inability of many to accept ambiguity and doubt—the prerequisite to the question. As a consequence, people rely on the primacy of the answer. Or perhaps it is true that they just aren't terribly interested in conversation anyway! As for myself, it has become custom that in interactions with my daughters the query, "Did you think of anything on down the line," a phrase I believe I learned from Arlo Guthrie, opened the conversation. That question creates the space for talk, and any response to the question is a legitimate one because any response to it has taken the question seriously and opened up space and time. Concerning conversation Thoreau notes that he had three chairs in his cabin: one for solitude, two for company, and three for society. Any hoped-for intimacy in conversation probably would avoid more chairs. Conversation is for thinking, which is why Thoreau says that sometimes he and his companion would have to move their chairs to opposite sides of the cabin in order to allow room for their sentences to unwind.

I think a similar relative conversational emptiness might be found in the more recent discursive practice of pronouncing "Love you" at the end of exchanges. I suspect that "Love you" (pointedly, I think, minus the pronoun "I") is coded and empty. It serves as a marker suggesting that the conversation is at an end. The phrase simulates affection but its ubiquity denies authenticity. Many years ago I remember reading Jerry Rubin's assertion in his book Do It that the word love had lost its human meaning because daily on the television and in advertising layouts one could read that "Cars love Shell!" Today, just as the opening "How are you?" pretends to begin an interchange, the concluding "Love you" seems to definitively close a conversation.

Though I do use the term too often, even as it has been defined in the previous paragraph, I don't actually know what the word "love" really means. Perhaps Bateson might suggest it is a means of avoiding argument. I know my partner likes to hear me say "I love you," but I am uncomfortable voicing the phrase because I really don't know to what it actually refers. I do so to comfort her, but I still do not know what comfort can be taken from the words if there had been nothing in my behavior that spoke of care and purposeful affection. I believe that in my attentions there had been such evidence, but this need of hers for the words remains a continuing issue between us. I think that in the absence of action the words are meaningless, though in the midst of sexual activity they can often serve as demand. I understand as well that like most words "love" has many related meanings: I love my daughters and I love pizza. What is similar to both uses of the word, I suppose, is the suggestion of a strong attachment to the object for which I express love, but that simple explanation doesn't help me distinguish the difference between the attachment to my daughters and to that of pizza. With the latter it is the consumption on which I focus, and I experiment with different venues in my quest for the perfect slice. But with my daughters it is their independence I celebrate and regardless of their distance from me I hold them close and continue to experience and express my care for them. I am not seeking perfect daughters: they are already good enough. But of the perfect pizza I say I am yet in quest, though I certainly have my favorites to which I regularly return. I have my favorites though I am not exclusive; I will sample pizza almost anywhere. With my daughters I am exclusive. Of course, I love pizza even when a specific slice disappoints me; the second-rate experience soon passes and it is on to the next joint. But to paraphrase Wordsworth, my daughters are with me late and soon! Whatever disappointment I experience speaks about me and not them! I try to always remember that. And finally, I would not sacrifice myself for any pizza but would not think twice of doing so for my daughters.

Erich Fromm writes in *The Art of Loving*, "Love is an attitude, an orientation of character which determines the relatedness of a person to the word as a whole, not toward one "object of love."[12] I am uncertain what exactly Fromm means, but he seems to hold that love is how I feel about love. Or maybe Fromm suggests that love is a matter of semantics, of a

---

12. Fromm, *The Art of Loving*, 46.

"relatedness" of an individual to the word itself. Love is how I think about love. But then it would seem to me that love as an orientation to the word "love" can only be perceived in action. As an orientation of my character love becomes how I approach the world. I can accept that, I think, but how I ought to approach the world remains an essential and existential question. And I still have to wonder why would I love Shell gasoline and not Exxon? Is it gasoline I love and not the particular brand? Why pizza and not ramen? Perhaps it is food that I love though as a detail I prefer pizza? Why this person and not another?

It interests me that in his voluminous journal Thoreau doesn't devote much thought to the topic of love, and perhaps that is a consequence of his failed proposal of marriage to Ellen Sewall. But on March 28, 1856, he does write "Enemies publish themselves. The friend never declares his love,"[13] and so his silence on the topic happens because he loves. And in *The Week on the Concord and Merrimack Rivers* in fact Thoreau does have this to say of his love for a friend: "I never asked thy leave to let me love thee—I have a right. I love thee not as something private and personal, which is your own, but as something universal and worthy of love, which I have found . . . you are the fact in a fiction. Consent only to be what you are. I alone will never stand in your way . . . Never to profane one another by word or action, even by a thought. Between us, if necessary, let there be no acquaintance."[14] I think this seems to approach Fromm's definition of love as an orientation around the word itself. Is Thoreau here defensive? Perhaps. Is Thoreau's orientation to love ideal? Certainly. But love for Thoreau means to be "kind to each other's dreams." I like that. It is an ideal with which I can live when awake.

For Thoreau love reveals itself in the silence. Though I think that this may be for Thoreau a defensive stance after the rejection of his spoken affection, I imagine also that Thoreau's strict principled belief must have made him a difficult companion and not one with whom it would be easy to maintain relationship, though I love to entertain fantasies of little Louisa May Alcott wending her way out to Walden to play with Henry David who I am convinced would have welcomed her warmly and innocently. One might not be apt to declare love to Thoreau, nor do I think that he would announce love for another. He writes, "If we would enjoy the most intimate society with that in each of us which is without, or above, being spoken

---

13. Thoreau, *The Journal, Vol. 8*, 232.
14. Thoreau, *A Week*, 336–7.

to, we must not only be silent, but commonly so far apart bodily that we cannot possible hear each other's voice in any case."[15] Interestingly, D.W. Winnicott in the next century suggested that the healthy existence of what he refers to as the True Self requires that the individual person know that it must never be communicated with or be influenced by external reality. Love might require silence to be heard. "Each individual," Winnicott writes, "is an isolate, permanently non-communicating, permanently unknown, in fact, unfound." Winnicott says, "I suggest that in health there is a core to the personality that corresponds to the self of the split personality. I suggest that the core never communicates with the world of perceived objects, and that the individual person knows that it must never be communicated with or be influenced by external reality."[16] Rather, that private self, defended ultimately by what Winnicott calls a false self, might be heard in the creative work of the individual as s/he enjoys the materials of the world because they are there to be found. Perhaps love is art. It speaks into the silence.

Silence has long frightened me, and that fear has had influence in my several environments: in the classroom when I peppered the air with questions and left too little time for thought; in my home where I played music almost continuously to disrupt the silence; about the dinner tables where I felt compelled to entertain the others and ensure social ease; in too many engagements where I filled the space almost obsessively with my talk. I had become known as one who facilitates conversation, but I believe that motives for my talk included the longing to entertain others and ensure I would be liked, and I talked as well as a means to avoid myself and others. My sound—a refusal of silence—prevents those daring, even dangerous thoughts from arising that would come to consciousness but for the presence of the noise. I invite sound to keep the silence away. I fear what might bubble up in the space that opens in the silence.

I think the first time I thought about silence was in 1964 with Simon & Garfunkel's recording "The Sound of Silence." The paradox intrigued me then—how could silence make a sound. What would the sound of silence sound like? I think I knew silence within my family: I cannot recall a single conversation outside of a few somewhat noisy arguments. People talking without speaking, people hearing without listening. We three children always ate alone and in a heavy silence. Eventually that experience of silence would define the times in which I almost matured. I became an

---

15. Thoreau, *Walden*, 152.
16. Winnicott, *The Maturational Processes*. 187.

angry existentialist. For Simon & Garfunkel the silence was like a cancer and therefore, potentially fatal: what it portended was spiritual alienation. I already knew that alienation in my home and in school. My compulsive movement to discourse sometimes represented an attempt to assert control, and what I would mean to control in my talk was the threat of abandonment. The opposite of sound would not be silence but loss.

In Nadine Gordimer's novel *Burger's Daughter*, a narrator says of Burger's daughter, Rosa, "She was mistress of her own silences."[17] I think this is a wonderful descriptive, even suggestive, phrase. To be mistress of her own silences indicates to me that Rosa controls comfortably the space that opens when conversation or really, any noise great or small ceases. Rosa's silence here seems to me more than a momentary cessation and avoidance of sound; it seems to me rather like an active decision not to further a line of discourse, not to make any response into a space that has been opened in and by the noise, not to be obliged to fill the ensuing silence with anything. Whatever follows subsequent to her silence has had no part in it; in her silence she was not organizing her thoughts to speak out from them. Her silence is complete in itself. But then, I think, Rosa does not fear the rising of her thoughts into consciousness; she appreciates her solitude even in the midst of assembly. She seems to me unafraid. Thus, to be mistress of her silence suggests that Rosa feels no need to address what might satisfy the other; to assert by sound her actual presence. I think she is not afraid of the space opened in and by her silence. Rosa remains satisfied to say nothing, unlike Hamlet, who could not master his silences, who complains bitterly that about his dear father has been murdered he can say nothing, and yet is never silent even concerning the death of his dear father murdered. Ironically, Hamlet continues to be very voluble and troubled and cannot seem to remain silent! Poe's Imp of the Perverse, rather than leave the void empty, stands precariously at the cliff's edge and is urged by something within to leap into the void, as if that void is an active presence that demands to be filled even if it is with his death. I think of silence as that void into which I am too often almost perversely and compulsively impelled to leap and to fill the emptiness that the silence oppressively presents to me. I would be a better master of my silences.

To linger peacefully in silence has become nearly impossible in our current frantic, frenetic environment: there is noise everywhere. Our noises are carried with us wherever we go: we avoid our silences with headphones

17. Gordimer, *Burger's Daughter*, 183.

and earbuds. Once our watches told us the time and now they obtrusively and noisily deliver us the busy world and track our every movement. Even in the yoga studios in which I have practiced, silence is rare: the sound of the heating units incessantly turns on and shuts off, and the clang of dropped weights in the gym adjacent to the studio floor disturbs the stillness I would learn to master. Everywhere the ring of a mobile phone intrudes on the potential silence as does someone's overly loud conversation either to the person immediately contiguous or to one miles and continents away. The internet encroaches noisily; a finger's flick too conveniently clicks away silence. When all else fails there are the televisions or radios to drown out the quietness. There remains no silence. I think again of Thoreau: "Society is commonly too cheap. We meet at very short intervals, not having had time to acquire any new value for each other. We meet at meals three times a day, and give each other a new taste of that old musty cheese that we are.... we live thick and are in each other's way, and stumble over one another, and I think we thus lose some respect for one another."[18] More, this thickness of our lives shows a disrespect for ourselves. Our noises suggest we would not be alone with ourselves; we need others to distract us from ourselves. Thoreau amusingly says that he who leaves the post office with the most letters has probably not heard from himself for quite a while.

*Into Great Silence* is a documentary about the lives of the Carthusian monks at the Grande Chartreuse Charterhouse in Southeast France. The Carthusian order, founded in the 11th century by St. Bruno of Cologne, is a community of hermits who in the mid-1990s gave to the film's director unparalleled access for six months to its daily life in the charterhouse. The film, almost three hours long, contains no more than a dozen sentences of dialogue: one spoken during the induction of a novitiate into the order, and a short statement toward the film's end offered by an elder monk declaring his fearlessness of death. There can be heard the occasional sound of the men at prayer, and the regular sounding of the bell calling the monks to these offices.

But mostly what is heard in the film is the silence in which these men live. The clearest sound heard is that of their footsteps as they move through the charterhouse, or of the sound of their activity in the process of maintaining their lives: chopping food or wood, turning the pages of their books; their kneeling in prayer in their cells or in the sanctuaries. The men do not usually leave the cells in which they individually and solitarily

---

18. Thoreau, *Walden*, 147.

reside, and on most days they engage wholly in study and prayer. Food is delivered through a small revolving compartment on the door of their cell; once a week, on Sundays, the men eat a communal meal in silence and once a week they take a walk on which they are allowed to speak to one another. Twice a year there is a community-wide day of recreation: the monks are seen sliding down a sharp incline in the mountain snow. In their simple joy during this activity they reminded me of children at play, and in the break of their practice of silence I could hear laughter as the "skiers" moved uncertainly and unbalanced down the slope. Once a year the monks' family members may visit.

I have often imagined the pleasures and rigors of the contemplative life. Years ago, I read with fascination the biography of the hermit Thomas Merton and have long wondered if the retreat into his hermitage was meant to be an engagement or an escape. But more than silence, seclusion and isolation was what I often sought. It was safe in there. But I learned that solitude need not necessarily entail silence; sometimes it was quite voluble. Emerson had said that a thinking man is always alone, but I wonder if that person is also silent. I had never imagined the perspective on silence offered by the monks portrayed in *Into Great Silence*. Their silence was absolute and full. They were, indeed, masters of their silence. Apart from the daily household chores, these men do little more than study, pray, and write every day of their lives but study, pray, and write every day of their lives. They tend to their own gardens outside the cells behind the monastery walls that keep them away from others; they may even do some manual work—one sees a monk repairing the sole of his shoe—but for the most part they live a completely solitary existence—except in companionship always with their God. They do no missionary work and they do not interact with the public.

As the film's title suggests, the silence into which these men enter and the silence in which they choose to live is as great as it is absolute, and the life that each man chooses—of prayer and study—consumes their whole existence. I considered how much of my life is taken up with concern and worry about the future: about what must be next done. I have remained much focused on what happens next. And I recognized that unlike myself consumed as I too often am by anxiety, for these monks there exists a great peace to their lives. There is one scene in the film that I have long cherished. An older monk walks solitarily down a cloister walk heading somewhere. He moves with considered slowness and deliberateness and with no sense of urgency at all. I remember thinking to myself that he ought to step to his destination with a livelier pace, but no, I then remembered thinking, this man is in no hurry to get anywhere. Indeed, there is nowhere he needs to be in any specific requirement of time. He is headed somewhere but going nowhere, and he is content wherever he might be in the life of the monastery. There is nowhere to which he needs be rushing; whenever he gets to wherever he is going it will be time enough when he arrives. I experienced a great peace watching the monk move down the cloister path perfectly at peace with himself and his life.

The Carthusian monks need not worry about anything except the present: they have nowhere to go and nothing with which they must engage except their study and prayer in the silent solitude of their cell and in the effort that maintains their physical lives. And so the monks move slowly and easefully throughout the charterhouse: they have nowhere else to be and nowhere else they would go. Indeed, their behavior offers a wholly other meaning to Estragon's complaint in *Waiting for Godot*: "Nothing to be done." For the monks, outside of study and prayer, that is exactly the point! During the screening of the film I found my breathing and pulse slowed, and I experienced (for me) a welcome calm. The regularity of the lives within the charterhouse occurred completely without incident or drama except that which took place in the presence of their spirituality. In a series of remarkable shots, at the film's conclusion the filmmaker offered portraits of each of the monks: for almost thirty seconds the camera looks at the face of each man and each man looks at the face of the camera and I could see in each individual gaze the peace that passeth understanding, a silence and a peace in which I think these men lived. I knew I could never enter such a life, but it was beautiful to watch the dedication and passion of these men to their Ideal. Each was master of his silences.

There is a line I have clung to since first reading it in Tillie Olsen's short story "Tell Me a Riddle." The old woman's family attempts to convince her to move with her husband into a retirement-like dwelling where she will have all her needs cared for: she need not cook or clean because all will be done for her. Nurses will care for her in her terminal illness. But the older woman absolutely refuses to leave her home. And she considers: "Enough . . . She would not exchange her solitude for anything. Never again to be forced to move to the rhythms of others . . . Being able at last to live within, and not move to the rhythm of others."[19] I have often been struck by the profundity of her demand and her wish. After a life devoted

---

19. Olsen, *Tell Me a Riddle*, 68.

to the needs of others—to the rhythm of others—to the imploring voices of others, she wanted now to live according to her own rhythms and to tend to her own needs, to become the master of her silences. Like the Carthusian monks, she chooses to move only at the deliberate pace that her desires demand; her desires, like theirs, are small.

I think in my retirement I would learn this peace—this peace that comes dropping slow—to do as the yogis teach, to slow and deepen my breathing, to move deliberately without hurry or anxious speed, to remain in balance. Thoreau teaches that it is a great art to saunter, and I would like to learn to saunter. I would not be a monk—Thoreau celebrated society, and I am naturally no hermit. But I would like to learn the art of sauntering and like that monk amble peacefully down my cloister path moving slowly going somewhere in my own rhythms and with no deliberate speed.

And yet . . . I recognize an alternative to this wholly contemplative life in the film *Of Gods and Men*, directed by Xavier Beauvois and adapted by him and Etienne Comar from a book entitled *The Monks of Tibhirine* by John Kiser. The film offers a portrait of lives informed by a deep spirituality and love of God, by a sincere commitment to communal engagement, and to expressions of true and guileless brotherly love. The monks of Tibhirine, following the teachings of St. Benedict, observe the qualities of charity, humility, and obedience within the community. The monks strive to purify [the] soul in preparation for union with God. In a very difficult world, the monks of Tibhirine aspire in their prayers and in their actions to a purity in their daily existence, an intense devotion to God, and a dedication to the community in which they live and which they serve. The film depicts the monks' decision to continue their lives in the village they serve despite the danger of violent deaths from the rebel group that terrorizes the land and daily threatens the monastery. The monks do not exist in the physical silence practiced by the Carthusian order, but they do maintain a spiritually full silence. They cannot be distracted from their prayer, from themselves, or from the community they serve.

The eight monks who live at the Monastery of Notre Dame d'Atlas serve both their God and the community in which the monastery is situated. Indeed, I think that they serve the former in their devotion to the latter. Abraham Joshua Heschel says, "What gives birth to religion is not intellectual curiosity but the fact and experience of our being asked." The lives of the monks of Tibhirine in Algeria give answer, having chosen to live amidst the poor whom they voluntarily and willingly serve. In the exercise of their daily lives the monks of Tibhirine achieve a life filled with a spirituality based in awe and wonder. "Awe, unlike fear," Heschel teaches, "does not make us shrink from the awe-inspiring object, but, on the contrary, draws us near to it. This is why awe is compatible with both love and joy."[20] Amidst the terrors of our daily lives, and in the face of our fears and doubts, awe promises us redemption and hope. "The meaning of awe," Heschel continues, "is to realize that life takes place under wide horizons, horizons that range beyond the span of an individual life and even the life of a nation, a generation, or an era. Awe enables us to perceive in the world intimations of the divine, to sense in small things the beginning of infinite significance, to sense the ultimate in the common and the simple; to feel in the rush of the passing the stillness of the eternal."[21] I think that feelings of awe inspire a profound silence.

And I think that this is what I saw in *Of Gods and Men*: in their engagement in the village of Tibhirine. There the monks experience the sense of awe that must have first brought them to the devotion that they practiced in the small impoverished Algerian village; their daily offices and public service offers them the strength to continue their effort in the face of the horror and violence that surrounds them and threatens their safety. Yet despite the terror that the film finally portrays, *Of Gods and Men* focuses on the expression of the monk's strong love for God, for each other and for the village, and the film gives expression to the joy that the monks realize in their commitment to the people of Tibhirine and of the love that the village returns despite the danger and adversities in which they all suffer. Such is the story of the film. I was mesmerized and deeply touched by the deep spirituality in which the monks' lives were lived, in which their purposes were fulfilled and in which they cared for each other. The monks' final communal dinner—which in fact does not allude at all in word or image to Jesus' reputed Last Supper—filled as their meal was by a silence and a deep holiness (I cannot find a better word) save for the strains of Tchaikovsky's Swan Lake that played on a venerable cassette player, and by the visibly overwhelming love they experience for each other and the work they do together, erased from my mind the violence in which the monks functioned and in which we now all live; in their faces had settled the image of a peace that passeth understanding. Shantih. Shantih. Shantih. At the film's end, I wept volubly and unashamedly though I do not cry easily anymore.

20. Heschel, *Between God and Man*, 53.
21. Heschel, *Between God and Man*, 52.

## GROW OLD ALONG WITH ME: AN ELEGY

Death: when we have shuffled off that mortal coil and then there are no more dreams. Death, when there is no consciousness and no sense that there is no consciousness. No darkness... not even a sense of nothingness, not an experience of nothingness but just an absolute nothing. To be dead and not even know one is dead: to know nothing! I have loved my dreams, those that occurred when I was asleep and those I have had when I am awake. I have experienced my share of nightmares but from even them I have always awakened. It is inconceivable now that at any moment I will die and not dream and not arise from even the not dreaming.

I had been rereading Virginia Woolf's *Mrs. Dalloway*, a novel very much concerned with time, death, and mortality. Though she is only in her 50s and I am well beyond those years, I feel a bit like Clarissa Dalloway. Like me, she fears death, and like me, Clarissa has issues with her heart that will in all probability kill her. I maintain anxious and regular visits to my cardiologist for checkups on my aging heart. Like me, Clarissa considers, "How unbelievable death was!—that it must end; and no one in the whole world would know how she had loved it all."[22] Unlike the monks of Tibhirine, Mrs. Dalloway seems not at all concerned with events outside of her own life and her parties, but then again, I suspect some might say I, too, have displayed a narcissistic self-absorption. *Mea culpa*. Nevertheless, the novel also speaks to an intense yet fragile love of life. From the opening pages the narrator, speaking clearly from within Clarissa's consciousness, declares "For Heaven only knows why one loves it so, how one sees it so, making it up, building it round one, tumbling it, creating it every moment afresh; but the veriest frumps, the most dejected of miseries sitting on doorsteps (drink their downfall) do the same... they love life."[23] Yes, Clarissa loves life though not always specific people in it: for example, she does not like Mrs. Kilman at all, and Hugh Whitbread seems rather stuffy, and Lady Bruton doesn't invite her to lunch though Lady Bruton does welcome Richard, Clarissa's husband. Mrs. Dalloway was, finally, a simple woman: "Nothing else had she of the slightest importance; could not think, write, even play the piano. She muddled Armenians and Turks; loved success; hated discomfort; must be liked; talked oceans of nonsense; and to this day ask her what the Equator was, and she did not know."[24] I, however, do know

---

22. Woolf, *Mrs. Dalloway*, 122.
23. Woolf, *Mrs. Dalloway*, 4.
24. Woolf, *Mrs. Dalloway*, 122.

the difference between the Armenians and the Turks and can define the Equator, at the moment can play no instrument; and like Mrs. Dalloway I love the idea of success and have achieved a small piece of it; do seek my comfort and would be liked though today I seem to have a bit less interest in seeking approval. And for the past seventy-four years I have misspelled "occurred" every time I write it.

I? Not a dull nor muddy-mettled rascal, but a mere man who was once a boy and at times yet remains so. I love to write and study while the sun shines, to take a short lie-down in the afternoons and then to enjoy my wines and my dinners in the evenings. I do love life with all of its many joys and difficulties and disappointments, perhaps more so aware as I am that my existence will end. I will miss being here. I am anxious to see what will happen next. I'm not all I thought I'd be, but I have achieved more than I ever expected. I have a few very dear, dear friends; I am for some a very dear friend. I have published ten books and this one, should it see some light of day, would be my eleventh. In Jewish practice a minyan consists of ten congregants praying together. My minyan sits now religiously on my shelf. I served happily in classrooms for forty-six years and helped not a few younger people through some troubles. I think that the time I spent in the schools helped me through my own difficulties. I have two beautiful socially conscious daughters who despite my many faults still talk to me! I have a home I would not leave and a partner who tolerates my **HOBBY-HORSES** and whose own stable I can abide.

Like me, Clarissa is very much aware of life's fragility. She "always had the feeling that it was very, very dangerous to live even one day."[25] Ah, I recall Yossarian! As Mrs. Dalloway walks through London on the day of her party she "felt very young; at the same time unspeakably aged." Engaged in the shopping and preparations for her party, Clarissa enjoyed the excitement of youth, but the inexorable tolling bells of Big Ben reminds her constantly of mortality. I think that Clarissa loves life so much that she understands the danger that at any moment it might be lost, as had happened to Septimus Smith whose experience in World War I had left him so permanently damaged that he threw himself out of the window to end his overwhelming despair. As it must happen at some time to us all, the bells will toll for me and thee. Mrs. Dalloway does not want to die though she is painfully aware that at some time she will do so. But on that day recorded in the novel she heads out happily to purchase flowers for her party amidst

---

25. Woolf, *Mrs. Dalloway*, 8.

the bustle and noise of the London that she loved. I remember that when I lived in New York City I enjoyed setting out from my apartment on the Upper West Side to amble down Broadway looking in the shop windows, stepping into the New York iteration of Shakespeare and Company and maybe purchasing a book I did not know that I would need; stopping for a potato knish slobbered with mustard at the kosher deli-restaurant, or stopping for a bagel and a schmear of cream cheese at H&H Bagels; shopping at Zabar's for everything culinary; visiting the West Side Judaica, where I first discovered the works of Primo Levi and from whom I purchased mezuzot for my home; window-shopping at the boutiques whose windows displayed clothes so expensive and beautiful that I couldn't imagine affording or deserving to wear; making my way casually down to Lincoln Center where in the summers I could sit by the fountain and watch the passing crowds; and then to cross east on Broadway to the Lincoln Plaza movie theater where I could almost always find a peace that passeth show. But, alas, at my back I still would hear time's winged chariot drawing near.

The news of Septimus Smith's suicide spreads at Clarissa's party, and she despairs, "In the middle of my party, here's death."[26] Perhaps the parties she organizes serve as a strategy to put off the idea of her inevitable demise. And perhaps her parties are her means of sharing joy for this life. When Clarissa wonders why she throws her parties, she acknowledges that the parties were "an offering . . . an offering for the sake of offering, perhaps. Anyhow, it was her gift." And yet, there in the middle of her party . . . . Engaged in study, perhaps, I might believe death can be held off.

And I wonder what my offering might be, what I can bestow as my gift. I wonder what will have been my equivalent of Clarissa's parties? My offering and my life seem to me inseparable. I think sometimes that my published works might serve as my offering. In them I have placed my thoughts, my intimacies, often my life. My classrooms? Sometimes an email comes to me to tell me how much my classes meant to him or her. But these late memorials were not what the classes were about at all: it was engagement first with beans and then with "such seeds, if the seed is not lost, as sincerity, truth, simplicity, faith, innocence and the like, and see if they will not grow in this soil and sustain us."[27] I think it was in the classrooms where I found whatever I would come to know about home. My daughters? I invited the children into my classrooms, and I brought my classrooms

---

26. Woolf, *Mrs. Dalloway*, 83.
27. Thoreau, *Walden*, 178.

to them. Like my students, the invitation was received sometimes with pleasure and sometimes with refusal. But today both of my daughters have subscriptions to the *New York Review of Books* that they read, and they frequent bookstores regularly and with enthusiasm. Unlike Mrs. Dalloway, they know the difference between the Armenians and the Turks.

Clarissa is class- and race-privileged, even as I have benefited from being the right color and gender and having been born by chance into the culture of the middle class; Mrs. Dalloway has sufficient means, and though I have my anxieties about money and though I am hardly rich, I have all that I need or could now want. Like me, Clarissa seems to understand the paradox at the center of her life. The suicide of Septimus Smith was "Somehow her disaster—her disgrace. It was her punishment to see sink and disappear here a man, there a woman, in this profound darkness, and she forced to stand here in her evening dress. She had schemed; she had pilfered She was never wholly admirable."[28] *Mea culpa*. I am myself indifferent honest; I have more offenses at my beck than I have thoughts to put them in. And yet . . . I believe that I have done good work. Clarissa Dalloway adores her immersion in the diurnal; that experience of happiness that would dissolve the reality of death and makes it well, implausible. It is not that Clarissa is completely oblivious to the world beyond her, nor even that she is not touched by sorrow and doubt. But at that moment, standing with her roses and just hours before her party, well, she loved it all . . . every single instant! What opposes and mediates her awareness of death is her immersion in and attention to the ordinary, the mundane, and the daily routines of her life. Her love of life is founded and expressed in the activities in which she daily engages. Love does not reside in the great passions enacted sometimes on the stage or the screen, or that is written about in even the great novels; love resides in the ordinary, sometimes even inarticulable expressions we haltingly make as we go through our daily lives, as in Richard's sudden desire and purchase of roses for Clarissa and yet his inability to say to her "I love you" when he gives them to her. But Clarissa knew from his gift what he was saying. Love exists in the quotidian. What Clarissa loved "was this, here, now, in front of her; the fat lady in the cab."[29]

With this reference to Clarissa's fat lady in the cab I am drawn to the conclusion of J.D Salinger's novel *Franny and Zooey*. Franny Glass has suffered a psychological crisis, a spiritual breakdown, and has returned home

---

28. Woolf, *Mrs. Dalloway*, 185.
29. Woolf, *Mrs. Dalloway* ,9.

and taken to her bed suffering the experience of existential angst and dread. She has sought comfort in the recitation of "the Jesus prayer," but really had received little comfort from it. In her search for some transcendent meaning to life she has lost touch with the diurnal. From a different room in the apartment to which she has come to suffer her depression, her brother Zooey calls her on the telephone. He points out to her that when she suffered her breakdown she did not search the world for a master spiritual guide; rather, in the midst of her crisis she came home! But in her anxious loss of meaning and desperate quest for ultimate guidance she had been blind to the holy that surrounded her there. He reproaches, "You don't even have sense enough to drink when somebody brings you a cup of consecrated chicken soup Bessie ever brings anybody around this madhouse. How in hell are you going to recognize a legitimate holy man when you see one if you don't even know a cup of consecrated chicken soup when it's right in front of your nose?"[30] Franny had taken no joy in the daily or found any goodness in the holiness contained in her mother's offering. It is to the diurnal that Zooey points Franny, and to the counsel not of some holy man but of her family. Her brother Zooey addresses the sacredness of the here and now.

He insists that Franny look to the seemingly ordinary activities of life as sources of joy and love. It is life and life only that must be loved. Once, Zooey reminds Franny, his older brother Seymour had advised Zooey that even though they performed on a radio show he ought still to polish his shoes: "He said to shine them for the Fat Lady," though Seymour had never revealed the identity of that Fat Lady. Franny remarks that she too has been counseled by her older brother, Seymour, to be funny for the Fat Lady also without identifying that individual. And Zooey says to Franny, who in her search for purpose and meaning in life suffers crushing anguish, "There isn't anyone out there who isn't Seymour's Fat Lady . . . Don't you know that—?"[31] The Fat Lady listening to the Glass children on the radio or sitting in the cab Clarissa Dalloway observes encloses the holy, and Franny's recitation of the Jesus prayer and search for ultimate spiritual guidance deflects her from attending with care and love to the Fat Lady listening to the radio—she misses the sacred that inheres to daily life. . . and cannot attend to the fat lady in the cab and or in her audience.

---

30. Salinger, *Franny and Zooey*, 194.
31. Salinger, *Franny and Zooey*, 200.

And what would I say is my diurnal and mundane. What would constitute my consecrated chicken soup? There is my morning coffee; my books and papers that cover the walls and litter the surfaces and floors about me; there is my exercise routine, once long-distant running and now extended walks. I have long taken my thoughts out on the roads and resolved not a few of my troubles and confusions there. There are my breads and muffins and scones that I bake on a too regular basis. I relish my cocktail hours and preparations for dinner. Attentions to my daughters. Nighttime reading and bedtime routines. Ben Pazi asserts that the verse that contains all of Torah reads, "You will sacrifice a lamb in the morning and another at dusk." Ben Pazi asserts that it is not the Devil that exists in the details: it is life that is found there. It is ritual—behavior and not belief—that sustains us. Ritual is commitment to the orders of our daily life and represents our responsibilities to it. Ritual is arising from my bed in the mornings; to my coffees; my writings; my running and now walks; my lie-downs; my cocktail hours; my attention to the difference between the Armenians and the Turks. There is another sentiment expressed in Nadine Gordimer's *Burger's Daughter* to which I am drawn: real loneliness is to live without social responsibility. Aimlessness and loneliness stem from a lack of ritual and responsibility. Outside of the commitments of the classroom I wonder if I have become lonely. I consider now how I might for the rest of my life be not lonely.

And so I come now to think again about Rabbi Ben Ezra, the speaker in Browning's poem of that name and from whom today I draw comfort and strength. He says, "Grow old along with me/The best is yet to be/The last of life for which the first is made."[32] I have wondered to whom he speaks in this invitation,; I am always interested in the narrator's audience, but today I think the rabbi speaks to me as I age. When first I read this poem, I was an English major at Roanoke College and too young to understand the implications of the rabbi's bidding. Studying Browning's poem then was a satisfying and wholly academic enterprise. When first I arrived on campus in the fall of 1965 the class of 1915 was gathered for their fifty-year reunion. I marveled at those gray-haired folk as they wandered the campus; I thought of them as very, very old, ancient even, though from my perspective now I understand that they were really at that moment only in their late sixties or early seventies as am I now. I was then amazed that so many people still managed to remain alive and I couldn't imagine that I would

---

32. Browning, "Rabbi ben Ezra," ll.1–3.

ever see my fiftieth reunion. Ah, I was so much older then. I'm seventy-four years of age now.

Browning's lines then sounded lovely enough to remember, and I have stored them in memory for this past fifty and odd years. And the words arose recently in my seventy-four-year-old mind and in that moment they possessed a different resonance than first they did on the campus of Roanoke College. I returned to the poem entire. Ben Ezra does not so much celebrate old age, though certainly for him it is a stage of life devoutly to be wished. He does, however, appreciate having earned its arrival: "Therefore, I summon age/To grant youth's heritage/Life's struggle having so far reached its term."[33] Age is an inheritance awarded to youth. As for me, I do love my life and would not want to leave it. As difficult as it has been at times and even now yet continues to be, I look forward to awakening each morning to realize all that is about me and to consider what lies on the schedule today. As the Weavers sing, "Though nations are warring and business is vexed/I'll still stick around to see what happens next." I accept Ben Ezra's belief that age may be a time for reckoning and acceptance. I have arrived here to this moment and I am content. I do not cling to regret for some refuge.

Like me, Rabbi Ben Ezra honors doubt. I think perhaps that what old age knows and enjoys is the certainty of doubt and the awareness that the ultimate paradox of life consists in the fact that what is important in life is not to measure the successes but its failures. The rabbi states, that "What I aspired to be,/And was not comforts me." It is not success that the rabbi values, but the failures in his youth that his effort achieved. To have failed is to have tried. Now, in his old age he can rest from the effort. To the ghost Hamlet says, "Rest, rest, perturbed spirit," but then Hamlet asserts that "The time is out of joint: O cursed spite/That ever I was born to set it right." Youth is the time for action. Aging may have been now extended, but it is comforting to know that at some point there will come a time to rest for just a bit. I have recently grown comfortable with an intellectual laziness that refuses constant study: my friend says, "Isn't it wonderful!" I turn very often to detective novels and I have left the classrooms. There is some comfort in leaving the torch for the next generation to assume, to step back from the struggle, and to acknowledge there are in this world differences of opinion but somewhere a truth. The rabbi asserts, "Let age speak the truth and give us peace at last!"[34] To my daughters I can only offer what I have learned

---

33. Browning, "Rabbi ben Ezra," ll. 73–4.
34. Browning, "Rabbi ben Ezra," l. 126.

and what I am, "A man, for aye removed/From the developed brute—a god, though in the germ."³⁵ I agree, and my death will finally complete that consent.

Wordsworth had said that the child is father to the man. What I imagine Wordsworth had in mind was that as the child was so becomes the man. But, Wordsworth suggested, as the child in experience enjoys a oneness and seamless joy with and in the world—that moment of splendor in the grass—and as the child does not think of death and does feel immortal, so in thought might the adult achieve that peace of the child. That visionary gleam, the immersion complete in the present in which the child exists can be experienced by the adult but only in thought. "We will in thought join your throng . . ." the poet says to the child. The wisdom the child possesses is total though inarticulate, and the child may live the truths for which the adults who "in darkness lost, the darkness of the grave . . ." achieve only in thought. And yet,

> We will grieve not, rather find
> Strength in what remains behind;
> In the primal sympathy
> Which having been must ever be;
> In the soothing thoughts that Spring out of human suffering;
> In the faith that looks through death
> In years that bring the philosophic mind³⁶.

For Wordsworth it would seem, age offers a return in thought to a childhood sense of oneness—Freud's oceanic feeling or Winnicott's return to stages of our primitive, or early selves: of senses of disintegration, depersonalization, and a relinquishment of an awareness of the outer world as objective fact. I appreciate that engagement in creative activity enjoys such returns. It comforts me to consider that thought has function—I have spent so much of my life in realms of thought. I trust in the powers of thought to give access and insight into life. Ironically, it is the past that Wordsworth's thought recovers.

Wordsworth's vision of the child is drenched in a romanticism of which I am skeptical. For too, too many children the world is too, too much with them late and soon and death always too near. When I consider Wordsworth's belief I think of Jake Barnes' comment to Lady Brett who has sighed that if only experience had not gotten in the way they "might have

---

35. Browning, "Rabbi ben Ezra," l. 78.
36. Wordsworth, "Ode" ll. 179-186.

had such a damned good time together." He punctures her illusions with his response, "Isn't it pretty to think so?" A realistic cynicism governs Jake's response, but I prefer to assume an ironic stance to my life and wait to see what happens next. I think my years have brought to me the philosophic mind, but my thoughts look not through death nor does my mind enjoy what Wordsworth refers to as "soothing thoughts that spring out of human suffering." Perhaps Wordsworth refers to my own personal sufferings of which I have experienced not a few, and he avers that those soothing thoughts derive from having endured that suffering and are now cognizant of my having flourished as a result. Perhaps. But when Rabbi Johanan went to visit Rabbi Hiyya who had fallen ill, he sat by his bedside and asked his friend "Are your sufferings precious to you?", and Rabbi Hiyya responded, "Neither they nor their reward." Then it seems Rabbi Johanan fell ill and Rabbi Hanina paid him a visit. Sitting by the bedside of his friend, he asked, "Are your sufferings precious to you?" Hanina answered, "Neither they nor their reward." And then Rabbi Eleazar fell ill and Rabbi Johanan came to visit him. In the midst of their conversation concerning mortality, Johanan asked Eleazar, "Are your sufferings precious to you?" Eleazar answered, "Neither they nor their reward."[37] For these rabbis, suffering does not serve to ferment anything. Suffering serves no purpose.

Perhaps it is that in the midst of suffering it appears pointless but when the present suffering subsides it inspires thought. Perhaps. I recognize that psychotherapy depends on this relationship, but despite a lifelong engagement in therapy, I remain somewhat skeptical. I have benefited throughout my life from my therapy encounters, and I know that I will continue to do so. But I have come to believe that what psychotherapy offers is a new story for my life and not a cure or sure fix for the one that has been lived. For me, at least, no thought sees anything past death: death is an end. A completion, I suppose,

I prefer the thought of Browning's Rabbi Ben Ezra who suggests that with aging comes the wisdom that youth, busy as it must be with experience, cannot achieve. For Rabbi Ben Ezra it would seem that old age is a stage to which I might arrive, the way my yoga teachers advise that to begin practice I might just lie on my back or come to a comfortable seated position and just "arrive." Ben Ezra suggests that though thought will validate and justify the days past, it is not a backwards longing at all nor is it some

---

37. Babylonian Talmud, *Bava Metzia*, 85a.

## Anxious Am I?

return to a past splendor. The present reflects on the past, proofs it and open the way to the future.

> Let me discern, compare, pronounce at last,
>   "This rage was right i' the main,
>   That acquiescence vain;
> The Future I may face now I have proved the past.[38]

Rabbi Ben Ezra suggests to me a different perspective on the life cycle than does Wordsworth. For the rabbi, the last of life was promised by the first of it but did not determine it. Youth may be the time of action and experiment and action, but old age offers the opportunity to rest, to contemplate, to prepare some understanding to his life. Rabbi Ben Ezra says,

> Youth ended, I shall try
>   My gain or loss thereby;
> Leave the fire ashes, what survives is gold.
>   And I shall weigh the same,
>   Give life its praise or blame.
> Young, all lay in dispute; I shall know being old.[39]

I do not imagine that now that I am well beyond youth I can really know, but I take comfort in the idea that at this time I can accept the occasions of my life and appreciate that what remains is finally valuable. Frost said that nothing gold can stay, but Rabbi Ben Ezra declares that only the gold survives. Whereas youth in its boldness and uncouthness strives to do, old age is "exempt from strife, should know . . . " Should know some peace, I think. I settle into my chair before the fire with a glass of wine.

I wonder how does one end a memoir when the life it remembers is not at an end? I suppose that a written memoir does not end but . . .

---

38. Browning, "Rabbi ben Ezra," ll. 99–102.
39. Browning, "Rabbi ben Ezra," ll. 85–90.

# Bibliography

Austen, J. *Mansfield Park*. New York: Barnes & Noble, 2004.
Bailyn, B. *Sometimes an Art*. New York: Alfred A. Knopf, 2015.
Balint, M. "Friendly Expanses—Horrid Empty Spaces." *The International Journal of Psycho-Analysis* (1955) 225–41.
Bateson, G. *Steps To an Ecology of Mind*. New York: Ballentine, 1972.
Becker, E. *The Denial of Death*. New York: Free Press, 1973.
Beckett, S. *Waiting for Godot*. New York: Grove Press, 1954.
Bennett, A. "Diary." *London Review of Books*, 2017.
Berger, J. *Bento's Sketchbook*. New York: Pantheon, 2011.
Bollas, C. *I Have Heard the Mermaids Singing*. London: Free Association Books, 2005.
Browning, R. "Rabbi Ben Ezra." In *The Victorian Age*, edited by John Wilson Bowyer and John Lee Brooks, 260–320. New York: Appleton-Century-Croft, 1954.
Calvino, I. *if on a winter's night a traveler*. Translated by William Weaver. New York: Harcourt, 1981.
Cavell, S. *Little Did I Know*. Stanford: Stanford, 2010.
Cercas, J. *The Impostor*. Translated by Frank Wynne. New York: Alfred A. Knopf, 2018.
Conrad, J. *Lord Jim*. New York: W.W. Norton, 1968.
Dead, G. "Uncle John's Band." Retrieved March 2021, from Genius Lyrics: https://genius.com/The-grateful-dead-uncle-johns-band-lyrics
———. "Scarlet Begonias." Retrieved January 2015, from Genius Lyrics: https://genius.com/The-grateful-dead-scarlet-begonias-lyrics
Eagleton, T. *Culture*. New Haven: Yale, 2016.
———. *Trouble With Strangers*. Oxford: Wiley Blackwell, 2009.
Eliot, G. *Middlemarch*. New York: Penguin, 1994.
Emerson, R. W. *The Complete Writings* (Vol. I). New York: W. H. Wise & Co., 1929.
Fromm, E. *The Art of Loving*. New York: Harper Colophon, 1956.
Gordimer, N. *Burger's Daughter*. New York: Penguin, 1979.
Heller, J. *Catch-22*. New York: Simon and Schuster, 1961.
Henry, O. *The Last Leaf*. https://americanliterature.com/author/o-henry/short-story/the-last-leaf. Retrieved August 2021
Heschel, A. *Between God and Man*. New York: The Free Press, 1959.
Housman, A. E. "Terence, This is Stupid Stuff." In *Chief Modern Poets of England and America*, edited by Gerald DeWitt Sanders et al., I-83–97. New York: Macmillan, 1967.
Kermode, F. *Not Entitled*. New York: Farrar, Straus and Giroux, 1995.

# Bibliography

Kiser, J. *The Monks of Tibhirine*. New York: St. Martin's, 2003.
Mantel, H. *A Place of Greater Safety*. New York: Henry Holt, 1992.
Melville, H. *Moby Dick*. New York: Hendricks House, 1962.
Mendelsohn, D. *An Odyssey: A Father, a Son and an Epic*. New York: Vintage, 2017.
Modell, A. M. *The Private Self*. Cambridge: Harvard, 1993.
Montaigne, M. *The Complete Works*. Translated by Donald M. Frame. New York: Alfred A. Knopf, 2003.
Olsen, t. *Tell Me a Riddle*. New York: Dell, 1961.
Phillips, A. *On Kissing, Tickling, and Being Bored*. Cambridge: Harvard, 1993.
Roth, P. *Reading Myself and Others*. New York: Vintage, 1985.
———. *The Facts*. New York: Penguin Books, 1988.
———. *I Married a Communist*. New York: Houghton Mifflin.
Rozema, P., dir. *I Heard the Mermaids Singing* [Motion Picture], 1987.
Salinger, J. *Franny and Zooey*. New York: Little, Brown, 1961,
Seneca. *Letters From a Stoic*. Translated by Robon Campbell. New York: Penguin, 2004.
Spinoza, B. d. *On the Improvement of Understanding, the Ethics, Correspondence*. New York: Dover, 1955.
Springsteen, B. "Independence Day." Retrieved December 2019, from GeniusLyrics: https://genius.com/Bruce-springsteen-independence-day-lyrics.
Sterne, L. *Tristram Shandy*. New York: W.W. Norton, 1980.
Sunstein, C. "Once Upon a time There Was a Big Bubble." *New York Review of Books*, January 14, 2021.
Szabados, B. "Autobiography after Wittgenstein." *The Journal of Aesthetics and Art Criticism* 50.1 (1992) 1–12.
Thoreau, H. D. *Collected Essays and Poems*. New York: Library of America, 2001.
———. *The Journal of Henry David Thoreau*. New York: Dover, 1962.
———. *Walden*. New Haven: Yale, 2006.
———. *A Week on the Concord and Merrimack Rivers*. New York: Thomas Crowell, 1961.
Tolstoy, L. *War and Peace*. Translated by Richard Pevear and Larissa Volokhonsky. New York: Vintage Classics, 2007.
Vincent, D. *A History of Solitude*. Cambridge, UK: Polity, 2020.
Vonnetgut, K. *Mother Night*. New York: Dial, 2000.
White, H. "The Aim of Interpretation Is to Create Perplexity in the Face of the Real: Hayden White in Conversation with Erland Rogne." *History and Theory* 48 (2009) 63–75.
Winnicott, D. *Home Is Where We Start From*. New York: W.W. Norton, 1986.
———. *The Maturational Processes and the Facilitating Environment*. London: Karnac, 1990.
Winterson, J. *Why Be Happy When You Can Be Normal*. New York: Grove Press, 2011.
Woolf, V. *Mrs. Dalloway*. New York: Harcourt, 1981.
Wordsworth, W. "Ode: Intimations of Immortality." In *English Romantic Writers*, edited by David Perkins, 167–367. New York: Harcourt, Brace & World, 1967.

www.ingramcontent.com/pod-product-compliance
Lightning Source LLC
Chambersburg PA
CBHW050148170426
43197CB00011B/2009